Race and
Police Brutality

SUNY series in Deviance and Social Control

Ronald A. Farrell, editor

Race and Police Brutality

Roots of an Urban Dilemma

Malcolm D. Holmes
and
Brad W. Smith

State University of New York Press

Published by State University of New York Press, Albany

© 2008 State University of New York

All rights reserved

Printed in the United States of America

For information, contact State University of New York Press, Albany, NY
www.sunypress.edu

Production by Diane Ganeles
Marketing by Anne M. Valentine

Library of Congress Cataloging-in-Publication Data

Holmes, Malcolm D.
    Race and police brutality : roots of an urban dilemma / Malcolm D. Holmes and Brad
W. Smith
        p. cm. — (Suny series in deviance and social control)
    Includes bibliographical references and index.
    ISBN 978-0-7914-7619-2 (hardcover : alk. paper) — ISBN 978-0-7914-7620-8
(softcover : alk. paper) 1. Police brutality—United States. 2. Sociology, Urban—
United States. 3. Minorities—Crimes against—United States. 4. United States—Ethnic
relations. I. Smith, Brad W. II. Title.
    HV8141.H95 2008
    363.2'32—dc22

                                                                        2007052570

                            10 9 8 7 6 5 4 3 2 1

CONTENTS

PREFACE

This book is the culmination of several years of thinking about the relationship of race/ethnicity and police brutality in America. We cannot recall with certainty what initially sparked our interest in the issue. Certainly questions about race/ethnicity and social control long have been central to our research agendas. We both vividly recall the video of the police beating of Rodney King in Los Angeles, an event that turned national attention to the issue of race and police brutality. We both read Jerome Skolnick and James Fyfe's (1993) *Above the Law*, which provided an insightful account of the cultural and structural characteristics of big-city police agencies that may contribute to such incidences. Most importantly for our future work, they presented a simple descriptive reanalysis of data from a controversial 1991 U.S. Department of Justice (DOJ) study of civil rights criminal complaints, which had claimed that no patterns of police brutality could be discerned. Skolnick and Fyfe countered that there are vast differences in the rates of complaints across agencies, and they called for further research. The DOJ complaints data, expanded to include variables from other data sources, became the focal point of our empirical work. A further search of the literature revealed a lack of reliable evidence concerning whether citizens' race/ethnicity plays a role in the use of police brutality, although the findings of existing research clearly pointed to that possibility. We sought to provide more definitive conclusions about these relationships with our analyses of the DOJ complaints data, which were published in two articles in *Criminology* (Holmes 2000; Smith and Holmes 2003). The findings of those studies indicate that the African American and Mexican-origin populations bear the brunt of police brutality.

During the course of conducting that research, it became increasingly clear to us that the relationship of race/ethnicity to police brutality is complicated. One question concerns what we mean by police brutality.

Minority citizens see a wide range of police misconduct as forms of police brutality, whereas legally it refers particularly to excessive force. The latter became the focus of our empirical research because the DOJ data comprise cases alleging criminal conduct by law enforcement officials. The employment of excessive force also is the focal point of the theoretical analysis we offer herein, but for a somewhat different reason. As we thought about the various types of police misconduct involving citizens, certain issues became progressively more evident. Existing theories seemed to offer plausible explanations for lesser police misbehavior, such as illegal searches and the use of racial epithets, yet police officers risk little by those actions. That misconduct is likely to go undetected and unpunished. Such practices are deeply embedded in the police subculture, comprising expedient informal means for establishing and maintaining control in disadvantaged minority neighborhoods, where police officers commonly perceive challenges to authority and threats from citizens. Excessive force is an altogether different matter, however. Whereas the police are empowered to use force to accomplish a legitimate duty, they risk severe punishment for using it gratuitously. Why would the police take such a chance? And why are minority citizens residing in impoverished neighborhoods the primary targets for excessive force?

These were the questions that intrigued us, and we found no compelling answers in the existing criminological literature. As we looked elsewhere, we began to find various strands of thought in the social psychological literature on intergroup relations, which proved highly useful in our effort to weave a more comprehensive account of the relationship between race/ethnicity and police brutality. Our synthesis draws on different perspectives that are not in full agreement on certain issues (e.g., the relative importance of cognition and emotion in human affairs). We do not seek to advocate any perspective over any other, attempting only to distill them into a cogent model by borrowing from the strengths of each. Above all, we endeavor to portray the immense complexities involved in acts of police brutality disproportionately targeted against disadvantaged minorities. While we are confident that we have identified the principal intergroup phenomena relevant to the questions we ask, we are under no illusion that our analysis offers the final word on the matter. Indeed, we hope, above all, that our arguments will engage others in a conversation about the issues at hand and possible avenues of resolving a problem that so profoundly affects the lives of America's most disadvantaged citizens. While the substantive focus is on a specific problem, the theoretical model has broader applicability to understanding untoward violence by those in positions of authority—police brutality in other nations, wartime atrocities, prisoner abuses, and so on. Hopefully others will find our work useful as they endeavor to understand such phenomena.

ACKNOWLEDGMENTS

Our undertaking was facilitated immensely by simultaneous sabbatical leaves from our respective institutions, the University of Wyoming and Wayne State University, as well as by support from the Humanities Center at Wayne State. We thank Ed A. Muñoz as well as the students in the spring 2007 seminar in crime and deviance at the University of Wyoming for their perceptive comments on drafts of the manuscript. The support and insightful comments of the anonymous reviewers for State University of New York Press are immensely appreciated. They contributed greatly to our endeavor. We thank Mary Shenouda and Shamsun Nehar for their assistance in the library and compilation of the references. The inspiration, support, and patience of our families during the writing of this book facilitated our work and are deeply appreciated. In particular, we wish to thank our wives, Michelle Deany Holmes and Sheryl Hansen Smith, for their support throughout our careers. Finally, we are grateful for the unflagging support and assistance of Ronald A. Farrell, editor of the SUNY series in Deviance and Social Control, and Nancy Ellegate, senior acquisitions editor for State University of New York Press, throughout this project. Of course we assume full responsibility for any errors in or omissions from the arguments presented herein.

CHAPTER 1

The Nature of Police Brutality

Belief in equal justice stands as a preeminent political tenet of American society. Yet abiding skepticism exists among many racial and ethnic minorities. Their mistrust is hardly surprising, given a history of differential treatment in the system of criminal justice, a problem especially apparent in police conduct. Scholars have long scrutinized police reactions to racial and ethnic minorities, offering ample evidence of minority disadvantage at the hands of police (e.g., Sellin 1930; Myrdal 1944; Westley 1953, 1970; Holmes 2000; Chambliss 2001). These investigations call into question various police strategies of coercive control, perhaps none more so than police brutality. Its utilization epitomizes the tensions between police and minorities that exist in America today (NAACP 1995).

Consider the events that unfolded in March 1991. Americans were transfixed by an amateur video showing Los Angeles police officers beating Rodney King, an African American citizen. The images seemed unambiguous. Most Americans were shocked by what they saw. Still, differences of opinion separated blacks and whites (Skolnick and Fyfe 1993; Flanagan and Vaughn 1996; Weitzer and Tuch 2006). The vast majority of blacks thought the police needlessly pummeled a citizen even as he lay helplessly on the ground. An appreciably greater share of whites believed the police acted properly to subdue an unruly, potentially dangerous black man. Their differences subsequently came to a head with the acquittal of four Los Angeles Police Department (LAPD) officers by a nearly all-white jury in Simi Valley, where the officers were tried on state charges after a controversial change of venue from Los Angeles. A devastating riot ensued as blacks took to the streets to express their outrage at the verdicts. Undoubtedly they saw confirmation of an unjust criminal justice system in the officers' acquittal, whereas whites witnessed evidence of black criminality in the race riots. In the end, over 2,000 injuries, more than fifty deaths, and an

1

estimated billion dollars of property damage were incurred (Useem 1997). This highly publicized case rekindled a long-standing, often fierce national debate about whether race is a factor in police brutality (Locke 1996).

Police-minority tensions are hardly new—during the 1960s, police-citizen interactions precipitated many of the race riots that plagued urban America. In response to the social unrest, President Lyndon B. Johnson issued an executive order to establish the National Advisory Commission on Civil Disorders (1968), better known as the Kerner Commission. The Kerner Commission was charged with investigating the disorders and making recommendations for averting future problems. The final report depicted a divided America, concluding that various long-term problems—unemployment, socially disorganized neighborhoods, lack of educational opportunities, poor health and sanitation conditions, and crime—were endemic to the ghettos of America's large cities. Ultimately the commission attributed the difficulties that blacks confronted to historical patterns of white racism and acknowledged that blacks see the police as oppressors protecting the interests of the white community. At the time, the great majority of police officers were white, and many were highly prejudiced, lending credence to blacks' beliefs. It is hardly surprising that many of the ghetto riots were triggered by confrontations between the police and citizens.

Police administrators did not help matters. They responded defensively to community concerns, asserting that citizens' complaints signified the impending breakdown of law and order (Locke 1996). Their defensiveness persists. Although LAPD Chief Daryl Gates condemned the beating of Rodney King, he explained it away as an aberration, despite clear evidence that police brutality was rampant in the LAPD (Skolnick and Fyfe 1993). In the eyes of many police administrators, police brutality is the exception, the collateral damage arising from the difficult challenges faced by police in urban areas. Yet African American and Hispanic citizens believe that it occurs more commonly (see Flanagan and Vaughn 1996; Weitzer and Tuch 2006), which fuels their mistrust and hostility toward the police.

While waxing and waning in intensity, the national dialogue is reengaged periodically as incidents of police brutality involving minority citizens surface. In 1979, a group of Dade County (Miami) police officers killed insurance agent Arthur McDuffie following a vehicle chase. Initially officers claimed that McDuffie's injuries were the result of falling off his motorcycle, but a subsequent investigation and coroner's report concluded that he was beaten to death after stopping (Kappeler, Sluder, and Alpert 1998). Following the acquittals of four officers, a three-day race riot ensued, resulting in eighteen deaths, hundreds of injuries, and tens of millions of dollars in property damage. McDuffie's family eventually received a $1.1 million settlement (*Washington Post* 1981).

In 1997, another high-profile incident shocked America and again revived the specter of police racism. Abner Louima, a married father of two, was viciously sodomized with a wooden handle in a Bronx precinct house restroom following a questionable arrest. His injuries were nearly fatal. Yet the case came to light only because an emergency room nurse informed Louima's family and the authorities (Alfieri 1999). The fallout from this horrific incident included a thirty-year prison sentence for the main perpetrator and the largest civil settlement ($8.75 million) against police in New York City history (Hays 2001).

More recently, in October 2005, news crews covering the aftermath of Hurricane Katrina videotaped four police officers in New Orleans beating a sixty-four-year-old retired schoolteacher, Robert Davis (Foster 2005). The video shows a police officer repeatedly punching Davis in the head before the group dragged him to the ground, where one kneed and punched him. A fifth officer ordered one of the camera crews to stop taping. When a news producer held up his credentials, the officer is seen grabbing him, slamming him into a parked car, and punching him in the stomach, all the while yelling profanities at him. Three police officers were indicted for their part in these events (Associated Press 2006). The incident has prompted a federal investigation, and the victim's attorney has stated that a civil suit is forthcoming. One could hardly be surprised if the familiar pattern—increased racial tensions, an undermining of the legitimacy of the police, and a drain on government resources as a result of a civil suit—plays out again in New Orleans.

African Americans are not the only victims in such high-profile cases. Consider twenty-three-year-old Joe Campos Torres, who was arrested by Houston police one night in May 1977 for disorderly conduct (Time 1978). Aside from possibly being drunk, Torres appeared unharmed when officers took him from the club where he was arrested. Several hours after his arrest, Torres arrived at the jail so badly beaten that intake officers refused to process him and instead instructed the arresting officers to take him to a local hospital. Six police officers then drove Torres a short distance to an area behind a warehouse next to Buffalo Bayou. Two officers later testified that they watched as Torres was pushed off a dock into the bayou by an officer, who said, "Let's see if the wetback can swim" (Curry 1978). Torres's body was found several days later. In a state trial, two officers were found guilty of negligent homicide and received suspended sentences (*Time* 1978). Later a federal trial resulted in guilty verdicts on federal civil rights violations for three officers.

Recently an immigration rally in Los Angeles ended when police officers, in response to a small group of provocateurs, decided to sweep the entire park and disperse a peaceful crowd of approximately 6,000 largely Hispanic demonstrators, including many women and children, with batons and foam-rubber projectiles (Archibold 2007; McGreevy and Winton 2007). The order by police to disperse was only given in English to a predominantly Spanish-speaking crowd. Videos show police in riot gear forcefully clearing the park of agitators, peaceful demonstrators, bystanders, and journalists alike. Numerous allegations of police misconduct have been filed and are under investigation. Irrespective of their final outcome, such cases provide ample evidence that police brutality remains a critical problem for minority communities today.

Such incidents remain deeply rooted in the racial and ethnic inequalities that exist in American society. Undoubtedly many Americans find it comforting to believe that the economic and social plight of minorities has improved since the 1960s. In reality, the racial divide depicted by the Kerner Commission not only endures, but it may be widening. Transformations in the American economy, for example, from goods-producing to service-producing industries, have resulted in an increased concentration of poor black and Hispanics in socially disorganized urban neighborhoods (Wilson 1987). Poor black residents of the inner city may have become even more isolated socially and spatially because of the exodus of relatively affluent blacks from inner-city neighborhoods. What remains are hypersegregated ghettos, which have "assumed even greater importance as an institutional tool for isolating the by-products of racial oppression: crime, drugs, violence, illiteracy, poverty, despair, and their growing social and economic costs" (Massey and Denton 1993, 217). Similarly disadvantaged barrios exist, particularly in cities near the U.S.-Mexico border, where many poor immigrants from Mexico relocate (see Alba and Nee 2003). At the same time, many poor whites in urban America also experience such disadvantages (Massey 2005), just as many relatively affluent minority citizens dodge them. But the afflictions of poverty, including various forms of discrimination, are without doubt borne disproportionately by racial and ethnic minorities.

In short, one side of America's economic and social chasm is inhabited disproportionately by whites, the dominant majority for whom the American Dream continually holds out the promise of opportunity. They do not routinely confront crime and social disorder in their comfortable suburban neighborhoods. The other side of the divide is populated disproportionately by impoverished racial/ethnic minorities for whom the American Dream offers little, for whom life is often a struggle merely to subsist. The disadvantages of their neighborhoods may spawn crime and social disorder (e.g., Skogan 1990; Sampson and Wilson 1995; Phillips 2002). In the middle of the two social worlds stand the police, the agents of social control officially charged with protecting all citizens equally.

Popular belief among the dominant group holds that the police do, in fact, uniformly enforce criminal laws that represent a consensus about the dangers confronted by the public and do not succumb to racial enmity in their treatment of citizens (see Weitzer and Tuch 2006). If the police exert greater coercion over some segments of society, it is only an objective response to real dangers posed by those parts of the community. Police brutality is an unfortunate corollary of the dangerous job of protecting society from its worst citizens, an anomaly attributable to characteristics of certain police officers and police departments. In many respects, this viewpoint parallels that of police administrators. Although more critical and nuanced, much of the scholarly work on police brutality also reflects this thinking. Black and Hispanic citizens see matters quite differently, however, expressing considerably greater skepticism about police practices (Weitzer and Tuch 2006). Those living in impoverished neighborhoods may be deeply cynical about the criminal justice system and hostile toward the police (e.g., Anderson 1999). Moreover, some scholars dispute the assessment that minority and dominant citizens are treated alike, arguing instead that the police protect the interests of the dominant group, by whatever means necessary, from the criminal threat allegedly posed by the disadvantaged (e.g., Jacobs and O'Brien 1998). In this view the police systematically and deliberately employ violence against impoverished minority citizens, knowing that white citizens are unlikely to interfere with efforts to control populations stereotyped as inherently criminogenic.

So which position is correct? Somewhat surprisingly, given the seemingly obvious significance of the issue, little empirical research has been accorded police brutality compared to matters such as the correlations between race and crime (Locke 1996). Undoubtedly the clandestine quality of police brutality makes research difficult. Still, criminologists seem more attuned to the dominant white community's concern with minority street crime. What little systematic research is available suggests that our society, particularly minority communities, has good reason for concern about police brutality (see Holmes 2000). But many more questions remain unanswered than answered. Is police brutality a matter of individual prejudice on the part of some police officers? Is it a problem of interpersonal antagonism between black citizens and the police? Is it an issue of the formal or informal organization of policing? Is it a reflection of whites' interest in maintaining the status quo? Or could there be causes of police brutality that have yet to be explored fully?

We examine this critical but little understood issue here, offering a distinctive and potentially controversial answer. Our line of reasoning stresses that police brutality is a grim symptom of intractable intergroup dynamics involving racial and ethnic minority citizens and the police officers who patrol their neighborhoods. The behavior of the police may implicitly represent dominant interests insofar as they enforce laws established to protect society as currently structured, but the police are far more attuned to the problems and dangers they personally confront in the course of their work in impoverished minority neighborhoods. In the eyes of minority citizens, the police symbolize an oppressive society. What is more, many minority citizens perceive the police as a real danger in their day-to-day lives. We delve into these intergroup dynamics with an eye toward what, if anything, can be done to heal the tensions between the police and minority communities.

What Is Police Brutality?

Many citizens define police brutality broadly to include a range of abusive police practices, such as the use of profanity, racial slurs, and unnecessary searches, not entailing the use of physical force (NAACP 1995; Locke 1996). Racial and ethnic minorities in particular perceive any degrading, restricting, or harassing practice as objectionable, and a number of studies indicate that the police disproportionately employ such practices against them. Observational studies of the police have provided evidence of the use of abusive language, including racial slurs (Westley 1970; Skolnick 1975; Anderson 1990). Research also suggests that minority males are disproportionately subjected to field interrogations and are more likely to be frisked or searched once they have been identified as suspects (Piliavin and Briar 1964; Black and Reiss 1967; U.S. Commission on Civil Rights 1970; Bogomolny 1976; Chambliss 1994). In a study of one city, a substantial proportion of black police officers, who are clearly knowledgeable about the relevant legal standards, said they personally had been stopped, questioned, or searched because of racial profiling (Barlow and Barlow 2002). Recently several states have confronted legal challenges to the inappropriate use of race in police stops, and observational data suggest that police searches often do violate constitutional principles of search and seizure (Gould and Mastrofski 2004).

Clearly such abuses may entail costs to the legitimacy of law enforcement in the eyes of minority citizens. While the theory of police brutality proposed here has relevance to each of these forms of police misconduct, we focus on excessive force, for several reasons. It is clearly at the heart of minority concern about police misconduct (Locke 1996; NAACP 1995; Reiss 1968). Moreover, other forms of misconduct do not rise to the legal standard defining police brutality. While citizens may apply that term loosely to various forms of police misconduct, from the standpoint of the law the use of excessive force most clearly defines police brutality (Locke 1996). Whereas other abusive practices constitute relatively minor infractions that carry little risk, excessive force potentially carries severe sanctions for offending officers. Thus the use of excessive force poses a conundrum that we seek to resolve: Why would the police employ excessive force when they are empowered by law to use the force necessary to accomplish a legitimate police duty?

Modern democracies employ domestic police agencies to control internal wrongdoers and maintain social order, and the legitimate use of force to protect citizens and officers from the dangerous people in their midst constitutes the essence of the police role (Bittner 1970). Even the use of deadly force by the police, which disproportionately involves minority victims (Brown and Langan 2001), is nearly always deemed legally justified (e.g., Fyfe 1980). At the same time, the reality that the police limit individual freedom requires that their authority be clearly circumscribed in democratic societies (Kania and Mackey 1977). Accordingly, the use of force by the police may be proper or excessive, depending on whether it is necessary to accomplish a legitimate police duty. Force that occurs "under color of authority, without lawful necessity" constitutes excessive force or police brutality (Locke 1996, 130).

Police officers receive extensive training regarding the proper use of force, as the employment of excessive force may entail severe criminal sanctions for police officers and substantial civil penalties for police departments. Despite the efforts of police departments to recruit and train professional officers who operate within the limits of legal standards, police officers periodically step well outside the bounds of the law. The quasi-military structure of policing, including the deployment of personal weapons arsenals and extensive training in the use of force, undoubtedly sets the stage for such transgressions (Chambliss 2001). What is more, within the subculture of policing, extra-legal force is considered a normal, essential instrument of control for handling those individuals perceived as threatening or who are otherwise discredited (Hunt 1985; Skolnick and Fyfe 1993; Van Maanen 1974; Westley 1970). The extra-legal quality of police brutality makes it expedient for situations in which legal responses are judged inappropriate or insufficient. Excessive force may be employed when no probable cause for arrest exists, or any time "justice" calls for informal sanctions in addition to formal ones. But can such observations about the customariness of the behavior explain why police officers periodically risk incurring harsh punishments by engaging in it?

How Can Police Brutality Be Explained?

The traditional approach to explaining police brutality comprises a set of propositions about (1) sociological or situational, (2) psychological or individual, and (3) organizational factors (Freidrich 1980; Worden 1996). The first approach suggests that situational exigencies, related to characteristics such as the race, gender, and demeanor of citizens, determine the use of excessive force. Emphasis is placed on the social dynamics of police-citizen encounters and the situational cues that officers use to decide how to handle an incident. The second approach identifies the characteristics of officers, such as racial identity, degree of prejudice, and personality attributes, which may predict the use of excessive force. In this view, individual variations among officers produce different responses to similar situations. The third approach maintains that organizational properties of police departments, such as administrative controls and the subculture of policing, determine the degree to which excessive force is employed. The focus is on formal and informal aspects of police organization that may influence officers' street-level behavior.

Elements of the various explanations are found in William A. Westley's (1953, 1970) seminal work on police violence. Drawing on observations and interviews conducted during the period 1949–1950, he examined a police department located in a medium-size industrial city with a large slum area and a large black population. Police behavior in the community reflected officers' concerns, grounded in informal organizational norms, about the maintenance of authority and respect. The police believed that blacks are naturally prone to criminality, and that they pose a particular threat to police authority. Thus situations calling for extra-legal violence frequently involved blacks being perceived as disrespectful of the police. Not only were blacks being particular targets of illegitimate violence, but also the police felt impunity from sanctions because blacks lacked political power.

Subsequent research has relied on a variety of data sources to investigate how situational, individual, and organizational variables relate to police brutality. An important source of systematic data for research on these relationships is observational studies of police officers on patrol. In response to the urban disorder of the 1960s, data for the President's Commission on Law Enforcement were collected in Boston, Chicago, and Washington, D.C., by observers who accompanied police officers on patrol in high-crime precincts (Black and Reiss 1967). A decade later, the Police Services Study (PSS), conducted by researchers at Indiana University and the University of North Carolina, observed police officers in twenty-four jurisdictions located in the metropolitan areas of Rochester, New York, St. Louis, Missouri, and Tampa-St. Petersburg, Florida. Multivariate studies of these observational data sets, which include variables pertaining to the various explanations of police brutality, provide somewhat mixed findings in regard to the influence of race (cf. Freidrich 1980; Smith 1986; Worden 1996). Still, it is noteworthy that more methodologically sophisticated recent studies indicate a link between race and the incidence of excessive force (Smith 1986; Worden 1996). In general, studies using these observational data sets buttress the situational explanation of police brutality insofar as black and antagonistic citizens were more likely to be the targets of improper force, whereas the individual and organizational explanations receive little support. Moreover, Smith (1986) found that the use of coercive authority was related to individual racial identity in interaction with neighborhood racial neighborhood composition; the police were most likely to use coercive authority against black suspects in neighborhoods that were primarily black.[1]

Further evidence that minorities are disproportionately the victims of excessive force comes from investigations sponsored by government agencies (e.g., Independent Commission on the Los Angeles Police Department 1991; U.S. Commission on Civil Rights 1970, 2000; Rampart Independent Review Panel 2000) and private organizations (e.g., NAACP 1995). Such commissions typically conduct interviews, review agency records, and hold hearings. Their conclusions uniformly emphasize that police misconduct predominantly affects members of minority communities. Taken together, these investigations provide a wealth of descriptive evidence concerning police misconduct, even though the data collection procedures do not involve rigorous methodological approaches that allow for reliable conclusions from any single inquiry. Such investigations regularly recommend organizational changes to rectify the problem of police brutality, revealing a deep-seated faith that changing police department policies and practices can alter the dynamics of police-minority relations (e.g., NAACP 1995).

Undoubtedly, methodological problems confound efforts to study the clandestine behavior of the police. Still, taken together, the findings of various empirical studies support the argument that racial/ethnic minorities are victimized disproportionately by police brutality. Even though research offers the most systematic support for the situational perspective compared to individual or organizational explanations of police brutality, the organizational approach remains especially significant with respect to policy proposals to reduce police brutality. Typically, calls for organizational reform focus on changing police personnel or increasing oversight of officers and agencies. Such recommendations reflect the unwavering belief that police organization affects officers' situational responses and individual predispositions. Presumably, with sufficient training and supervision, police officers can control their behavior, even in the most incendiary circumstances.

An alternative to the traditional theoretical approach, derived from the conflict theory of law, argues that crime control is an instrument used by powerful groups to regulate threats to their interests, thereby maintaining existing social arrangements. In this view, the police function to control the "dangerous classes" of immigrants, racial minorities, and the poor (e.g., Turk 1969). The structural characteristics of society, manifested via the formal and informal organization of police departments, produce a propensity for the misuse of force against minorities (Chambliss 2001). Police-minority tensions stem, inevitably, from the enduring

racial/ethnic divisions in American society that cannot be addressed simply by altering the organization of policing (Smith and Holmes 2003).

Several scholars, notably Allen E. Liska and his colleagues, have developed the structural-level threat hypothesis to test empirically the argument of conflict theory. The threat hypothesis stipulates that "the
greater the number of acts and people threatening to the interests of the
powerful, the greater the level of deviance and crime control" (Liska
1992, 18). Popular stereotypes conflate race/ethnicity and violent criminality (Quillian and Pager 2001), and the public attributes urban violence
primarily to racial and ethnic minorities (Chiricos, Welch, and Gertz
2004). The presence or mere perception of a large minority population is
sufficient to heighten whites' fear of crime (Chiricos, Hogan, and Gertz
1997; Liska, Lawrence, and Sanchirico 1982). Public authorities believe
that racially and culturally dissimilar minority groups threaten the social
order (Turk 1969), and a relatively large minority population may be
seen as posing a substantial problem of social control (Liska and Yu
1992). Thus the dominant white citizenry and local authorities may mar-
shal their political power to forge public policy that assuages their concerns about crime.

Tests of the threat hypothesis that focus on policing have used aggre-
gate-level data to examine how the percent of nonwhite and economic inequality affect the allocation of police resources (e.g., Jackson and Carroll
1981; Kent and Jacobs 2005; Holmes, Smith, Freng, and Muñoz 2008), arrests (e.g., Liska and Chamlin 1984; Liska, Chamlin, and Reed 1985), and
homicides by the police (Jacobs and O'Brien 1998; Liska and Yu 1992;
Smith 2003; Sorensen, Marquart, and Brock 1993). In addition, our previous work tests the threat hypothesis using civil rights criminal complaints alleging police brutality that were investigated by the Federal Bureau of
Investigation (FBI) and reported to the Civil Rights Division of the U. S. Department of Justice (DOJ). A DOJ (1991) analysis of the data revealed no
discernible pattern in police brutality complaints in cities with an average of
two or more complaints annually during the period 1985–1990. Extending
the DOJ data to include sociodemographic characteristics of cities and organizational characteristics of police departments, our research included all
cities of 150,000-plus population. One study found that the percent of
black, the percent of Hispanic (in the Southwest), and majority/minority in-
come inequality in cities were related positively to civil rights criminal complaints (Holmes 2000).[2] A subsequent reanalysis of those data, in a study
that added organizational variables, showed virtually the same effects for
the percent of racial/ethnic minority variables and revealed stronger support
for the threat hypothesis than for the organizational approach (Smith and
Holmes 2003). These studies validate and extend the findings of earlier investigations of police brutality by demonstrating a broad pattern of civil

rights criminal complaints in large cities with relatively large racial/ethnic minority populations.

Findings from tests of the threat hypothesis generally support its predictions, but they also reveal complexities in the relationships between measures of threat and measures of crime control by the police. For example, a study of race-specific arrest rates showed that the percent of nonwhites was related negatively to nonwhite arrest rates (Liska and Chamlin 1984). The researchers concluded that intraracial crimes increase as the percent of nonwhite in the population increases, and that the police and minority victims alike see such crimes as personal or family matters in which formal intervention is not required. Such crimes pose no threat to dominant group members or police officers. In contrast, consistent support for the threat hypothesis comes from studies of homicides by the police and police brutality criminal complaints.

The most plausible explanation of these divergent findings is that threat has multiple dimensions, involving the interests of both dominant group members and the police. Following the conflict theory of law, work on the threat hypothesis emphasizes that mechanisms of coercive control are mobilized to protect the dominant classes of society. Resource allocations to policing and police department policies may reflect perceived threats to dominant interests, but police officers on the street are hardly automatons blindingly following dominant group imperatives. Minority attitudes and actions in particular may be perceived as directly threatening a police officer's well-being or challenging an officer's authority (Chevigny 1969; Skolnick 1975; Westley 1970). Moreover, police behavior is characterized by a high degree of discretion and a low degree of visibility and thus may be open to extra-legal influences (e.g., Smith and Visher 1981). In light of these considerations, it makes sense that salient threats perceived directly by the police should be more important than distal threats to or political pressures from the dominant group in predicting their street-level responses to racial/ethnic minorities—the disproportionate rate of minority victimization in instances of police violence may reflect reactions to situations in which officers personally perceive minority threat (Holmes 2000; Liska and Yu 1992).

Building on this argument, we contend that conflict theorists place too much emphasis on the interests of the dominant group in society without adequately recognizing the role of the police as an independent social group whose street-level behavior is influenced by the threats police personally confront. Conflict theorists sometimes acknowledge that the police are responding to personal risks when they resort to violence, asserting that the powerful groups of society ignore clandestine "dirty work" that represents their interests (e.g., Jacobs and O'Brien 1998). But this approach only superficially deals with the underlying causes of brutality, and it downplays the reality that police officers risk severe sanctions for engaging in illegal violence, even though the larger society may tacitly approve of it. No doubt the larger society lives in willful ignorance of big-city police practices, and dominant-group citizens may be suspicious of the veracity of any revelations of police misconduct. Yet while citizens may deceive themselves by coming up with every conceivable rationalization for police misconduct, when these justifications become untenable, they may define the case as aberrant and the offending officer(s) as deserving of severe punishment. This raises a critical question: Why would the police risk using coercive strategies that primarily benefit a powerful group peripheral to the day-to-day world of policing?

Our argument takes a different tact, suggesting that police behavior ultimately represents a complex interplay involving various dimensions of intergroup relations. Police officers are hardly likely to accede to implicit dominant group demands that may contradict their personal well-being. Put simply, even though coinciding to some degree with dominant interests, the street-level behavior of police is not informed by reference to dominant values and interests nearly so much as to the exigencies of their unique position. While this line of reasoning parallels the situational approach, the social-psychological dynamics of police-minority interactions remain woefully underdeveloped in research that relies on situational explanations of police brutality. Here we undertake the task of developing a comprehensive account of the behavior.

Outline of an Alternative Theory

In developing a multifaceted social-psychological model, we begin by analyzing the properties of intergroup conflict. Relying on the seminal insights of scholars such as Georg Simmel (1908/1955) and George B. Vold (1958), we reason that humans are naturally group-involved organisms, and that group conflict is a fundamental form of human interaction. Groups are said to arise from common interests and needs that can be furthered most effectively by means of collective action. Conflict occurs when group interests encroach on one another, which produces perceived intergroup threat and solidifies ingroup cohesiveness. We demonstrate that the normative interests of minorities living in poor neighborhoods and the police who work those neighborhoods are fundamentally at odds. Yet while that argument provides an important first step toward better understanding police brutality, we question whether differing interests are sufficient or necessary to produce police brutality. The conflict approach highlights enlightened self-interest (Liska 1992), an assumption that appears at odds with the reality that police brutality may convey severe costs that far outweigh any benefits. After all, the police control the legitimate means of violence and need not resort to extra-legal force to protect themselves when confronted with danger.

Much of our argument, while recognizing the insights of the group-conflict approach, focuses on the conundrum posed by the seemingly irrational nature of police brutality. A more general theory must consider other dimensions of intergroup relations. We take into account contemporary theory and research on three additional social-psychological factors—social identity, stereotypes, and emotions—that produce intergroup tensions and solidify group memberships.

Social identity and stereotypes involve related cognitive processes that determine how people categorize and respond to ingroup and outgroup members. These processes do not require conscious deliberation and thus facilitate rapid responses to others. Research on social identity reveals that the mere perception of ingroup membership, even when the group is designated arbitrarily, may induce ingroup favoritism and concomitant outgroup discrimination (see Brewer and Brown 1998). This effect is most pronounced when group membership is salient. Policing is an all-encompassing occupation, and race/ethnicity likewise constitutes a deep-seated basis for social identity, which suggests that a source of intergroup bias other than shared interests exists. The closely related literature on information processing reveals that people rely heavily on stereotypes when responding to others. Stereotypes comprise cognitive categorizations that simplify the world and permit rapid responses in the face of complex and demanding social environments (see Fiske 1998). Pejorative stereotypes of outgroups generally consist of anecdotal exaggerations that predispose adverse behavioral responses to outgroup members. The police stereotypically perceive minority citizens as criminal threats, whereas minority citizens stereotype the police as authoritarian and racist. Social identity and stereotyping processes may heighten intergroup tensions well beyond those produced by the existence of any actual conflicts of interest.

Basic emotions such as fear and anger may play an even more fundamental role in fostering ingroup/outgroup distinctions and instigating violent behavioral responses to members of outgroups. Until relatively recently, social psychologists have given short shrift to the power of emotions, instead giving primacy to cognitive processes and assuming that emotions arise from conscious appraisals of experience (see LeDoux 1996; Zajonc 1998). It is becoming increasingly apparent that emotional responses need not rely on cognitive processes. Conversely, cognitions are always "tagged" with emotions that influence behavioral responses. The challenging conditions of minority neighborhoods may arouse powerful emotional, as well as cognitive, responses among police and citizens alike, helping set the stage for violent encounters.

The independent but highly interrelated mental systems of emotion and cognition operate in parallel to produce intergroup behavior that seems at odds with mere self-interest. These cognitive and emotional bases of group life may elicit myriad behavioral responses, intergroup aggression representing but one manifestation. Completing the groundwork for our theory of police brutality, we examine two dominant theories of aggression—cognitive neoassociationism and social learning theory—to show how emotional and instrumental forms of aggression are influenced by intergroup dynamics (see Geen 1998). Consistent with our emphasis on the seemingly irrational quality of police brutality, research reveals that aggression often is triggered by unconscious emotional and cognitive responses to threatening stimuli. Conscious deliberation may or may not alter the course of events should immediate aggressive tendencies be tempered, depending on influences such as cognitive appraisals of emotions and beliefs about the deservedness of the target of aggression.

We culminate this theoretical overview by systematically integrating these social, emotional, and cognitive ingroup/outgroup dynamics into a model of police brutality. It identifies the social and psychological background conditions, targets, mental processes, motives, temporal sequences, and mediating factors that may interact to produce incidents of excessive force. While seemingly irrational acts of excessive force comprise the theoretical focus of the investigation, the analysis sheds light on the many less injurious forms of police misconduct directed toward minority citizens. The complexities revealed by the model also point to a key question: What are the prospects for reducing police-minority tensions via organizational change in police departments, the staple of policy recommendations to curb the problem? Our analysis suggests that excessive force involves inescapable social psychological processes that make it virtually inevitable in light of the difficult social conditions that exist in urban America. Organizational modifications may provide some laudable outcomes and are worth pursuing, but we maintain that simply altering police organizations will have relatively little palliative effect on the obdurate reciprocal antagonisms existing between police and racial/ethnic minorities. Acknowledging the mutual involvement of police and citizens in the production of the behavior implies neither blame for nor justification of it, only the recognition that complicated and unyielding influences are at work that are not resolvable through simple formulae. Real improvements in police-minority relations demand other avenues of change, ones that challenge existing social arrangements.

We conclude our work with an assessment of how meaningful change may occur, focusing on the structural roots of the problem. In so doing, we explore the broader implications of our analysis. For example, the increased spatial concentration of poor whites in urban neighborhoods raises questions about the influence of race versus class and whether the social-psychological dynamics outlined herein may operate with respect to cultural markers (e.g., speech, clothing, demeanor) more than physical ones (e.g., skin color). We consider the possibility that the increasing segregation of poor whites will make them more vulnerable to police abuses in the future. Another issue is the increasing racial and ethnic diversity of American society. We focus the analysis on the relatively large African American and Mexican-origin populations, because historically they have experienced profound discrimination and have been the primary targets of police brutality. Given America's changing racial and ethnic mosaic, we consider the implications of the theoretical model for the treatment of other minority groups at the hands of the police.

CHAPTER 2

Social Threat and Police Violence

A defining element of political states is the capacity to exercise force in conflicts with internal and external adversaries (Weber 1922/1968). The police visibly symbolize the coercive resources of domestic rule. In modern democracies, the state grants the police a virtual monopoly on coercive force to control internal law violators and dissidents who challenge existing social arrangements (Bittner 1970). While the coercive power of the police is hardly the only means employed by the state to ensure domestic tranquility, it is indispensable for the maintenance of social order. To the extent that social inequalities characterize a state, maintaining social order implies protecting arrangements that advantage some segments of society but disadvantage others.

The conflict theory of law contends that coercive crime control mechanisms expressly aim to regulate threats to the interests of the powerful (e.g., Turk 1969; Chambliss 2001). Privileged members of society benefit greatly from the existing social and economic order, whereas many other citizens, especially poor racial/ethnic minorities, experience profound disadvantages. Preservation of the differential reward structure demands exercising coercive power to control the threat posed by disadvantaged groups that have much to gain and little to lose (Jacobs and O'Brien 1998). Police-minority relations thus embody the social divisions, deeply rooted in the social structure, that separate dominants and subordinates. While policing may represent the legitimate interest of all citizens in controlling crime and its deleterious effects, empirical research provides considerable support for the argument that both the resources and the coercive strategies of policing are linked to the racial and ethnic makeup of communities (e.g., Jackson and Carroll 1981; Liska and Chamlin 1984; Liska, Chamlin, and Reed 1985; Liska and Yu 1992; Holmes 2000; Smith and Holmes 2003; Kent and Jacobs 2005; Holmes et al. 2008).

Although politically powerful citizens may exert considerable influence over the distribution of resources for policing by state and local government, they cannot directly dictate the street-level actions of police officers. Still, police authorities must remain cognizant of resource disadvantages that might befall an agency should influential citizens become displeased with the operational practices of the organization. Moreover, the powerful can exercise political influence and employ attorneys to defend their interests in the face of police action (Chambliss 2001). Thus rather than following the official policy of administering justice impartially in a value-free framework, police agencies substitute goals and implement policies that accommodate these organizational imperatives (Chambliss and Seidman 1971). The day-to-day operations of law enforcement agencies involve policies and practices that maximize rewards and minimize strains for the organization—it is organizationally expedient for police to refrain from processing the powerful and to focus on the powerless instead.

In this view, then, the differential mobilization of street-level coercive control reflects the organizational imperatives of policing, protecting dominant interests while simultaneously assuaging concern about minority crime. White citizens associate minorities with the threat of urban violence (Chiricos, Welch, and Gertz 2004), and authorities believe that racially dissimilar minority groups threaten the social order (Turk 1969; Chambliss 2001). Police violence may be seen as an essential means of maintaining social order, and privileged citizens avoid interfering with police methods that comport with their stereotypes of criminals and protect their interests (Jacobs and O'Brien 1998; Chambliss 2001). Given that police authorities and the dominant group perceive relatively large, impoverished minority populations as posing the greatest criminal threat, police violence is most commonly employed in cities with heavy concentrations of poor blacks and Hispanics (Jacobs and O'Brien 1998; Holmes 2000; Smith and Holmes 2003). The clandestine and extra-legal nature of police brutality provides a means of violence that can be employed against the powerless in situations where formal sanctions cannot be justified, giving it a unique niche in the coercive control arsenal of the police. Such practices do not ordinarily elicit close scrutiny by dominant group members, whose willingness to ignore the behavior of society's "dirty workers" helps explain why much official brutality remains concealed (see Hughes 1964).

Despite its apparent effectiveness, police brutality occurs relatively rarely in modern democracies. More extensive deployment would undermine the legitimacy of government. Yet the fear-provoking quality of police brutality may render it particularly effective. Even though its use remains hidden from the majority of citizens, the racial and ethnic minorities most affected by police brutality are acutely aware that they may be subjected to it at the whim of the police, knowledge that generates feelings of fear and hopelessness among the residents of impoverished minority neighborhoods. The impact of such extra-legal violence is illustrated poignantly in Richard Wright's (1945, 150–1) *Black Boy*, his compelling story of growing up in the Jim Crow South, which portrays the vicarious effect of lynching:

> The things that influenced my conduct as a Negro did not have to happen to me directly; I needed but to hear of them to feel their full effects in the deepest layers of my consciousness. Indeed, the white brutality that I had not seen was a more effective control of my behavior than that which I knew. The actual experience would have let me see the realistic outlines of what was really happening, but as long as it remained something terrible and yet remote, something whose horror and blood might descend upon me at any moment, I was compelled to give my entire imagination over to it, an act which blocked the springs of thought and feeling in me, creating a sense of distance between me and the world in which I lived.

Research on how minorities perceive the police likewise reveals that much is learned vicariously, not just through direct contact or actual observation (Brunson 2007). Attitudinal research shows that many more citizens claim to have heard of brutality than to have actually seen it, and that minority citizens in particular believe police brutality occurs (Weitzer and Tuch 2006). The sharing of atrocity tales about police brutality within minority communities undoubtedly distances citizens from the police and the larger society that the police are seen as representing. By isolating minority citizens psychologically, such stories facilitate preservation of the existing social order, even though severe police brutality may rarely be brought into play.

It might be reasonably surmised from this line of reasoning that police brutality implicitly defends the welfare of privileged whites. Certainly instances of its use would be challenged more vigorously if this were not true. Yet this argument suffers from inattention to the police as a distinct social group. Would the police risk employing brutality against powerless minorities purely because those citizens lack the political wherewithal to retaliate effectively and the powerful implicitly approve of using coercive controls against the allegedly dangerous elements of society? The interests of the police may not always coincide with those of the dominant group in the larger society, whose sensibilities may be shocked by police practices that overtly compromise their widely held belief in equal justice. Police misconduct may occasion serious legal ramifications for "deviant" officers. Unsurprisingly, police brutality frequently and deliberately occurs in situations that shield officers from detection, yet it always involves criminal behavior that may be detected and punished. These points raise important questions: Why would the police rely on coercive strategies that primarily benefit the dominant group while placing themselves at risk of legal sanctions? And why do they sometimes employ excessive force in situations that invite detection? How, then, can the traditional approach of the conflict theory of law explain the street-level behavior of the police?

In part, the answers to these questions may lie in a seemingly obvious observation. Coercive power used to control minorities not only protects the interest of dominants who fear the criminal threat allegedly posed by minorities, but it also protects police officers on the frontlines of America's racial divide. The salience of threats perceived directly by the police should figure prominently in their street-level behavior (Liska and Yu 1992; Holmes 2000). In contrast to the traditional argument of the conflict theory of law, this observation emphasizes that the police are not mere minions of the powerful. It downplays the role of the police as protectors of dominant group interests, instead portraying them as a unique social group with its own interests. By focusing on the police and minorities as distinct social groups with divergent interests, the alternative approach highlights the dynamic vitality of intergroup relations that has little to do with the wishes or interests of the powerful beyond their silent complicity in police misconduct. Such an argument does not imply that police behavior occurs without reference to community political influences, only that a complete picture of policing must also recognize that the police possess unique interests and the power to act on them independently of external constituencies. Nowhere is the validity of that observation more apparent than in the deployment of excessive force.

A historical analysis of policing in American cities reveals that both external and internal exigencies have influenced police behavior since the inception of the institution of public policing. The origins of public policing clearly reflect the interests of influential classes. At the same time, street-level policing has always been influenced by factors unrelated to external interests. Moreover, the history of the institution reveals an inexorable movement toward organizational independence from external demands and increased internal organizational cohesion within police agencies. In making this historical case, as well as in subsequent treatments of contemporary policing, we focus on urban areas as police brutality is a problem particularly in big-city policing (Holmes 2000). As we shall demonstrate, the spatial concentration of poor minorities in urban neighborhoods plays a key role in setting the stage for acts of excessive force.

Police Organization and
Police Violence in American History

Rural and small-town early America was characterized by a high degree of homogeneity and close relations among citizens (Walker 1998). Communities relied on personal relationships and family ties to establish informal systems of social control. Community members shared the obligation to monitor and protect others. But with the growth of towns and the development of cities, informal means of social control began to weaken as personal ties gave way to the impersonal relationships of city life. As society became increasingly anonymous, more formal means of policing were implemented. Still, early law enforcement duties were performed largely by common citizens who served as constables and night watchmen on a part-time and voluntary basis. The constabulary charged with carrying out law enforcement functions actually spent relatively little time controlling crime and social disorder. Civil duties held primacy over law enforcement because constables were often paid on fee schedules that provided more certain remuneration for services such as inspecting taverns and serving papers. Night-watch systems were designed to deal primarily with problems of nighttime disorder, such as fires and drunkenness. Male citizens typically shared a civil obligation to serve on the night watch. But lack of pay, combined with responsibilities to families and jobs, meant that many actively avoided service. Despite the prevalence of crime and disorder in American cities and the widely held belief that they were ineffective at resolving those problems, these loosely structured systems of social control persisted well into the nineteenth century.

Around that time, the acceleration of industrialization, urbanization, and immigration was radically changing the nature of life in American cities. Large influxes of immigrants resulted in increased racial and ethnic tensions as culturally and religiously diverse groups competed for scarce resources in densely populated neighborhoods. Historic animosities between ethnic and religious groups were transported to the United States and often erupted in urban violence. Large-scale disorder and riots were commonplace in the American cities of the mid-1800s (Lundman 1980; Walker 1998; Monkkonen 2002). The business elites and middle class of American cities increasingly feared for the stability of society (Silver 1967). They attributed the roots of social disorder to those commonly referred to as the "dangerous classes," which comprised the poor, ethnic immigrants, and blacks (Lundman 1980). Frequent reference was made to the threat posed by this "unmanageable, volatile, and convulsively criminal class at the base of society" (Silver 1967, 3). Elites' fear of riots and civil disorder, combined with their interest in protecting property, prompted the desire for a mechanism to control those seen as threats to the stability of society. Their fear of the dangerous classes was the major factor motivating the establishment of city police departments (Silver 1967; Hahn and Jefferies 2003).

Voluntary and part-time means of social control such as the night watch proved inadequate for responding to the perceived problems of urban disorder. The night watch of most towns was poorly organized and inadequately staffed (Langworthy and Travis 2003). The military, although capable of handling riots, responded slowly and risked inflaming ethnic and class tensions. Elites increasingly came to believe that a formal public institution backed by the coercive power of the state provided the best option for controlling large-scale disorder among the dangerous classes (Silver 1967). Urban elites, middle-class citizens, and business owners stood to benefit from the creation of a bureaucratic police system in a number of ways. Such a system could protect property and control the urban underclasses and at the same time shield the privileged from direct participation in social control. The new institution also would benefit the dominant classes by transferring the hostility of the dangerous classes to the police, who ostensibly served larger societal interests (Silver 1967; see also Lundman 1980; Hahn and Jefferies 2003).

Despite being "created by and for elites" (Lundman 1980, 31), the police were never an instrument monopolized by a single powerful faction; rather, they were a tool fought over by competing interest groups. Local political machines, often a product of immigrant neighborhoods, ensnared big-city police in the mid-1800s. Police officers were political appointees beholden to politicians for their positions, which were awarded through a system of patronage (Walker 1977). Early city police departments were geographically and administratively decentralized. Often this organizational structure intimately involved the police in local neighborhood affairs, where they could readily serve the politicians to whom they were beholden. Administratively, police chiefs were appointed to run departments, but in reality local politicians controlled precinct appointments, leaving chiefs with little practical power over officers on the beat (Fogelson 1977; Langworthy and Travis 2003).

Given that the police were a prize for whichever local political machine was in power, turnover was high (Monkkonen 2002). For example, in 1880, Cincinnati dismissed 219 of 295 members of its police department (Walker 1977). Policing was largely viewed as a temporary job rather than a career, and police officers frequently were recruited from the neighborhoods in which they would work. Requirements often were minimal, one needing only the right political connections or willingness to pay a fee to obtain a position. A new police officer was provided a club and badge but little or no training.

With little training and minimal supervision, police officers of the nineteenth and early twentieth centuries had considerable freedom in carrying out their duties. Indeed, many historians agree that early police officers spent a great deal of time avoiding their job responsibilities altogether (see, e.g., Haller 1976; Walker 1998). Nonetheless, police agencies provided a wide variety of services directly out of precinct houses, and police officers were expected to maintain a degree of order on their beats. Insofar as police were neighborhood based and heavily influenced by dominant local political powers, the type of policing that citizens received depended largely on the neighborhood in which they lived. The police "maintained a paternal surveillance" in ethnic neighborhoods, whereas in more affluent areas "police spared no effort or force to locate the culprit" of a crime (Hahn and Jefferies 2003, 8). Possessing little political influence, black neighborhoods were largely ignored. Police were not drawn from within those neighborhoods, and they paid scant attention to the needs of residents (Williams and Murphy 1990). In short, police activity reflected the racial and ethnic composition of neighborhoods. Police-citizen conflicts often had an ethnic or a racial character, the police sometimes representing one ethnic group over another (Walker 1998).

It is hardly surprising that controversy often surrounded policing in the nineteenth century (Walker 1998). Lack of training, minimal supervision, public hostility, and ethnic tensions compelled the police to rely heavily on personal authority to obtain compliance and respect. Brutality and corruption plagued urban police agencies. Citizens often complained about police clubbing people with nightsticks or blackjacks (Johnson 2003). For their part, citizens frequently challenged police authority, and officers resorted to brutality to establish control (Walker 1998).

Impetus for police reform began during the late nineteenth and early twentieth centuries, when public attention turned to various forms of police brutality and corruption. The National Commission on Law Observance and Enforcement, better known as the Wickersham Commission, issued a "scathing indictment of police brutality" (Walker 1998, 155). In addition, commentators of the day often complained about corruption within big-city police agencies (see, e.g., Johnson 2003). The red-light or vice districts of cities were often considered choice assignments, providing a steady source of payoff money for the police. They gladly accepted bribes from operators of illegal establishments to ignore the activities of patrons who did not seriously disrupt the public peace.

Middle-class, native-born whites became increasingly incensed by frequent corruption scandals and accounts of brutality, motivating a political movement to reform the police (Langworthy and Travis 2003). External reformers, however, were not the only ones interested in changing policing. Police administrators held accountable for the failures of their agencies, even though they had little control over precinct commanders or street-level police officers, began to look for a means to attain greater control and respect. The movement to reform city police departments evolved into a coalition of progressive outsiders and police insiders. Progressives sought to remove a powerful tool from political machines, and police administrators aimed to gain independence and control.

Reform of the police centered on narrowing organizational focus, increasing centralization and control, and upgrading personnel (Fogelson 1977). The police began to concentrate more on the enforcement of laws and the control of crime, moving away from maintaining order and providing services. The decentralized structure of early police organizations became more centralized, giving greater control to the police chief and weakening the power of local neighborhood commanders and the politicians who had appointed them. Changes in recruitment, selection, and training sought to make the police officer a professional. Civil service reforms, such as the use of examinations for hiring/promotion and upgraded entry requirements, ended patronage appointments and helped weed out unqualified applicants. New training programs prepared police recruits to perform their jobs. Greater supervision and methods of accountability aimed to ensure that officers carried out their duties appropriately while avoiding the temptations of corruption. In addition to these reforms, police departments adopted the latest technologies and business practices to ensure organizational efficiency (Uchida 2001).

The movement toward professionalism dramatically altered American policing. By the late 1950s, urban police departments had achieved a great deal more political autonomy. They had become centralized bureaucracies composed of police officers who viewed themselves as a distinct occupational group responsible for fighting crime, anonymous professionals impartially enforcing the law. Officers no longer came from their neighborhood beats. They now patrolled in cars, keeping in steady communication with supervisors through two-way radios. The police as we know them today had emerged.

Despite all the changes in the organization and technology of policing, a number of forces converged in the 1960s to call public attention to the police once again (Uchida 2001). Crime rates increased precipitously, despite the claim that professional police could control crime. In addition, police were called upon to deal with widespread civil unrest, including antiwar protests, civil rights protests, and race riots, which brought them into direct conflict with citizens. For example, police officers beat civil rights marchers and set dogs upon them. A shocked public saw such aggressive police responses to civil unrest reported in newspapers and on television. The National Advisory Commission on Civil Disorders (1968) charged that police actions and unequal justice sparked outbreaks of urban race riots. The commission reiterated a laundry list of the seemingly inexorable problems seen throughout the history of policing, including police brutality. The reforms of previous decades had hardly eliminated one of the most enduring and destructive problems of urban policing.

Ironically, an unintended by-product of the century of reform was the development of a distinct occupational subculture embodying the unique interests of the police (Uchida 2001). Whether appointed through patronage or civil service, the primary concern of the police has always been the challenges they face in their day-to-day work on the streets. While the new police professional no longer catered to local politicians, the problems of policing the "dangerous classes" remained virtually unchanged. Much of the street-level behavior of police still revolves around maintaining authority and identifying potential threats (Skolnick 1975; Crank 1998). Informal norms and policies frequently outweigh the departmental regulations and statutory codes that govern policing. These unofficial procedures are passed to new recruits through informal socialization on the job, not during the formal training of the police academy. Above all, the police subculture reflects the shared group interests of those responsible for protecting society from its wrongdoers. It is the existence of a powerful subculture with norms that form without reference to external constituencies or departmental policies that affirms the importance of understanding the street-level actions of officers as reflections of the unique circumstances they confront on the job. While other factors influence their behavior, the normative framework for action is located in the subculture.

Group-Conflict Theory

Clearly the traditional approach of conflict theory, emphasizing the role of policing in protecting the dominant classes, accurately describes the political demands implicated in the origins of policing. Undoubtedly, external political influences still determine the crime control capacity of police agencies via the processes for allocating public resources (e.g., Jackson and Carroll 1981; Kent and Jacobs 2005; Holmes et al. 2008). But the day-to-day behavior of the police on the streets is another matter entirely. There the dominant group played little direct role in controlling the police historically, an observation that is even truer today. Thus the traditional conflict theory of law is found wanting, particularly when applied to acts of excessive force that may incur significant costs for offending officers. An approach that better comprehends the complexities of group interests may contribute significantly to a more compelling account of such seemingly inexplicable behavior.

One variant of conflict theory may offer considerably more promise with respect to explaining the incidence of police brutality. Group-conflict theories hold that complex societies comprise numerous interest groups, and that conflict is an inevitable social process with predictable consequences for social organization and behavior. Rooted in the seminal work of Georg Simmel (1908/1955), this approach examines the causes and consequences of both intragroup and intergroup conflict. It has been recast in structural-functional terms (Coser 1956), applied to criminological issues (Vold 1958), and used to analyze race relations (Blumer 1958). Despite their nuances, the formulations all point to several dimensions of intergroup relations key to understanding police-minority relations.

The basic premise of the approach is that humans are fundamentally group-involved beings. People's lives are part and product of group affiliations, which provide the vehicle for collective (i.e., socially coordinated) action that aims to protect their shared interests (Vold 1958). The elemental principle of social organization is that groups form when people possess common interests and needs that can be best furthered through collective action. Intergroup conflict occurs when their interests overlap, encroach upon each other, or become competitive. Serious conflict between groups never takes place when their collective actions can be performed satisfactorily and their interests can be protected without moving in on one another's domain of common interests and purposes.

The social process of conflict generates far-reaching consequences for group affiliation and behavior. Notably, intergroup conflict serves as an integrative force in its own right (Simmel 1908/1955). Conflict enhances group identification and loyalty. Whereas group bonds derive originally from shared interests, conflicts with other groups possessing opposing or overlapping interests reinforce members' bonds to their own group. Even the mere perception of threat from another group, irrespective of its objective existence, may be sufficient to promote group cohesion (Coser 1956). Conflict also highlights the basic rights and duties of group members, and groups in conflict become intolerant of their members' deviations from group norms (Simmel 1908/1955).

Whenever members vest their identity in a group, conflict takes on an intransigent quality. Yet considering society in its totality, the group-conflict approach argues that intergroup conflicts tend to establish and maintain a balance of power (Coser 1956; Vold 1958). Only rarely does unbridled conflict take place, as even the most severe disputes (e.g., wars) give rise to regulatory norms. Adherence to common rules allows predictable outcomes and the calculation of likely consequences from warlike acts. At the same time, while an established balance of power emerges and stabilizes the social system, society always remains

a congerie of groups held together in a shifting but dynamic equi-
librium of opposing group interests and efforts. . . . The end result
is a more or less continuous struggle to maintain, or to defend,
the place of one's own group in the interaction of groups, always
with due attention to the possibility of improving its relative status position. (Vold 1958, 204)

In the shifting sands of group life, prospects for maintaining power and
status are generally enhanced by intergroup alliances (Simmel 1908/1955;
Coser 1956). Coalitions formed against a shared enemy may develop,
even when mutual antagonisms prohibit other forms of unification. Such
alliances may be quite minimal, however, representing nothing more than
an instrumental response to a common threat.

Group-conflict theories suppose that a considerable part of human
conflicts involve violent resolution, an observation that finds ample
support throughout history. One might reasonably inquire as to what
the causative psychological motivations underlying intergroup aggression, with its often grave costs, might be. Formulated at the structural
level, group-conflict theories pay scant attention to underlying psychological processes that produce aggression, either relying on relatively
simplistic assumptions or dismissing such processes altogether. For example, in a seminal synthesis of what he terms "realistic-group-conflict
theory," prominent social psychologist Donald T. Campbell (1965) eschewed the need for a specifically psychological theory of motivation to
explain intergroup conflict and its outcomes. In his view, individual psychological characteristics can no more explain these processes than physical properties of building stone can explain architectural styles. He
argues that intergroup conflict arises as a *collective* reaction to real
threats to group interests that elicit the psychological perception of
threat among individuals. Real threats and perceptions of threat are generally, albeit not necessarily, synonymous. Summarizing the various formulations of the group-conflict model, Campbell maintains that the
existence of real threats causes hostility to the source of the threat, ingroup solidarity, ingroup identity, tightened ingroup boundaries, punishment of ingroup defectors and deviants, and increased ethnocentrism.
An ancillary prediction of special significance to our analysis is that "the
strongest and most threatening outgroup should be the target of the
most ethnocentric hostility from an ingroup" (Campbell 1965, 292). In
this perspective, then, it is hardly surprising that members of America's
largest minority groups disproportionately become victims of excessive
force at the hands of the police who directly perceive minority threat
(Holmes 2000).

Clearly, a fundamental similarity between the traditional conflict theory of law and the group-conflict model is discernable. Both approaches conceptualize coercive police behaviors as instruments for controlling members of threatening outgroups. Their fundamental difference lies in the conceptualization of whose interests are being protected by coercive controls. The group-conflict model hardly dismisses the fundamental assumption of the conflict theory of law, that policing represents the interests of the powerful (see Vold 1958, 207–209), but it alters the image of the relationship between society's dominant group and the police, as well as between minorities and the police. Rather than depicting the police as subordinate to dominant imperatives, the group-conflict perspective suggests the presence of a more egalitarian, sometimes uneasy, alliance between police and dominants against the common threat allegedly posed by racial/ethnic minority groups. Tensions certainly exist between these ostensible allies, as the police do not get along well with the public generally (Skolnick 1975). For example, affluent white citizens commonly break certain laws (e.g., traffic violations) and express hostility toward those with authority to enforce them. Whereas the conflicts of interests between white citizens and the police are hardly as severe as those existing between them and minority groups, they are real nonetheless, suggesting the existence of a relatively unidimensional alliance. Above all, police and white citizens share popular stereotypes that conflate race and criminality and identify minorities as an appreciably greater mutual threat. By considering the police as an interest group in its own right, however, a more nuanced and sophisticated analysis of police behavior becomes possible. Fundamental questions for such an analysis concern the interests of police and minorities and how they frame the conflict between them. Thus, we ask: How and to what extent do the interests of police and minority groups conflict?

Police-Minority Conflict

Many residents of impoverished minority neighborhoods share the concern of the police with crime control and order maintenance. Yet many are dissatisfied with what they perceive as lackadaisical efforts by the police to address these problems (Barlow and Barlow 2000; Weitzer and Tuch 2006). Furthermore, the police mandate involves intrusive practices that infringe upon individual freedom. These conditions produce distrust and antagonism toward the police. For their part, the police must patrol dangerous minority neighborhoods, where they seek to resolve the immediate problems of crime control and order maintenance. While police engage in similar tasks regardless of jurisdiction, one should not mistake the job of policing poor minority neighborhoods with that of working in more affluent locales. Descriptions of policing often stress uniformity, frequently painting a picture that masks important variations in the atmosphere of police work in different neighborhoods. The police continually confront the potential for violent encounters and affronts to their authority in poor minority neighborhoods, challenges that are far less common in more affluent locales. Thus unique conflicts of interests and expectations frame interactions between police and citizens of impoverished minority neighborhoods.

To illustrate these arguments, we look to the ghettos of inner cities and the barrios of southwestern cities. Certainly problems of police-minority relations are not limited to America's black and Mexican-origin populations. That notwithstanding, the relationships between the police and the citizens of the ghetto and barrio are profoundly strained and clearly highlight the dynamics of intergroup conflict that may contribute to police brutality. Our research suggests that the citizens of those areas bear the brunt of police brutality, demonstrating that the incidence of civil rights criminal complaints alleging brutality in large cities is related positively to the percent of blacks, as well as to the percent of Hispanics in southwestern cities (Holmes 2000; Smith and Holmes 2003).[1]

The race riots of the 1960s and the more recent upheavals in Miami (1980, 1982, 1989), Los Angeles (1992), Cincinnati (2001), and Benton Harbor, Michigan (2003), provide poignant examples of the antagonisms existing between black citizens and the police. Civil disorders in the Southwest likewise reveal tensions between those of Mexican origin and the police. Undoubtedly the most prominent instance is the "zoot-suit riots" of 1943 Los Angeles. During a week of anti-Mexican violence, inspired by "public hysteria" over a rumored crime wave, American servicemen rampaged through the barrio (Escobar 1999). The police followed behind them, sometimes even joining the servicemen, arresting youths victimized in the attacks. Hundreds of Mexican youths were incarcerated. The servicemen instigated the disorder, but only a few were arrested. The media and public authorities attributed the violence to youth gangs and Mexican criminality, whereas barrio residents saw the hand of racism at work. Riots that occurred throughout the Southwest in the early 1970s, often in conjunction with the Chicano political movement, involved many of the same dynamics as the ghetto riots a few years earlier—persistent ethnic disadvantages and conflict with police seen as symbols of white power and racism (Morales 1972).

Without a doubt, the histories of America's African American and Mexican-origin populations reveal similar legacies of oppression. Both groups entered the United States involuntarily via force, both are physically and culturally different from the dominant society, both are relatively large, and both are economically dispossessed. The traditional conflict perspective describes their shared experiences in terms of "internal colonialism," a model that emphasizes the economic interests of the dominant group and the role of the police in subordinating potentially troublesome populations (see, e.g., Blauner 1972; Mirandé 1987). In this view, police brutality is simply another tool of oppression. Although we argue that the intergroup dynamics motivating police brutality are appreciably more complex than suggested by such an approach, the internal colonialism model identifies the historical roots of the difficult conditions found today in America's ghettos and barrios.

The Creation of the Ghetto

Nearly all of the black population of the United States can trace its ancestry to those who arrived from Africa via the slave trade (Massey 1993). Slaves provided essential labor to the plantation economy of the South. Until the turn of the twentieth century, the substantial majority of blacks remained in the rural South, enduring harsh tribulations under the Jim Crow system of legalized segregation that emerged in the aftermath of slavery. Ultimately, persistent patterns of subjugation and the mechanization of southern agricultural production pushed blacks to northern cities where their labor was increasingly in demand as industrialization escalated (Massey and Denton 1993). Between 1890 and 1970, black out-migration from the South created a largely urban population residing in non-southern cities. But life in the North hardly proved a panacea to the harsh conditions existing in the South. Blacks often were employed as strikebreakers, engendering lasting hostility between themselves and white workers. Rampant discrimination in labor and real estate markets concentrated blacks in impoverished ghettos. The riots of the 1960s, combined with the promise of the civil rights movement, led to a migration reversal starting in the 1970s, when blacks began moving back to the South. Still, one third of America's black population now lives in conditions of "hypersegregation" in the inner city, cut off from contact with the larger society and its culture, "among the most isolated people on earth" (Massey and Denton 1993, 77).

The social and cultural isolation of the black "underclass" generates crime, social disorder, and hostility toward white society (Wilson 1987; Skogan 1990; Massey and Denton 1993; Anderson 1999). The conditions of the ghetto, not the characteristics of the people living there, produce these deleterious outcomes. Structural economic changes and the exodus of relatively affluent blacks have worsened the desolation of urban black neighborhoods and eroded the social institutions, such as family and church, upon which social stability is built (Wilson 1987). Such dislocations have been described in terms of structural social disorganization and cultural social isolation, factors said to be the most important determinants of the relationship between race and crime (Sampson and Wilson 1995). Structural social disorganization refers to the interaction of macrosocial forces (e.g., segregation, economic transformation) and community-level characteristics (e.g., concentrated poverty, family disruption) impeding the realization of community values and social control. Cultural social isolation denotes separation from mainstream culture and the existence of value systems supportive of crime and deviance. While many ghetto citizens denounce the deviant behavior characteristic of inner-city neighborhoods, their children are commonly exposed to crime and violence and incorporate them into their "cognitive landscape" of appropriate conduct. Even the children of "decent" families, who are taught adherence to conventional values and lifestyles, must learn to survive on the streets by relying on interpersonal violence to secure respect and personal safety (Anderson 1999). Among "street" families, the most desperate and alienated of the inner city, crime and violence are part of everyday life. That such values emerge in the social isolation of the ghetto does not imply that they possess a "life of their own" and would persist in contexts other than areas of concentrated poverty (Sampson and Wilson 1995). Rather, they arise as a psychological defense mechanism in opposition to the collective and enduring experience of racial oppression (Massey and Denton 1993).

The Creation of the Barrio

The Hispanic population is more diverse than the black population, including people of various national origins who share some common ancestral connection to the Spanish settlement in the Americas (Massey 1993). Beyond that, considerable differences in physical characteristics, social class, timing of arrival, and history of discrimination exist. Among the various peoples making up the Hispanic population, those of Mexican origin (58.5%) far outnumber all others combined (Guzmán 2001). Although the Mexican-origin population is increasing throughout the United States, and large enclaves exist in other areas (e.g., Chicago), the vast majority of Mexicans reside in the Southwest, a region ceded to the United States in the aftermath of the U.S.-Mexico War.[2]

The Treaty of Guadalupe Hidalgo formally ended the war in 1848, hostilities that had been instigated by the United States. Apart from ceding the land now recognized as the American Southwest, the treaty contained certain provisions intended to protect Mexicans incorporated into the United States after the conquest of Mexico (Acuña 1988). Mexicans living in the Southwest had the option of emigrating to Mexico, but few did. Instead, they preferred to remain on what they rightfully considered their land. Their property and water rights were guaranteed under the treaty, guarantees that did not withstand the devices employed by Anglo (non-Hispanic white) settlers to circumvent their intent. A variety of legally dubious strategies, along with the imposition of American title standards, resulted in mass land transfers during the 1800s (Barrera 1979; Mirandé 1987; Acuña 1988). Mexicans displaced from their generations-old land grants became the backbone of an internal colonial labor system, subordinated to low-paying jobs in agriculture, ranching, mining, and railroad building. By the early 1920s, the displacement of Mexicans from their land and the burgeoning industrialization in the region were contributing to the urbanization of the Mexican population, concentrating it in impoverished and dilapidated barrios (Mirandé 1987; Acuña 1988; Escobar 1999). Discrimination in housing, labor, and education was rampant, creating profound poverty and lack of opportunity.

Today, the Mexican-origin people of the Southwest reside primarily in urban areas where they continue to experience significant segregation and economic disadvantage (see Alba and Nee 2003). While not rising to the level of hypersegregation experienced in many black neighborhoods, moderate to high levels of Mexican-Anglo segregation exist in most southwestern cities (Massey and Denton 1989). Yet compared to the ghetto, economic disadvantage may not be as severe in the barrio, and some have questioned whether a true "underclass" exists among those of Mexican origin (cf. Moore 1989; Massey 1993). Barrio residents certainly confront disadvantages, but conditions that foster social organization coexist. Barrio residents have a high rate of formal and informal labor force participation, albeit often in low-paying jobs, and a shared cultural legacy of language and religion that is constantly reinforced through ongoing immigration from Mexico (Martinez 2002). They thus may experience a higher degree of social integration compared to blacks in inner cities, which suggests that the adverse consequences of poverty would be less acute.

Perhaps the conditions of the contemporary barrio do not compare to the grinding poverty of the inner-city ghetto. Still, a large influx of poor immigrants from Mexico is continually moving into the barrios of the Southwest, which remain segregated enclaves of concentrated disadvantage (see Portes and Rumbaut 2001; Alba and Nee 2003). Cities such as El Paso (Holmes 2003) and San Antonio (Valdez 2006) contain large and profoundly impoverished barrios, and people throughout urban areas of the Southwest face many social problems. For example, central El Paso, located directly across the border from Ciudad Juárez, has a population density, poverty level, and crime rate that far exceed any other area in the city (Holmes 2003). The homicide rate in this and other such deeply impoverished barrios is higher than in more affluent neighborhoods (Martinez 2002). Moreover, drug markets have flourished in the barrios of San Antonio over the past several decades (Valdez 2006). The structural disadvantages and isolation of such neighborhoods may provide an ecological context that creates a link between ethnicity and violent crime, just as it does in impoverished black neighborhoods. Such conditions may explain the generally higher homicide rates of Latinos compared to whites in the United States (Phillips 2002). Overall, the severity of the Latino crime problem may be less acute than for blacks, but it is appreciably greater than commonly experienced in Anglo neighborhoods.

Policing Minority Neighborhoods

Citizens residing in poor African American and Mexican-origin neighborhoods may call on the police to resolve a variety of problems relating to crime and social disorder. Frequently they request help with service and minor disorder problems, issues that patrol officers see as less important than fighting crime (Van Maanen 1978b). Irrespective of how police view their problems, citizens want them handled effectively, fairly, and respectfully (Stoutland 2001). Yet police officers enter into encounters with citizens constrained by formal and informal guidelines regarding productivity and safety, issues significantly more pronounced in high-crime, minority neighborhoods, where police receive a larger number of calls for assistance.

Usually dispatched by radio to a location and provided with limited information, the first concern of police officers upon arrival at the scene is establishing control and ensuring their personal safety, especially in neighborhoods or circumstances they perceive as dangerous. Their immediate reactions to a situation often conflict with the expectations of citizens. Citizens may find themselves the target of suspicion as police officers attempt to determine the nature of the situation. Even those who summon the police may find themselves face down on the concrete until officers determine who is dangerous and who is in need of assistance. Only after they have taken charge of the situation do officers begin dealing with the problem at hand. Police concerns regarding safety unique to poor minority neighborhoods may thus set the stage for confrontational encounters with already distrustful citizens. They may take fewer and less aggressive protective measures in middle- and upper-income neighborhoods.

Urban police officers rarely spend much time and effort responding to citizen requests that do not involve serious crimes. Patrol is not intended to deal effectively with such calls but to ensure that officers can respond rapidly to major crimes in progress (Lundman 1980; Bayley 1994). While relatively rare, every police supervisor knows the consequences of failing to respond quickly with adequate resources to a major problem; patrol is a place to store reserve capacity for such occasions. Added to these pressures, the occupational culture places great value on patrol officers handling their share of calls and being available to back up fellow police officers (see Smith, Novak, and Frank 2001). Should something serious happen, officers do not want to be tied up with an "unimportant" call that slows their response. Patrol officers strive to resolve quickly the immediate problem at hand, quieting the noisy party or quelling the dispute, but rarely do they attempt to resolve persistent problems. In busier urban areas, calls may be handled hastily rather than with the care and attention that may be paid in other locales (Bayley 1994).

The conflicting interests of police officers and citizens of minority neighborhoods are evident in everyday encounters. Citizens want police to resolve their unique problems, sometimes long-standing ones of crime and disorder, with appropriate solicitude. Police officers desire to get their work done quickly, maintain ties with colleagues, and return home safely, concerns amplified by the conditions in minority neighborhoods, where call volumes may be higher and where police perceive greater threats to their personal safety.

Police-Minority Conflicts and Police Violence

We have seen that the lives of the police and minority citizens are characterized by different, often conflicting concerns about crime and its victims. To the police, minority attitudes and actions symbolize danger; therefore, the police pejoratively characterize and differentially respond to citizens of impoverished minority neighborhoods. Their "working personality" in such areas comprises cynicism, mistrust, and hostility (Skolnick 1975; see also Westley 1970; Anderson 1990). For their part, minority citizens distrust the police, whom they see as threatening representatives of an oppressive power structure (Chamlin 1989; Feagin 1991; Locke 1996; NAACP 1995). They may be antagonistic toward the police and even direct extra-legal violence against them, ranging from pummeling the police with any available object to lethal assault (Chamlin 1989; Chambliss 2001). The antagonism of minority citizens may, in turn, increase the severity of the informal and formal sanctions levied against them by the police (e.g., Smith 1986; Smith and Visher 1981). Given a climate of mutual distrust and threat, the mere presence and day-to-day visibility of minority citizens may amplify the risk perceived by the police and, consequently, their willingness to employ excessive force (Holmes 2000).

In light of the group-conflict model, it becomes clear that real threats perceived by officers may be a principal cause of police brutality. This theoretical approach is important, because it directly addresses the behavior of the police rather than treating them merely as political appendages of the dominant group. At the same time, it recognizes that racial/ethnic minorities constitute salient political groups whose interests in some degree oppose those of the police. This pattern of reciprocal antagonism is one key to the analysis developed here. The police and minority group members see one another as ongoing threats. While they pose real dangers to one another, perceptions of threat may be amplified appreciably beyond the bounds of objective reality. These subjective perceptions of danger reaffirm group identity and reinforce group cohesion, thus perpetuating conflictual intergroup relations. Interactions between group members may escalate to extra-legal violence because of real and perceived threats from both parties.

It is at this juncture, however, where we again confront the contradiction that drives our analysis. The group-conflict model assumes that humans are rational actors whose behaviors are motivated by enlightened self-interest. Thus the employment of excessive force again raises this difficult issue: Why would highly trained professional police, who have various means of legitimate force at their disposal, engage in behavior apparently at odds with their interests? The structural-level theory of group conflict, while in some respects making an important contribution to a more accurate understanding of police-minority relations, seems ill equipped to answer that question completely. Consider that the rules of engagement for the police are clearly defined (e.g., in codes of criminal procedure), and much of police training focuses on employing the means of violence within the limits of the law. The great majority of police behavior falls within prescribed limits. Nonetheless, egregious transgressions occur periodically. Perhaps these offenses represent altruistic expressions of group interests that take precedence over individual interests. Yet it is not clear why individuals would risk sacrificing themselves for some ostensible good of the group, even though the group may ultimately achieve primacy over its individual members. And it remains unclear that police brutality serves the group interests of the police, insofar as it poses potentially great costs to their legitimacy and status. Moreover, it is not at all apparent that the real conflicts of interests separating minorities and the police are sufficiently severe to provoke extra-legal violence. What strategic advantage accrues from the use of excessive force?

Another possibility is that most police brutality is not an expression of rational, self-interested behavior, at least not in the way postulated by group-conflict theory. In reality, "Such theory does not serve to explain many kinds of impulsive, irrational acts of a criminal nature that are quite unrelated to any battle between different interest groups in organized society" (Vold 1958, 219). While the exercise of excessive force is certainly related to group interests, those interests alone are not sufficient to explain the behavior. In light of this concern, we now part company with the assumption that complex individual psychological dynamics are unnecessary to explain intergroup conflicts. In recent years, the social psychology of intergroup relations and interpersonal aggression has developed around theory and research regarding the individual cognitive and emotional propensities of humans. Consideration of these developments in no way diminishes the important insights of the group-conflict model. As we have seen, that approach calls attention to the complexity of intergroup interests and dynamics lost in analyses that presume the hegemony of society's dominant group. Undoubtedly, it tells us a good deal about lesser abusive practices that widen the police arsenal of social control while conveying little risk. But other social-psychological theories of intergroup relations promise to advance considerably our understanding of the bonds between group members and the intergroup dynamics that produce extra-legal police behavior.

CHAPTER 3

═══

Social Identity and Ingroup Bias

We aim to develop a comprehensive explanation of the relationship between race/ethnicity and police brutality, which we conceptualize as a specific instance of the general class of phenomena comprising human aggression. Relying on various social-psychological perspectives, our analysis builds on theory and research concerning the dynamics of intergroup relations. One way social psychologists conceptualize the problem of intergroup relations involves different dimensions of category-based reactions to people. These include cognitive, affective, and behavioral components (Fiske 1998). As we proceed through our analysis of the relationship between race/ethnicity and police brutality, we seek to disentangle the connections among these elements of category-based reactions. Ultimately we seek to explain a discriminatory pattern of aggression, but it is impossible to do even a passable job without recourse to the cognitive and affective dimensions underlying the behavior. By treating those facets of the problem (e.g., racial stereotypes) merely as by-products of historical patterns of discrimination, explanations of police brutality based on sociological conflict theories have failed to comprehend fully the intricacies of intergroup bias underlying the behavior. Our approach certainly does not ignore the emergent properties of social organization that constitute the theoretical focus of macro-level theories such as the group-conflict model. At the same time, we see considerable value in the insights of micro-level perspectives that identify human mental characteristics implicated in the production of aggression.

The social-psychological approach we develop here assumes that humans' category-based responses to others are deeply rooted in the structures and processes of the brain. Nonetheless, whereas some basic mental processes that influence intergroup relations appear to operate universally among humans, a highly plastic brain capable of acquiring and using information from the environment bestows tremendous advantages for dealing with the diverse, complex environments humans inhabit. Humans may come inherently prepared to learn some things more easily than others, but their behavior is highly malleable and heavily influenced by information acquired from the environment via social learning (Machalek and Martin 2004). For example, stereotyping appears to be a universal cognitive means of rapidly categorizing and responding to others, but particulars of myriad stereotypes are encoded in specific cultural milieus and inculcated in individuals via processes of socialization (Fiske 1998). Individual and collective intergroup behavior involves a complex interplay of ordinary psychological processes and the social contexts that drive them. An understanding of how psychological processes influence police brutality thus demands consideration of both the psychological phenomena and the social environments that shape the lives of police and minority citizens.

Cognitive Perspectives on Intergroup Relations

The social psychology of intergroup relations emerged in the aftermath of World War II (Brewer and Brown 1998). Over the past half century or so, social psychologists have increasingly moved away from purely individual explanations of intergroup bias to focus on group-level phenomena that express underlying human psychological propensities. That is, intergroup behavior may possess superordinate properties irreducible to interpersonal behavior but explicable in terms of individual psychological processes (Turner 1982). This line of reasoning relies on the fundamental conceptual distinction between ingroups and outgroups originally articulated by sociologist William Graham Sumner (1906), who argued that ethnocentrism—ingroup attachment and preference over outgroups— is a universal characteristic of human life. The social-psychological offshoot of Sumner's argument, that humans cognitively categorize their social world in terms of ingroup/outgroup memberships and act on the basis of those categorizations, is now taken for granted among intergroup relations researchers (Brewer and Brown 1998). As we shall see, work using this cognitive approach reveals that intergroup tensions involve far more than just realistic conflicts of interest.

A number of theoretical milestones from the early period of intergroup relations research influenced the emerging emphasis on groups, but Gordon W. Allport's (1954) classic, *The Nature of Prejudice*, provides the foundation for much of the later work in the cognitive tradition (Fiske 1998). Allport argued that generalization and hostility are universal characteristics of the human mind. In regard to the former, categorization is necessary in human life, providing the basis for orderly living. Humans must rely upon mental categories to handle efficiently the vast number of events they encounter daily. Mental categorizations simplify the world through coarse overgeneralizations, enabling quick responses to the various situations people routinely confront. But humans are highly prone to erroneous generalizations, with irrational categories (i.e., those lacking empirical validity) forming just as easily as rational ones. People selectively admit new evidence, usually that which supports existing categories. Contradictory evidence also may be admitted as an exception that does not require modifying the existing generalization. To varying degrees, the mental categories that people form have feelings associated with them.

Ingroup categorizations are essential to human existence, which depends on living within groups. Allport maintained that by age five, children are capable of recognizing that they belong to various groups. The existence of ingroups implies the existence of outgroups, but the former holds psychological primacy. People's physical survival and psychological self-esteem demand ingroup partisanship and ethnocentrism. The presence of a threatening outgroup may strengthen ingroup bonds but is not a requisite for its existence.

The rejection of outgroups constitutes the hostile component of categorical thinking. Even the very young child, one only a few months old, may display anxiety over an approaching stranger. Symbols of difference become salient indicators that convey negative messages about outgroup members. Stereotypes comprise the exaggerated, fixed, and often derogatory beliefs that people attach to categories designated by sensory cues such as skin color. These beliefs require no basis in reality, though they may contain elements of truth. Support for stereotypes derives from the human tendency to select, accentuate, and interpret evidence in ways that simplify the world and leave existing beliefs intact.

Allport's analysis suggested that cognitions involving ingroups and outgroups are analytically separable, and, correspondingly, two distinct but closely related research traditions have developed (cf. Brewer and Brown 1998; Fiske 1998). One concerns the consequences of social identification with a group. That is, how does the recognition of belonging to a group affect behavior toward fellow group members and, secondarily, toward those seen as not belonging? Theories addressing these issues, which we discuss under the rubric of the *social identity model*, center on the creation and maintenance of social identity as part of the overall self-concept. Identification with an ingroup involves self-stereotyping, people's belief that they share characteristics representative of the ingroup, and produces favoritism toward the ingroup. The other tradition focuses on the negative perceptions of outgroup members held by members of an ingroup. How do people cognitively distinguish among various other types of people, and how do their cognitions bias behavior toward outgroup members? Theories that address these questions, which we discuss under the rubric of the *information processing model*, focus on stereotypes that derogate the members of particular outgroups. Stereotypes of outgroup members generally highlight the negative characteristics thought to characterize a category of people and tend to bias behavior against members of the category.

These are analytically separable questions that we will examine in this chapter and the next, but work on these issues is linked closely by reliance on the ideas of cognitive social psychology, and both are essential to describing intergroup behavior (Schaller, Rosell, and Asp 1998). Each approach assumes that social categorization involves stereotype-based interpretations of and reactions to group members that minimize perceived ingroup differences and exaggerate perceived outgroup differences (e.g., Taylor 1981; Turner et al. 1987). They highlight ordinary cognitive processes of social categorization driven by social context rather than by individual psychological variations (Fiske 1998). The complementary approaches allow a more in-depth understanding of taken-for-granted insights about police-minority relations, such as the "us-versus-them" mentality of the police (Skolnick and Fyfe 1993) and the existence of "symbolic assailants" in the working personality of the police (Skolnick 1975). Such knowledge promises to contribute to a more comprehensive explanation of why the police periodically employ excessive force that serves no apparent self-interest.

The Social Identity Model

Each individual possesses a self-concept comprising the psychological processes and cognitive structures that define her or him. Cognitions concerning the self fall into two large classes. One subset includes personal or individual attributes, such as physical characteristics, intellectual concerns, and personal tastes. The other comprises memberships in various social groups, such as political affiliation, ethnic background, and occupation. The social identity model defines the sum totals of the two subsets as personal and social identity, respectively, and hypothesizes that the self-concept constitutes a relatively enduring, multidimensional cognitive system that fosters the perception of unity and consistency among highly differentiated parts (Turner 1982). In any given situation, different parts (personal or social) may operate, depending upon which is most relevant to the circumstances at hand. Personal identity may fully determine some interactions between two or more individuals, whereas social identity may completely dominate other interactions (Tajfel and Turner 1979). When cognitive functioning shifts from personal to social identity, a corresponding shift from interpersonal to intergroup behavior occurs (Turner 1982). Thus the cognitive mechanism of social identity is said to underlie intergroup behavior.

Two fundamental questions arise from this conceptualization of social identity. Under what circumstances is social identity relevant? That is, when do people act as group members rather than as individuals? And how does social identity influence behavior toward ingroup and outgroup members? In particular, why do we favor ingroup members and, concomitantly, discriminate against those in outgroups?

Early empirical insights into these questions come from the field studies of intergroup conflict by Muzafer Sherif and colleagues (Sherif 1967), which were important precursors to subsequent work employing the social identity model (Turner et al. 1987). Three experiments were conducted between 1949 and 1954, at different locations in the United States. The participants in the studies were eleven-to-twelve-year-old white, middle-class boys attending ostensibly normal summer camps. The researchers posed as camp authorities, and camp activities comprised experimental manipulations designed to test various hypotheses about group formation and intergroup conflict. In the first phase of each study, camp-wide activities and living arrangements allowed the development of normal friendships between the boys. Then the boys were divided into two groups, which resided in separate dormitories and participated in separate activities. The groupings created in this second phase intentionally split up the spontaneous friendships that had developed among the boys. Assigned activities and work duties required cooperation within the groups, which led to strong intragroup bonds. Friendships realigned, most (about 90%) now coming from within the boys' experimentally created ingroups.

The third phase is of special interest here. It involved intergroup competitions in which the winners received prizes. Initially the between-group rivalries were friendly, but they rapidly became overtly hostile. Perceptions of outgroup members included negative attitudes and stereotypes, whereas heightened solidarity and pride existed within the groups. In the final phase, only included in the last study, the groups were given a series of goals unachievable by the efforts of either alone, demanding intergroup collaboration. The cooperation necessary to achieve those goals broke down intergroup hostility and fostered positive bonds between the groups.

Findings from this program of research provide considerable support for the realistic-group-conflict model (see, e.g., Campbell 1965), and they remind us of the important role of conflicts of interest in determining intergroup discrimination. Yet subsequent studies building on this research tradition reveal that realistic conflicts of interest are not necessary for the phenomena of social categorization, group formation, and intergroup discrimination to take place. The early studies of Henri Tajfel and his colleagues (Tajfel 1970; Tajfel, Billing, Bundy, and Flament 1971) added to the emerging paradigm of intergroup psychology by investigating the minimal conditions necessary for intergroup discrimination to occur. Intending to build on a skeletal baseline condition for group categorization, the researchers created groups ostensibly using a trivial criterion. In reality, they randomly assigned the participants to groups stripped bare of normal characteristics, including face-to-face interaction, norms, and intergroup relationships. Participants were asked to make private decisions in tasks requiring that they award money to others identified only by a personal code and group membership. Unexpectedly, discrimination favoring the ingroup occurred in this minimal group setting, in which the groups existed merely as cognitive categories and nothing more.

Subsequent research employing this *minimal group paradigm* provides a robust body of evidence that clearly contradicts the assumptions of the realistic-group-conflict perspective (Brewer and Brown 1998). In the absence of objective conflicts of interest or prior intergroup competition, the mere perception of group membership, even when designated arbitrarily, may be sufficient to produce biased judgments and discrimination. Moreover, research using the minimal group paradigm shows that intergroup bias results from ingroup favoritism rather than outgroup derogation. That is, the disadvantages experienced by outgroup members are ancillary to the favoritism shown to ingroup members. What could motivate such behavior?

One possibility is that the tendency to evaluate the ingroup positively derives from the need for positive self-esteem or positive social identity (Tajfel and Turner 1979). Positive comparisons of the ingroup to an outgroup increase subjective status and prestige, motivating individuals to identify and enhance the positive distinctiveness of the ingroup. In other words, the perception of one's group as superior implies that the individual is superior as well, motivating people to make invidious distinctions between groups. Low ingroup distinctiveness threatens social identity, and ingroup members strive to differentiate themselves from similar comparison groups. Thus simply perceiving oneself as a member of a social category may be sufficient to produce ingroup favoritism.

By way of illustration, consider social fraternities on college campuses. While they generally comprise organizationally and socially similar groups, students who are members of different fraternities may see themselves as distinct from each other, espousing the superiority of their fraternity and showing considerable ingroup favoritism in their behavior. Members define each other as brothers, and secret rituals set them apart from other fraternities. Here we see clearly how a need for positive self-identity might create a measure of intergroup bias, even when the ingroup and outgroup share similar social characteristics and interests.

Perceived differences between more dissimilar groups also may produce intergroup bias and conflict in the absence of competing interests. Extending this line of reasoning to the development of a more general theory of self-categorization, John C. Turner and colleagues (1987) maintain that intergroup dynamics involving social identity occur whenever group memberships are salient and group comparisons are made. Building on several conceptualizations of category formation, self-categorization theory articulates the *principle of meta-contrast*. It stipulates that in any situation involving a clear-cut set of psychologically important stimuli, a collection of stimuli will more likely be categorized as an entity when the differences on important dimensions of comparison *within* that class of stimuli are perceived as less than the differences *between* that class and other classes of stimuli that are present. In situations where salient social categorizations involve group comparisons, people tend to perceive greater homogeneity within categories (social groups) as the average perceived between-category differences on relevant dimensions of comparison increases. This meta-contrast ratio is defined as the mean perceived intercategory difference over the mean perceived intracategory difference. Heightened meta-contrast gives rise to the process of depersonalization or self-stereotyping, whereby individuals perceive themselves more as undifferentiated, interchangeable parts of a group and less as unique persons characterized primarily by individual differences. In other words, social identity becomes paramount.

Perceived ingroup similarity enhances elements of group cohesiveness—mutual attraction, esteem, empathy, and cooperation—among members of the ingroup (Turner et al. 1987). A corollary of ingroup cohesiveness is the existence of ethnocentrism, or the attraction to and positive value placed on the ingroup in comparison to relevant outgroups. Ethnocentrism forms the basis of positive self-identity and ingroup favoritism. In contrast to theories that postulate the role of interests in group formation, self-categorization theory views "ingroup identification as an adaptive social-cognitive process" that creates pro-social relations among humans, impelling them to operate as group members rather than as unique individuals unfettered by the demands of group life (Turner et al. 1987, 67).

The applicability of this theory includes both the emergence of groups based on spontaneous social categorizations in immediate situations and the large-scale, preexisting social groups that individuals internalize into their social identity when they become members (Turner et al. 1987). Translating this line of reasoning into terms of existing social groups, the upshot of self-categorization processes is that (1) the more people perceive that factors such as race or occupation differentiate two collectivities of people, (2) the greater will be the perceived contrast between members of the two groups, (3) the more the self- and other-categorization will be used by members of the groups, and (4) the greater the likelihood of category-based reactions, namely, ingroup favoritism and concomitant intergroup discrimination. Examining police-minority relations using this argument, we begin with a consideration of the occupation-based self categorizations employed by police officers and the race/ethnicity-based self categorizations used by minority citizens. As we shall see, police occupational identity and racial/ethnic identity are quite different, hence salient, when perceived in relation to one another.

Social Identity and Policing

Observers of the police frequently note that police officers are uniquely bonded to one another, sharing common beliefs and attitudes about themselves, their work, and those they police. Indeed, the police themselves acknowledge their distinctiveness from the public and the strong bonds they share with one another (Van Maanen 1978b). The strength of this bond is illustrated by the terms used to describe the police—clannish, brotherhood, and family—expressions the police often apply to themselves. This is not to suggest that all police everywhere are the same. They are not. Unique cultures develop in different departments and even within departments. Yet cops everywhere share some common views and beliefs (Crank 1998). Different aspects of the occupational culture may be more pronounced in certain agencies, particularly those in larger cities, but many core themes characterize American policing. Despite variations across and within agencies, the occupational culture of big-city police patrol officers is pivotal to explaining police behavior. It may be the most distinct occupational culture in modern American society.[1]

Early scholars portrayed the culture of policing in terms of a closed society. Many features were seen as central to the occupational culture of police patrol officers: solidarity and group loyalty; isolation from the public; suspiciousness and secrecy; intense concern with danger and personal safety; a singular focus on crime fighting; and a pronounced tendency to stereotype citizens (see, e.g., Westley 1970; Van Maanen 1974, 1978a; Skolnick 1975; Crank 1998). Above all, police officers show an unusually high degree of group solidarity and group loyalty. In addition to the time they spend together at work, officers socialize extensively with one another outside of work (Skolnick and Fyfe 1993). They generally rely on one another, rather than on civilians, for friendships and support. In comparison to other occupations, police officers are highly active in fraternal organizations (Skolnick 1975).

Police look out for one another in many ways. For example, their loyalty to the group manifests itself in traffic stops of off-duty police officers, handling of citizen complaints, and the ritual of police funerals. Police officers may rarely ticket fellow officers, except for very serious violations. A particularly controversial norm involves police officers protecting or covering for one another when faced with citizen complaints or other rule violations, a practice labeled as the "blue wall of silence" or "code of secrecy" (Skolnick and Fyfe 1993; Crank 1998; Kappeler, Sluder, and Alpert 1998). The code of secrecy personifies the group loyalty that exists among officers. Police funerals publicly display the loyalty and solidarity of the group (Crank 1998). These highly ceremonial events may attract thousands of police officers wholly unconnected to the deceased, often from other departments and even other states. Police officers sense that they belong to something special, and they share a bond that only other police officers can fully understand.

An "us-them" worldview highlights the bonds of group solidarity (Skolnick and Fyfe 1993). Police often believe that they are misunderstood and unappreciated by the public. They divide the world into two camps—fellow officers who can be trusted, and all others who cannot (Van Maanen 1978a; Kappeler, Sluder, and Alpert 1998). Their worldview strongly emphasizes suspicion of outsiders, secrecy, and negative attitudes toward outgroups, including the public and police administrators. In the extreme, the police believe that most of society is against them. The belief system promotes social isolation and feelings of distinctiveness (Kappeler, Sluder, and Alpert 1998).

Suspiciousness and concomitant secrecy comprise two oft-noted attributes of the police (Westley 1970; Van Maanen 1978b; Skolnick and Fyfe 1993; Crank 1998; Kappeler, Sluder, and Alpert 1998). Police are suspicious of those they encounter on the job (suspects, witnesses), but their mistrust extends to all citizens, as well as police supervisors and the media. For example, while working as a researcher observing patrol officers, one of the authors was present during the telling of a story clearly meant to warn fellow officers about outsiders. According to the story, a previous observer/intern from a university complained about an officer, who was subsequently fired and sued. The story had a clear message that could not possibly have been lost on anyone present: Don't trust this guy! This observer, like the previous "outsider," may cause problems. Officers remain circumspect and reserved—trust and rapport with outsiders develop slowly.

Scholarship on the police occupational culture consistently stresses the value police place on crime fighting (Lundman 1980; Van Maanen 1974, 1978a, 1978b; Westley 1953). The occupational culture, along with organizational rewards and training, creates and continually reinforces the image of police as crime fighters, an image that completely ignores the more time-consuming but pedestrian aspects of the job. Police organizations, and hence officers, are evaluated based on crime rates and other quantitative measures related to law enforcement, including number of arrests, number of tickets, and amount of drugs seized. Police organizations spend a great deal of time and resources training police to handle such law-enforcement-related matters, and officers receive formal and informal rewards for "big" arrests. They receive nominal rewards for handling more routine problems; indeed, no record may exist of a more routine encounter or its resolution. The enforcement of laws and crime fighting not only provide officers with tangible rewards, but they also derive personal satisfaction and esteem from catching criminals. Other aspects of the job are not viewed as "real" police work (Van Maanen 1978b).

The culture of policing not only provides a perspective on citizens and police work, it also imparts an occupational self-concept (Kappeler, Sluder, and Alpert 1998). Policing bestows a heroic self-perception (Van Maanen 1978a). Officers see themselves as critically important to safeguarding society, a force for good, a "thin blue line" between anarchy and civil order. They protect good and decent people against the dangerous, predatory, and evil in society. Defining their work as inherently moral and themselves as warriors against evil, a sense of mission is cultivated among officers. Policing is more than just a job—it is a social imperative (Skolnick and Fyfe 1993; Herbert 1998; Kappeler, Sluder, and Alpert 1998).

The working environment of the police undoubtedly fosters a strong occupational identity, but understanding police culture and identity also requires attention to certain aspects of the quasimilitary bureaucratic structure of large police departments, including formal and informal methods of training and socialization. The process of occupational socialization begins in a police academy, where recruits are introduced to their new role (Van Maanen 1973). The quasimilitary training academies of many departments encourage recruits to work together and think of themselves as a group, promoting solidarity from the outset (Lundman 1980). Myriad rules and their inconsistent enforcement produce cooperation and cohesion. The sheer number of them makes it impossible for recruits to avoid all violations, encouraging them to join together to avoid mistakes and punishment. As a consequence, police recruits develop a sense of solidarity and an us-versus-them mentality early on (Lundman 1980; Van Maanen 1973).

Academy training disproportionately focuses on crime fighting and law enforcement. Recruits spend a great deal of time learning about laws and methods of arrest. Formal instruction highlights the inherent dangers of the job through extensive weapons and self-defense training that includes scenarios and warnings explicitly portraying various threats (Crank 1998). Reinforcing the formal skills training are war stories that convey the themes of danger, distrust of outsiders, and secrecy. Such stories provide concrete, "real-life" examples of how different types of situations were handled by others, thus imparting practical advice on handling threats. Formally and informally, police academy instruction exaggerates the dangers of policing and may misinform recruits about the actual threats that they will confront on the streets (Kappeler, Sluder, and Alpert 1998). Training that emphasizes danger, suspicion, and distrust of outsiders, along with recruits' reaction to extensive rules, further germinates the us-versus-them culture of policing (Lundman 1980; see also Kappeler, Sluder, and Alpert 1998).[2]

On the street, most new police officers discover a rather different reality than what they anticipated. Field-training officers pass on the informal norms of the police subculture to each new generation of recruits. But much like the academy experience, new officers confront a very rigid, control-oriented bureaucracy with numerous rules that seem to provide little useful direction while creating a minefield of potential disciplinary actions. The large number of rules, combined with the varied situations officers encounter, almost guarantees violations. The end result is that officers break rules, others know it, and all must cover for one another or risk exposing their own transgressions. Thus a strict code of silence regarding rule violations and a "cover-your-ass" mentality exist among patrol officers (Van Maanen 1973, 1974, 1978b). Officers learn that they can be punished for seemingly petty rule violations, and they become wary of everyone, as it is believed that anyone can create problems for them (Kappeler, Sluder, and Alpert 1998). The control-oriented military model of the police bureaucracy helps cultivate the occupational solidarity and the us-versus-them mentality that police officers share (Skolnick and Fyfe 1993; Van Maanen 1978b).

Even more than organizational factors, the nature of police work isolates police from citizens and fosters the occupational culture of policing. For example, new officers quickly discover that often odd work schedules render personal relationships outside policing problematic (Crank 1998; Langworthy and Travis 2003). Maintaining a police presence every hour of every day requires patrol officers to work nights, weekends, and holidays, times that most people spend with family and friends. Furthermore, many departments use rotating schedules, requiring officers to work one shift for a period of time (commonly one month) and then switch to another one. Outside friendships are difficult to establish and maintain. The easiest friendships to sustain are with other police officers who share rotating shifts and odd hours.

The most distinguishing feature of the police—coercive authority—also hinders interpersonal relationships with nonofficers. The power of the police often makes citizens uncomfortable, as both parties are well aware of their unequal relationship (Langworthy and Travis 2003). No matter how law abiding they may be, people are keenly aware that the police have the power to control their behavior, and thus they fear them. Few are entirely comfortable in their presence. For example, even when committing no traffic violations, most citizens become uneasy with a police car behind them. Police officers quickly learn that other drivers are afraid to pass a police car, even one traveling below the speed limit. Compounding the problem, police may not always obey the laws they enforce on the job. Aware of this fact, citizens often resent police authority (Skolnick 1975). In the end, most citizens only want the police around when they really need them.

Off-duty interactions with the public are problematic given that police authority exists with or without the uniform (Skolnick 1975). Consider the predicament that police may face at social gatherings. While charged with enforcing laws related to public morality (e.g., public intoxication and driving under the influence), they too may wish to drink alcohol at social gatherings. They are aware, however, that citizens watch them and know that they may be held to a higher standard of conduct. Will they be accused of hypocrisy if they have a few drinks and drive home? The fear of censure makes social gatherings awkward. Police find solace in the company of other officers, where such issues do not arise.

Police officers develop many work-related traits that also strain relations with citizens, furthering their social isolation. For example, they are taught to be suspicious (Crank 1998; Skolnick 1975; Skolnick and Fyfe 1993). In many situations, police must sort through the details of incidents as recounted by citizens, some of whom have good reason to distort their accounts. Even law-abiding citizens may portray events to police in a manner slanted to produce a desired outcome (Goldstein 1977). Police come to believe that virtually all citizens try to deceive them, perhaps an assumption with some merit. Their suspicion is frequently apparent to citizens, who may be offended by the implication that they are untruthful (Crank 1998). The problematic qualities of police-citizen interactions amplify the isolation and distrust felt by police.

Social isolation, an us-versus-them outlook, and a pervasive sense of danger cultivate a remarkably strong bond among police officers. The belief that only other police officers can be trusted encourages a degree of secrecy foreign to other occupations. The focus on crime fighting and danger encourages officers to maintain an edge at all times, further isolating officers from the public and encouraging stereotypic perceptions of fellow officers and citizens. The police see themselves as members of an exclusive club, separate from and better than ordinary citizens (Bonifacio 1991; see also Van Maanen 1973; Crank 1998; Langworthy and Travis 2003). With its sense of mission and strong ingroup solidarity, police work provides officers with more than a job—it is the core of their identity (Skolnick and Fyfe 1993). "The day the new recruit steps through the doors of a police academy, he leaves society behind to enter a 'profession' that does more than give him a job; it defines who he is. For all the years that he remains . . . he will be a cop" (Ahern 1972, 3).

Racial and Ethnic Identity

Peoples' social identities generally tend toward complexity, involving multiple group memberships. Social identity is fluid, and various identities may come into play at different times. Which identity is salient depends on the situation and the characteristics of the people with whom one is interacting. Occupations clearly provide one basis for social identity but rarely one that envelops the individual so completely as policing. Religious and political memberships are relevant in some situations. Social class also is an important point of reference. Social categorizations based on occupation, religion, political partisanship, or social class often are not so openly displayed or situationally relevant as racial and ethnic identities, which may be more clearly visible and salient across a range of social settings. Still, racial and ethnic identities comprise dynamic, multidimensional categorizations (Phinney 1990). They may incorporate cultural, political, religious, familial, class, and national orientations that build complexity into group categorization. They often include various nuances that are contingent on audience, the social group that is providing the standard of comparison (Daudistel, Hosch, Holmes, and Graves 1999). Even so, race/ethnicity provides a prominent starting point for categorizing self and others, one that poses a special problem for positive social identity among members of groups with low social status (see Phinney 1990).

Our discussion of the impoverished conditions of black ghettos and Mexican-origin barrios highlighted shared aspects of their histories, aspects that also are germane to the development of their respective social identities. Their contemporary experience with segregation and employment in urban areas can be traced to migration patterns that shifted populations from rural, agrarian locales to urban, industrialized ones. Presumably, exposure to different kinds of people in cities could break down parochial ties fostered by the relative social isolation of rural life, creating an amalgamation in which various ethnic identities dissolve as immigrants assimilate into the dominant culture and its institutions (see, e.g., Gordon 1964). Yet such a process hardly describes the experiences of those who are physically distinct, who initially entered the United States involuntarily, and who provide cheap labor, in short, the most oppressed peoples in America (e.g., Blauner 1972; Barrera 1979). Deliberately segregated from the larger society by a range of discriminatory machinations (see, e.g., Massey and Denton 1993), these groups have not been permitted (nor do they necessarily desire) full assimilation. Moreover, the conditions of urban life may activate and magnify their racial and ethnic identities and boundaries (Nagel and Olzak 1982). Ethnic affiliations ease the difficulties that confront in-migrants to the city; ethnic differences provide a basis for organizational development in urban areas; and urban labor markets are often divided along ethnic lines. Even European Americans, many of whom now have pan-ethnic identities, retain distinct ethnic enclaves in many cities. The segregation of the black and Mexican-origin populations is far more extensive, their racial and ethnic memories far more cohesive.

Social Identity in the Ghetto

We have seen that industrialization in the North provided a stimulus for the in-migration of blacks from the rural South (Massey and Denton 1993). As blacks left the South, they relied on their established predecessors for assistance in finding jobs and housing in northern cities. Deeply troubled by the arrival of large numbers of rural blacks, whites were not so welcoming. Middle-class whites found blacks' appearance and demeanor coarse and repugnant, whereas working-class whites saw them as economic competitors. Earlier patterns of black-white integration in the North began to give way to racial segregation and antagonism during the early 1900s. Blacks became victims of willful discrimination in labor and real estate markets, and they were targets of intense racial violence paralleling what they had experienced in the South. By the 1970s, black segregation was deeply entrenched in the inner city, and the subsequent out-migration of more affluent blacks established an underclass that rarely interacts with people of other racial or social-class backgrounds (Wilson 1987).

The harsh conditions of ghettos, where opportunities for education and employment are in short supply, make it difficult to abide by societal values concerning work and family (Massey and Denton 1993). An alternative system of social status and values has emerged in the ghetto, one that is defined in opposition to values of the broader society, one that values lifestyles seen as deviant by the larger society. This *oppositional identity*, a sense of collective identity or peoplehood that overtly repudiates the social values of the dominant group, commonly develops as a psychological defense mechanism against the rejection of the larger society whenever a minority group experiences systematic subordination. Black street culture thus legitimates behaviors commonplace in the ghettos, behaviors condemned by whites.

> This [oppositional] culture, especially among the young, gains strength and legitimacy by opposing the dominant society and its agents. But such opposition produces ever more alienation, and lines become hardened, polarities develop. And people, particularly young black males, become demonized. Those who experience contempt from society often cannot enjoy self-respect without dishing out contempt in return. (Anderson 1999, 318)

Most people living in inner-city neighborhoods poignantly sense their shared distance from the rest of America, but social identity varies among them. Certainly not all share an oppositional identity. Elijah Anderson (1999) describes their value orientations or codes as ranging from "decent" to "street," labels that residents use themselves to make evaluative judgments and to confer status. Individuals may adopt either identity, but decent families, who accept mainstream values, must still learn to adopt street culture to get by in public. Decent people learn to "code switch" as the situation dictates, allowing them to navigate the dangerous streets in which they reside. Children of the inner city have little choice but to come to grips with the harsh realities of the streets. No matter the values instilled at home or how protective their parents, all children must eventually mingle on the streets, and campaigning for respect there means learning to stand up for oneself, fighting when called upon for self-protection and self-respect. Conventional values about school success, hard work, and marriage often are rejected because they signify "acting white" and carry the risk of derogatory labeling, or worse. For their part, street people subscribe more wholeheartedly to deviant values and behaviors that are legitimated precisely by their opposition to those of the larger society. A sizable number of them engage in drug use and marketing, assaults, and robberies, among a laundry list of street crimes, activities certain to draw attention from the police.

Social Identity in the Barrio

Similar dynamics of urbanization and identity creation characterize the Mexican-origin barrios of the Southwest. During the early 1900s, as industrialization took hold and attracted Mexicans dispossessed of their rural lands, barrios burgeoned throughout southwestern cities. The conditions in these neighborhoods were generally appalling (see, e.g., Escobar 1999). Discrimination in employment and housing markets, combined with the attraction of familiar cultural traditions, concentrated urban in-migrants in those enclaves, as they do to this day.

A key difference between the black and Mexican experiences is ongoing immigration from country of origin (Massey 1993; Martinez 2002). Much of the American Southwest borders Mexico, a permeable international boundary that does little to impede migration in either direction—a large foreign-born population exists all along the border (Malone, Baluja, Costanzo, and Davis 2003). Employers in the region have always relied on cheap Mexican labor, more or less so depending on the vicissitudes of the economy, with workers often enduring substandard working conditions and various strategies of labor oppression (Barrera 1979; Montejano 1987; Acuña 1988). Despite the many disadvantages facing those of Mexican origin, their experiences also cultivate social integration (Martinez 2002). This population shares a common cultural legacy, notably the use of Spanish and the practice of Catholicism, cultural patterns continually reinforced by seg-regation and ongoing immigration. Proximity to the homeland and the ex-istence of a prominent Spanish-language media in the Southwest further buttress their cultural heritage. Many radio stations, television stations, and newspapers use Spanish exclusively.

The social identity of the Mexican-origin population in the South-west may have deep roots in a commonly shared and continually rein-forced traditional cultural legacy, one that clearly distinguishes Mexicans from the larger culture, but the impoverished conditions of barrio life also spawn elements of an oppositional identity. Prejudice and discrimi-nation by the dominant society may engender feelings of isolation and alienation and promote solidarity among younger members of this popu-lation in opposition to the discrimination experienced (Portes and Rum-baut 2001). The pachucos of Los Angeles during World War II exemplify the creation of an oppositional identity. Their distinctive argot, attire (the zoot suit), and lifestyle, "*la vida loca*," displayed their "hostility toward and scorn for white society" (Escobar 1999, 166). These were the Mexi-can-American youth most likely to engage in criminal and antisocial behavior. Relatively few became full-fledged pachucos, but many adoles-cents adopted at least some element of the distinguishing zoot-suit style of dress. This oppositional identity emerged among second-generation chil-dren of immigrants, a "phenomenon [that] resulted primarily from the racism, discrimination, and extreme poverty that people of Mexican de-scent faced in the southwestern United States" (Escobar 1999, 167). Today, this reactive process of social identity formation remains common among many second- and third-generation Chicano and *cholo* adoles-cents, leading them to reject values that signify "acting white" (Portes and Rumbaut 2001).

Social Identity and Police-Minority Relations

Clearly the occupation of policing and the lives of minority citizens engen-der quite different bases of social identity, spawning ethnocentric world-views and ingroup favoritism made explicable in terms of the social identity model. The occupational subculture of policing provides a barrier between the police and other segments of society. Militaristic uniforms and training clearly separate the police from the larger society. In big cities, much of their work takes place in impoverished minority neighborhoods, where the social identity of many citizens contrasts dramatically with that of the po-lice. An oppositional identity prevalent in the ghetto and barrio arises in re-sponse to discrimination and repudiates cultural conventions of white society, many of which the police are bound to uphold. Thus the contrast between police and minorities is stark, prompting the activation of social identity processes that will create ingroup cohesion and ethnocentrism in situations where they face one another. The principle of meta-contrast postulates that the more people see factors such as race and occupation differentiating two groups, the greater their perception of contrast between the groups and the more they rely on self- and other-categorizations (Turner et al. 1987). Category-based reactions that favor the ingroup and, concomitantly, discriminate against outgroup members become more likely. Even when no obvious conflict of interest is evident in a situation, the mere perception of ingroup similarity and outgroup dissimilarity may create discord any time the police and minority people interact with one another.

The intergroup conflict produced by social-identity processes may be amplified by various conditions characteristic of police and minority groups. Two related factors are commitment and threat (Ellemers, Spears, and Doosjie 2002). When people are highly committed to a group, the various responses specified by the social identity model are amplified. This condition applies rather uniformly to the police and in varying degrees to racial/ethnic minorities. However, those who acquire an oppositional identity appear committed to their deviant lifestyles. Threats to group status or moral values may further intensify cognitive, affective, and behavioral biases among highly committed group members, as they strive to reassert their group's reputed superiority. While the police challenge the values and status structure of street culture, those who live by street values contest the moral authority and social status of the police. The existence of group commitment and symbolic threat may amplify self-stereotyping, ingroup loyalty, and readiness for collective action among the police and minorities.

Intergroup bias also may be affected by group size, power, and status (Hewstone, Rubin, and Willis 2002) in ways that are readily apparent in police-minority relations. Groups in a numerical minority show more bias than do groups that constitute a numerical majority (Mullen, Brown, and Smith 1992). Moreover, numerical minorities with a high degree of power tend to demonstrate especially strong bias (Bouhris 1994; Sachdev and Bourhis 1991). The interaction of small group size and high group power may contribute significantly to the strong ingroup bias that exemplifies the subculture of policing. Minority populations of cities typically far outnumber the police numerically, and the coercive authority of the police, combined with their considerable firepower, makes them very powerful relative to the citizens of poor minority neighborhoods. On the other hand, members of low-status groups may exhibit greater bias when status differentials are seen as illegitimate and group boundaries as impermeable (Ellemers, Wilke, and Van Knippenberg 1993). The severely disadvantaged minority citizens of American society undoubtedly question the legitimacy of existing social arrangements that maintain the marked barriers between them and the larger society (see Massey and Denton 1993).

Research on social identity processes plainly reveals the ineluctability of the ingroup biases that differentiate police and minority citizens. Apart from implications for relations between minority groups and the police, it is important to recognize that relations between groups that are moderately dissimilar, such as the police and the dominant group, may entail intermediate levels of intergroup bias. The relative lack of bias allows the limited, sometimes uneasy, alliance between the police and the dominant group with respect to their shared interest in controlling the threat allegedly posed by racial and ethnic minorities. At the same time, the perceived contrasts between the allies may help maintain a wall of mistrust between them, even in the absence of any vital differences of objective interests.

Clearly the social identity model offers fresh insights into the tensions between the police and citizens. Conflict may occur simply because of the ethnocentric biases produced by identification with their respective social groups. Perceived within-group similarities and between-group dissimilarities may foster intergroup conflict in situations lacking competing interests. Consistent with Turner's (1987) self-categorization model, which postulates that greater perceived differences between groups arouse stronger ethnocentrism, research consistently shows that group distinctiveness is related positively to judgmental differentiation (Jetten, Spears, and Postmes 2004). That is, ingroup favoritism that occurs relative to greatly dissimilar outgroups takes the form of positive judgments of the ingroup. On the whole, research in this tradition provides evidence of such relatively mild forms of ingroup favoritism, said to be rooted in the mutual interdependence and cooperation essential to human survival (Brewer 1999, 2001). Put differently, rather than focusing on the corrosive effects of overt hostility directed against outgroups, the social identity model concentrates on more subtle intergroup biases resulting from the lack of positive sentiments toward outgroup members. But is favoritism toward ingroup members sufficient to explain acts of police brutality directed against minority citizens? While a more comprehensive understanding of the underlying dynamics is made possible by applying the social identity model to the problem, other intergroup processes surely are at work.

Taken together, the realistic group conflict and social identity models provide a more satisfying explanation of the social and psychological forces underlying ingroup solidarity and outgroup discrimination. These processes highlight the intransigent quality of police-minority tensions—obdurate normative conflicts of interest and robust ethnocentrism are clearly evident in the juxtaposition of the police subculture and the oppositional identity of some minority citizens. Certainly those conditions exacerbate police-minority tensions and set the stage for police brutality. While the insights of these theoretical models move us closer to a comprehensive explanation of police brutality, important issues remain unaddressed by them. The side of the ingroup/outgroup equation that we examine next, namely, stereotyping of outgroups, involves more active components of derogation critical to triggering incidents of excessive force.

CHAPTER 4

====

Stereotyping and Outgroup Bias

Stereotypes of racial and ethnic minorities pervade the popular culture and the world of policing. Explanations of police brutality commonly identify the police subculture and the stereotypes embedded within it as key contributors to the behavior (e.g., Westley 1970; Skolnick and Fyfe 1993), but such work does not incorporate an in-depth analysis of the social-psychological dynamics underlying intergroup conflict. The social identity model yields important insights about the processes of cognitive categorization involved in intergroup relations, but it focuses on ingroup biases and pays relatively little heed to stereotypes that may trigger discrimination against certain outgroups. An examination of social psychological research on stereotyping promises to broaden the contributions of the subculture of policing and social identity approaches to provide a more complete account of how cognitive biases influence police behavior.

Our perspective on stereotyping is best described as an information processing model (see, e.g., Schaller, Rosell, and Asp 1998). This line of reasoning emphasizes that stereotypic categorizations involve normal "cognitive shortcuts" that people use to simplify a complex world (Fiske 1998). In many respects the cognitive processes identified in this model also apply to the self-stereotyping dynamics specified in the self-identity model (cf. Taylor 1981; Turner et al. 1987). These two cognitive perspectives share fundamental assumptions but emphasize different aspects of intergroup relationships. The information processing model specifies the ways in which stereotypic thinking about outgroups, rather than ingroups, is psychologically functional.

David L. Hamilton's (1981a) volume, *Cognitive Processes in Stereotyping and Intergroup Behavior*, provides the general framework for investigations of stereotypic cognition that have proliferated over the past quarter century (Fiske 1998). Contributors to the collection relied heavily on Allport's (1954) seminal ideas regarding the normality of stereotyping and Tajfel's (e.g., Tajfel 1969; Tajfel et al. 1971) insights into the inevitability of group categorization. Their overarching theme is that people are cognitive misers who strive to conserve limited mental resources in the face of complex and demanding social environments. For example, Shelley E. Taylor (1981) argued that cognitive categorizations "tag" information using the physical and social characteristics of people, including race and gender. These categorizations minimize within-group differences and maximize between-group differences and generate stereotypic attributions about group members' behavior. Although generally simplifying the world, cognitive categorizations may become more sophisticated as one's familiarity with a group develops, capturing multiple characteristics that distinguish subtypes of a larger social category (e.g., the "street-smart black"). Still, even sophisticated stereotypes reduce the world to simpler terms and trigger cognitive processes that preserve mental resources. While achieving mental efficiency, such simplifications also produce misperceptions. One noteworthy example is the phenomenon of illusory correlation, the propensity to overestimate the strength of the relationship between undesirable behaviors and group membership (Hamilton 1981b). People tend to generalize anecdotally the objectionable behavior of certain individuals to all members of a social category.

Building on such ideas, subsequent work using the information processing approach has documented the cognitive processes employed in day-to-day life, particularly the shortcuts that facilitate rapid decisions when time and resources are limited. That conception of cognitive responses has been extended to offer a more complete account of cognitive processing, one that acknowledges that people habitually rely on cognitive categorizations to make decisions rapidly but maintains that they also are "cognitive tacticians" who devote more time to appraising a situation carefully when motivated to by their current goals (Fiske and Taylor 1991). But the capacity to sort through things without reflection may convey tremendous advantages in certain situations. The ability to choose an appropriate line of action quickly becomes critical in the face of potential threats. Humans use various cues to identify rapidly those who pose danger when the situation prohibits more extensive appraisal and careful response. Police officers often confront such circumstances, and they rely heavily on stereotypic categorizations to guide their street-level behavior. Citizens' racial/ethnic identities provide readily accessible and highly salient cues about alleged behavioral propensities and appropriate courses of action.

The Information Processing Model

Human social life is often complex and demanding, requiring attention to both invariant and novel stimuli in the social environment (McCrae and

Bodenhausen 2000). While much of everyday life consists of orderly and predictable events, people must be prepared to deal with unexpected occurrences as well. Thus an adaptive mind needs to be highly flexible and capable of rapidly digesting various types of stimulus events (Johnston and Hawley 1994). Two complementary learning/memory systems (see McClelland, McNaughton, and O'Reilly 1995) endow humans with the cognitive flexibility needed to traverse effectively through the social world. The slow-learning neocortical system contains generic information that accumulates through repeated exposure to various stimuli. The beliefs, expectancies, and norms encoded in this system resist change and address the need for stable representations of the social world. Ideally these cognitive structures (often termed *schemata*) are simple, coherent, and relatively stable; they provide a priori organization for interpreting new experiences (Markus and Zajonc 1985). While purposive action relies on the enduring knowledge stored in the neocortical system, survival also hinges on the ability to respond speedily and adaptively to novel and unexpected stimuli (Shallice 1988). The fast-learning hippocampal system enables humans to form transient representations of unique stimuli, but barring repeated exposure such experiences have little impact on cognitive schemata. Together the independent but complementary learning/memory systems endow humans with the balance of "stability and plasticity it requires if [one is] to chart a smooth passage through life's potentially turbulent waters" (McCrae and Bodenhausen 2000, 94).

When encountering someone new, people call upon their cognitive schemata to guide social interaction (McCrae and Bodenhausen 2000). Initial perceptions of people derive from old and general beliefs that simplify and structure the person-perception process. People rely on their stock of knowledge concerning social category memberships, such as race and sex, rather than attending to unique characteristics of others. Once activated, such cognitive categorizations guide information processing (e.g., Bodenhausen 1988) and produce stereotype-based judgmental outcomes (e.g., Brewer 1988). In short, categorical reasoning is the cognitive shortcut that streamlines information processing in general and the person-perception process in particular.

Several important issues arise from this conceptualization of cognitive shortcuts. The view that automatic category activation inescapably influences the person-perception process dominates the field (Fiske 1998). Accounting for the advantages that accrue to the seemingly automatic activation of cognitive categories, including stereotypes of other groups, poses a central concern. Given that stereotypes simplify a complex social world, inaccurate attributions and responses must inevitably occur, and people may incur significant social costs as a result of their misperceptions. Yet we will see that automatic categorical processes may bestow significant advantages that outweigh such potential costs. Another issue is the degree to which automatic category activation influences behavioral responses. Automatic activation is unintentional; it requires no conscious effort and remains beyond individual control. But information processing also involves a controlled component; it demands conscious effort and provides for flexible responses (Devine 1989). Even though personal beliefs can influence whether people inhibit or control responses occurring subsequent to automatic stereotype activation, the influence of stereotypes appears inevitable in many situations. A closely related concern is the conditions conducive to triggering automatic categorical reasoning. Certainly situationally specific demands and goals affect a perceiver's ability to evaluate a situation and determine an appropriate line of action. Research shows that some conditions elicit rapid, automatic responses, whereas others permit activation of higher-order cognitive processes that give rise to more careful assessments and deliberate reactions (McCrae and Bodenhausen 2000). Careful consideration of these matters provides considerable insight into the street-level behavior of the police in minority neighborhoods, as well as the perceptions of the citizens who inhabit those locales.

Advantages of Automatic Stereotype Activation

Automatic categorical reasoning undoubtedly bestows immense advantages, not the least of which is the ability to respond rapidly to environmental stimuli that pose threats or proffer opportunities. For example, the ability to identify swiftly potential adversaries (outgroup members) and allies (ingroup members) could have enhanced individuals' prospects for survival in the simple societies where nearly all of human evolution took place. Evolutionary psychologists argue persuasively that natural selection shaped the cognitive structure of human brains to solve problems that our ancestors confronted regularly (e.g., Tooby and Cosmides 1992). For example, the division of learning functions between the neocortical and hippocampal systems discussed earlier is not a biological metaphor for describing capacities of the human brain; it is a literal anatomical description of the independent but interrelated regions of the brain responsible for processing and storing different kinds of information (McClelland, McNaughton, and O'Reilly 1995). Such hard-wired circuitry facilitates rapid information-processing abilities such as face recognition and threat recognition without conscious effort, capabilities that would be highly adaptive given the problems posed by life in ancestral societies (see Tooby and Cosmides 1992). In short, humans possess cognitive structures that process certain types of salient social information effortlessly and rapidly, because natural selection "designed" the brain to work that way.

In complex societies, day-to-day life is simplified greatly by the automatic activation of stereotypes. For example, numerous studies demonstrate that people use cues about race and gender to categorize others rapidly (see

Fiske 1998; McCrae and Bodenhausen 2000). Once activated, stereotypes of outgroup members provide expectancies that guide subsequent information processing in two ways. First, activated categorical representations guide the assimilation and integration of subsequently encountered information, producing a greater emphasis on stereotype-consistent information (e.g., Fyock and Stanger 1994; McCrae, Milne, and Bodenhausen 1994; McCrae, Stangor, and Milne 1994). Second, in the absence of evidence clearly contradicting stereotype-based expectancies, category activation leads to more stereotypic judgmental and memory effects (e.g., Bodenhausen 1988). Thus stereotypic categories are cognitively functional because their use preserves mental resources by channeling information into preexisting categories and demanding little conscious cognitive effort. Routine interactions habitually invite quick appraisal and minimal effort, with more strategic action taken when one's current goals motivate the extra cognitive effort (Fiske and Taylor 1991).

Attributions about members of stereotyped groups clearly manifest stereotypic expectancies, revealing elements of both ingroup favoritism and outgroup derogation (Fiske 1998). People tend to perceive the good qualities of the ingroup and the bad ones of a disliked outgroup as personal and dispositional (e.g., genetically determined), whereas the bad characteristics of the ingroup and the good ones of the outgroup may be attributed to situational circumstances or seen as exceptions (Pettigrew 1979). In other words, people tend to perceive the allegedly negative qualities of outgroup members and the good ones of ingroup members as inherently residing within individuals; bad qualities of ingroup members and good ones of outgroup members are explained away by various circumstances that do not reflect people's essential attributes. Such attributions allow the perceiver to assimilate stereotype-inconsistent information without challenging his or her stereotypes about groups. Moreover, essentialist explanations of group qualities may be rooted in a popular biology that promotes the belief that race and sex differences are meaningful and immutable (see Martin and Parker 1995). These lay theories about the social world engender stereotyping (Levy, Stroessner, and Dweck 1998) and rationalize existing social arrangements (e.g., Jost and Banaji 1994).

The implications of this line of reasoning are profound (Devine 1989). Racial and ethnic stereotypes pervade society, and no one can escape learning them (Ehrlich 1973). Stereotypes become well established in children's memories long before they acquire the ability to assess critically the validity of stereotype content (e.g., Allport 1954; Katz 1976). Stereotypical conceptions of race/ethnicity may acquire cognitive primacy for various reasons (see Fiske 1998). An individual's race/ethnicity provides visual cues (physical features and customary attire) that allow ready identification of putative category membership; it symbolizes a person's position in the social hierarchy; and it indicates reputed behavioral propensities, as in the association of blacks with violence. In regard to the latter, studies of both adults (Duncan 1976) and schoolchildren (Sagar and Schofield 1980) show that interpretations of an ambiguous shove or a bump in a hallway depend on the race of the actor. Presumably the presence of a black actor automatically primes (i.e., stimulates) activation of the stereotype that associates blacks with violence. Consistent with that assumption, these studies show that white participants (as well as black ones in the schoolchildren study) perceived a black actor's ambiguously aggressive behavior as more hostile and threatening than the same behavior by a white actor. Put simply, acts that seem innocuous when performed by a white person seem threatening when performed by a black person.

It appears that all people are exposed to racial and ethnic stereotypes, and they may exert considerable influence on people's judgments of others. But knowledge of them does not necessarily signify belief in their validity. Most social psychologists, for example, are keenly aware of pejorative racial stereotypes, but they rarely accept them as truths. Thus a fundamental concern about the activation of racial/ethnic stereotypes is the degree to which their automatic activation may be controlled by effortful cognition.

Controlling Automatic Stereotype Activation

The dominant view maintains that automatic category activation is an inescapable part of the person-perception process, and that prejudice is an unavoidable consequence (e.g., Allport 1954; Hamilton 1981c; Tajfel 1981). Challenging this *"inevitability of prejudice* perspective,"* Patricia Devine (1989) designed an influential study that broadens insights into the automatic and controlled components of stereotype activation. She contends that high- and low-prejudice people are equally knowledgeable of stereotypes of blacks; that stereotypes comprise a set of well-learned associations; and that stereotype activation is equally strong and automatic among both high- and low-prejudice individuals. She posits, however, that high- and low-prejudice whites possess different beliefs about blacks. Stereotypes and beliefs constitute conceptually separate cognitive structures. The personal beliefs of the highly prejudiced are congruent with stereotypes, whereas the beliefs of those with low levels of prejudice consciously reject them. But given that the stereotype has a long history of activation compared to personal beliefs that may develop later in life, the low-prejudice person must intentionally inhibit an automatically activated stereotype to avoid prejudiced responses. Whether these automatic and controlled processes can be dissociated is critically important to understanding how stereotypes shape people's responses to outgroup members.

Devine's study first examined whether high- and low-prejudice participants (white introductory psychology students were employed in all of the experiments) differed in their knowledge of cultural stereotypes of blacks. No statistically significant differences were found in sixteen categories capturing various stereotypical traits of blacks, such as aggressive/tough, criminal, and low intelligence, findings that support the hypothesis that stereotype knowledge is unrelated to prejudice. In the next experiment, lists of various racial identity or stereotypic associates, along with neutral words, were used to subliminally prime participants at a low level (20% prime words) or high level (80% prime words). Later the participants completed an impression-formation task that involved reading a paragraph that described ambiguously hostile behavior by a person of unknown racial identity and then rating that person on various trait scales. The procedures were designed to preclude conscious monitoring of stereotype activation by the participants. Findings from the experiment indicate that stereotype-congruent encoding and interpretation of behavior is equally strong and inescapable in both high- and low-prejudice participants. The final experiment used a conscious thought-listing protocol that required participants to generate labels descriptive of blacks, and each participant's proportion of pejorative and nonpejorative labels was calculated. Responses were classified as negative-belief, positive-belief, negative-trait, or positive-trait. Whereas the responses of high-prejudice participants emphasized stereotypic traits, those of low-prejudice participants emphasized beliefs negating stereotypes. These findings indicate that in circumstances permitting controlled thinking, disassociation of stereotypes and beliefs can occur among those with low levels of prejudice. Still, Devine (1989, 15) makes clear that "in situations in which controlled processes are precluded or interfered with, automatic processing effects may exert the greatest influence on responses."

Obviously humans living in complex societies encounter many situations that permit careful assessment of different lines of action and deliberate decision making. Stereotypic reasoning might be more of a hindrance than an expedient in such situations. Under other circumstances, automatic preconscious responses to stimulus events in the environment might signal the difference between life and death. Police officers often confront ambiguously threatening situations that demand rapid decisions. Does a brief glimmer of metal signify a weapon in the hands of a potentially dangerous suspect? An erroneous conclusion may convey a terrible cost, the injury or death of an unarmed citizen or a police officer. But can responses to such situations permit careful appraisals?

Consider the case of Amidou Diallo, a black West African immigrant shot by New York City Police Department (NYPD) officers who were searching for a rape suspect on the night of February 19, 1999 (Haberman 2005). Police officers mistakenly identified Diallo's wallet as a gun. The four officers on the scene fired forty-one shots, killing him on the spot.

Ultimately, the officers involved in the shooting were acquitted of criminal charges, their actions justified as a mistake based on a reasonable assumption about the suspect's behavior at the time. But would the officers have fired had the suspect been white? Yet again the specter of police racism ignited a national debate.

The Diallo case also kindled the interest of scholars concerned with automatic cognitive processes. One investigator conducted a study that assessed the automatic and controlled processes involved in misperceiving a weapon (Payne 2001). Two experiments were devised to examine the relationship between the prime of black versus white and the target type of gun versus tool. Participants in the studies were nonblack undergraduates. In the first study, the participants were primed by exposure to photos of black and white faces with features that varied systematically only with respect to racial identity. Then they were asked to identify, as quickly and accurately as possible, either a gun or a tool from a second set of photos. Participants identified guns faster when primed with black faces. The second experiment replicated this procedure but added a response deadline, which shifted racial bias from response time to accuracy. Participants primed with black faces were more likely to incorrectly identify a harmless tool as a gun than when they were primed with a white face. The addition of the response deadline in the second experiment reduced the effect of controlled cognitive processes but not the effect of automatic processes, resulting in the racially biased error rate in gun identification. Taken together, the findings indicate that biased error rates require two conditions: the presence of stereotypic cues, and the limited opportunity to contemplate and control one's response. "Unfortunately, these may often be precisely the conditions present when police officers enter into a confrontation with a stereotyped suspect" (Payne 2001, 190).

A subsequent study extended this line of inquiry by examining the effect of racial primes on "shoot/don't shoot" decisions (Correll et al. 2002). Noting that expectancies about social categories guide the interpretation of ambiguous events, the investigators more directly addressed the question of whether the NYPD officers' decision to shoot Diallo could have been affected by the stereotypic association of blacks with violence. The study comprised a series of four experiments using a simple video game that simultaneously presented a prime (black or white) and an object (gun or no gun). Ten young white men and ten young black men served as targets in the video game, which used twenty diverse physical backgrounds. Each model appeared twice in a gun condition and twice in a no-gun condition, creating a total of eighty target images. The object of the game was to "shoot" armed targets and not "shoot" unarmed ones. The first three experiments used college students (almost exclusively white) as study participants and employed payoff matrices and monetary rewards to make their participation meaningful. For the last experiment, both white and African American participants were recruited in heavily trafficked public places (e.g., malls) in the community.

In the first experiment, the participants were instructed to shoot/not shoot as quickly as possible. They fired more quickly at a black armed target than at a white armed target, and they decided not to shoot an unarmed target more quickly when he was white than when he was black. The second experiment imposed a time constraint that produced errors in shooting decisions. Participants were more likely to shoot black than white unarmed targets, and they were more likely to fail to shoot a white than black armed target. The findings of the first and second experiment parallel those from the aforementioned studies, demonstrating that people use race to interpret an ambiguously threatening target. The third experiment replicated the response time protocol and findings of the first experiment but also considered racial attitudes. Shooter response bias was more pronounced among participants who believed that there is a strong cultural stereotype of blacks as violent and among those who reported more contact with African Americans, but neither prejudice nor personal belief in the stereotype affected response bias. These findings suggest that widespread knowledge of the cultural stereotype of African Americans could lead to automatically activated shooter bias in anyone exposed to the stereotype, irrespective of their personal beliefs. The fourth experiment examined that possibility by including both white and African American participants and testing reaction time and error rates with the protocols used previously. This study replicated the former findings and found that response time bias and error rate were *not* dependent on the participants' race. White and African American participants exhibited equivalent levels of bias.

Obviously the participants in the studies of weapon identification and shooting decisions had not received the extensive training of actual police officers in tactical firearms use. A recent extension of that work addresses this issue by including police officers in the study (Correll, Park, Judd, Wittenbrenk, Sadler, and Keesee 2007). The participants included a sample of police officers from the Denver Police Department, a sample of civilians from the Denver community, and another sample of police officers from fourteen states, who were attending a training seminar. The samples were racially/ethnically diverse. Like the previous work, this investigation examined biases in reaction time and shooting decisions. In general, the findings reveal that police officers were similar to the community participants with respect to the speed in which they reached shoot/don't shoot decisions. They made decisions more rapidly for stereotype-congruent targets—armed blacks and unarmed whites—and more slowly with stereotype-incongruent ones—unarmed blacks and armed whites. Moreover, correlational analyses of the data for national officers revealed the following:

Officers serving in districts characterized by a large population, a high rate of violent crime, and a greater concentration of Black people and other minorities showed increased bias in their reaction times . . . these environments may reinforce cultural stereotypes, linking Black people to the concept of violence. (Correll et al. 2007, 1014)

However, stereotypic interference with performance did not affect police officers' decisions to shoot, whereas civilians were more likely to mistakenly shoot unarmed black targets. The researchers attributed the lack of bias in officers' shooting decisions to the extensive training they receive regarding holding their fire if they are uncertain about their target. They tested that possibility in an experiment with undergraduate participants. The findings indicate that practice (playing the video game twice a day for two days) reduced stereotypic interference in the decision to shoot. While suggestive, the results concerning lack of bias in the decision to shoot observed for police and the "trained" undergraduates may have limited external validity. Can these findings be generalized to actual situations that confront the police, which may entail fatigue and stress, involve real dangers, and elicit powerful emotions such as fear? After all, video games cannot shoot back.

This line of research suggests that the psychological sequence underlying the decision to shoot requires perception of the object (gun), interpretation of the object as a gun, and decision to shoot when some degree of certainty about the target is reached (see Correll et al. 2002). When a target stimulus possesses African American characteristics, stereotypic associations with violence stored in cognitive schemata produce faster, more automatic cognitive processing, whereas a target stimulus with white features produces slower, less automatic processing. Thus people may respond more quickly and may make more mistakes when the target is African American, because cultural stereotypes implicitly affect information processing. This pattern of differential cognitive processing leads to the prediction of tragic interference with performance in police encounters involving unarmed black suspects and time pressures (Payne 2001), an observation that directs attention to the more general issue of what demands on cognitive resources may elicit stereotypic responses among police officers.

Conditions Eliciting Automatic Stereotypic Activation

Current conceptualizations of information processing suggest that automatic category-based thinking is an ordinary human cognitive process driven largely by social context rather than by individual differences

(Fiske 1998). Various contextual factors may play a role in generating stereotypic judgments and responses in interpersonal interactions. The need for cognitive closure during an interaction freezes the search for additional information and thus educes the use of stereotypes. Situational pressures and individual motives may encourage one to close one's mind. When lacking time, motivation, or cognitive capacity to think about others, people rely more heavily on their cognitive categorizations (Fiske 1998; McCrae and Bodenhausen 2000). The aforementioned shooting studies clearly demonstrate how racial stereotypes may influence decisions that must be reached quickly in situations where time limitations are imposed. That people normally use cognitive shortcuts in the face of time constraints is often taken for granted, but individuals also may strategically choose which situations deserve more or less cognitive effort, choices that often may be "made on the fly, tactically, in the course of a busy social interaction" (Fiske 1998, 363). The expenditure of additional cognitive energy depends on one's goals; for example, the effort may be warranted when one seeks to get along with another person. At the same time, one's cognitive load may be affected by conditions such as complex and competing environmental stimuli that tax cognitive resources and encourage stereotypic responses in routine situations lacking novel features to which one must attend (see McCrae and Bodenhausen 2000).

The cognitive preeminence of racial stereotypes and the conditions that activate their use are particularly evident in encounters involving the police and minorities in impoverished locales. Complex demands and constraints typify street-level policing in those environments, circumstances that inescapably stress officers' cognitive resources and thus may habitually elicit stereotypic responses in interactions with citizens. There is no strategic advantage in wasting precious time and cognitive resources on the humdrum problems that provide the mainstay of their day-to-day work. Indeed, they are generally less concerned with getting along with citizens than they are with protecting their authority and personal well-being. Racial/ethnic identity allows swift dispositional inferences useful for predicting likely outcomes of interactions in neighborhoods where omnipresent dangers and challenging social conditions exist. Moreover, beliefs about racial inferiority are endemic to police culture, reinforcing their proclivity to stereotype. Clearly the environment of street-level policing yields fertile ground for stereotypic judgments, ones that may trigger gratuitous acts of violence. We begin our substantive analysis of the issue with an overview of the stereotypes about race and crime pervading American society, images that are central to understanding the cultural baggage that police recruits bring to their new job.

Cultural Stereotypes of Race and Crime

Stereotypes derogate members of groups perceived as somehow fundamentally different from one's own group. Following Erving Goffman's (1963) seminal work *Stigma*, it is generally assumed that socially constructed beliefs about a stigmatized attribute such as race, rather than the objective facts about it, comprise the essence of pejorative stereotypes (see Crocker, Major, and Steele 1998). People may perceive those with stigmas as less than human, characterized by discrediting qualities thought to pass hereditarily through family lineage (Goffman 1963). One such persistent but questionable belief, which pervades not only popular discourse but also some scientific analyses, alleges racial differences in criminality and aggression. For example, Cesare Lombroso, generally acknowledged as the founder of modern positivist criminology, argued that blacks in the United States posed a social danger attributable to their inherent savagery and were responsible for an increasing crime problem (Horn 2003). Similarly, political apologists for lynching maintained that free blacks created a special threat as they reverted to their naturally primitive and brutish ways in the absence of slavery's coercive control (Kennedy 1997). In particular, blacks were thought to possess a nearly uncontrollable lust for white women. These popular stereotypes were reinforced in early films, such as *Birth of a Nation*, which depicted blacks as demented, bloodthirsty, white haters (Noble 1970).

Such depictions continue to flavor the media accounts that provide the primary source for most people's information about crime (Rome 2000; Chambliss 2001). The media not only report stories about race and crime that reflect dominant crime stereotypes, they also shape them by disproportionately reporting the crimes committed by blacks (see Dorfman and Schiraldi 2001). The highly questionable belief that race and crime are innately linked persists in some scientific analyses of crime causation (e.g., Rushton 1997), giving further credence to social stereotypes. Today, popular ideology portrays the common criminal as a poor, young, black male (Chambliss 2001).

Yet blacks hardly hold a monopoly on stereotypes conflating race and crime. Popular images of the Mexican-origin population also incorporate ideas of biological inferiority and inherent propensity for criminality and violent behavior (Bender 2003). Sociohistorical research has documented the development of various stereotypes of Mexican criminality. The mid-nineteenth century Mexican bandido, who allegedly usurped Anglo land, property, and women, was later joined by the violence-prone macho alcoholic early in the twentieth century, during the first major wave of Mexican immigration (Rosales 1999). As southwestern industrialization took hold, urbanizing more and more Mexicans, the "pachuco zoot-suiter" came to be seen as a scourge to American culture and social order by the mid-twentieth century (Escobar 1999). Now popular images of Mexican criminality have evolved to include such hyperboles as the ruthlessly violent gangbanger (Bender 2003) and the Mexican immigrant "superpredator" (Martinez 2002).

Highly contestable assumptions generally provide the building blocks of such racial/ethnic stereotypes, but an element of truth may inform some. Consider, for example, higher crime rates among blacks for certain violent crimes, which may be held out as evidence of criminal proclivities. Yet even those who are not culpable may be perceived as a threat because they otherwise fit a broad stereotype.

> [Oppositional] behavior becomes all the more complex when the whole community is victimized. In this context the community may get a bad name, while residents themselves, notably black males, are demonized. The resulting stereotypes are then so broadly applied that anyone from the community who dresses that way, who looks that way, is thereby placed at odds with conventional society. This underscores the huge communication gap between different urban neighborhoods . . . and the broader society. The stereotyped person is often caught in a horrendous bind, because, though completely decent, he or she may take up this way of dressing, this way of looking, this way of acting, in order not only to preserve a measure of self-respect but to survive the street. (Anderson 1999, 318–19)

Here we see how anecdotal generalizations about criminality among certain racial/ethnic groups may greatly exaggerate the robustness of any underlying evidence, seriously challenging the validity of popular stereotypes conflating race and criminality.

Perhaps more importantly, the alleged biological bases of violence among minorities rest on some dubious assumptions about racial variation. Certainly average between-group differences on certain physical characteristics exist. Yet common racial classifications based solely on *visible* physical traits are challenged by recent genetic evidence (Bamshad and Olson 2003; Bamshad, Wooding, Watkins, Ostler, Batzer, and Jorde 2003). While a few genes dictate outward physical differences commonly used to designate races, the distribution of myriad other genes may vary considerably among individual members of a racial category. Group categorizations based on genetic information may not correspond well to the predefined categories of race in common use, because such racial designations involve social constructions largely unrelated to genetic differences (Zuckerman 1990). Even people of predominantly European ancestry may be classified as black because of the stigmatizing quality of some African heritage. For example, such designations in the antebellum South may have required but a tiny fraction of African ancestry. In reality, the hue of one's skin is little more than a stigma that subjectively identifies alleged differences in the essential qualities of various humans.

The relationship between stereotyping and differential treatment in the criminal justice system is an especially troubling matter. Belief in racial differences of intelligence, aggression, and criminality may produce harsher outcomes for minorities throughout the criminal justice process. A notable example is found in the literature on crime stereotypes and differential adjudications by criminal courts. Theoretical and empirical research has elaborated the role of racial stereotypes in criminal court decisions, suggesting that they play a prominent role at even this most deliberate point in the adjudication process (Swigert and Farrell 1977; Farrell and Holmes 1991; Steen, Engen, and Gainey 2005). Popular stereotypes and ideologies likewise permeate the police subculture (e.g., Bolton and Feagin 2004), where they may be reinforced by selective interactions with minority citizens. Unbridled of the constraints of public proceedings, police officers possess wide-ranging discretion that invites category-based decision making. The utility of stereotypes in making inferences about potential outcomes of interactions with racial/ethnic minority citizens makes them especially useful to the police officer on the street, even though such outcomes often turn out to be self-fulfilling prophecies initiated by stereotype activation.

Stereotyping and the Working Personality of the Police Officer

The use of stereotypes by the police is well documented (Bittner 1967; Kappeler, Sluder, and Alpert 1998; Piliavin and Briar 1964; Skolnick 1975; Van Maanen 1978a; Waegel 1981). Police recruits arrive at the academy with a knowledge of popular stereotypes that conflate race and crime stowed in their mental baggage, and the depersonalization that occurs in the academy encourages the use of stereotypes early in their socialization (Lundman 1980). Once on the street, patrol officers confront problems that elicit the use of stereotypes. They encounter a wide variety of people and situations, yet they have little time to sort through things and resolve people's unique problems. In addition, they must often make decisions with limited, sometimes ambiguous, information. Officers seek to perserve their authority and personal safety under uncertain circumstances that may pose potential dangers.

Police patrol work involves a great deal of uncertainty (Bayley 1994). Officers assigned to patrol are frequently dispatched to the location of a problem knowing little about what awaits them. In their attempts to learn more about the situation at hand, they may receive differing, and often conflicting, accounts. The situations that require police intervention frequently involve interpersonal conflicts in emotional and stressful circumstances. For example, responding to a call about an assault, officers may be unsure who to identify as victim and perpetrator. One of the authors once observed a situation involving a woman, apparently in the throes of a psychotic episode, who jumped from a second-story apartment, fortunately receiving only minor injuries. Her boyfriend called 911 from a cell phone for medical and police assistance while restraining the woman by sitting on her. Upon arriving on the scene, the officers immediately identified the boyfriend as the perpetrator of a crime because of his behavior and the woman's injuries and allegations of victimization. Only after observing the woman's erratic behavior and receiving witness accounts did the police recognize what had actually transpired and release the altruistic boyfriend.

Proactive encounters, those initiated by police officers, also may involve ambiguity. When officers observe people or situations that seem out of place, they may initiate an interaction (see Skolnick 1975). Frequently they are uncertain about with whom they are dealing, but they clearly suspect something untoward is occurring. Yet they often have nothing more than a hunch supported by little or no objective information regarding the suspect or activity in question. Stereotypes help frame their interpretation of and reaction to the situation.

In short, the work of patrol officers, while often routine, involves many ambiguous situations. Given the complexity of interpersonal conflict and the inability of officers to readily verify people's accounts, uncertainty is a staple of patrol work. Stereotypic reasoning provides an expedient for resolving the ambiguity inherent in day-to-day policing:

> Typifications of others and events serve to structure interaction in a provisional way, rendering it more predictable, minimizing its problematic character, and enabling the actor to better manage an ambiguous social environment. Typificatory schemes are used as resources from which to construct a practical solution to the problem at hand. (Waegel 1981, 264)[1]

Time limitations further infringe upon police officers' handling of most calls. They spend much of their day waiting for "real" police work, the exciting and sometimes dangerous duties related to the "big" call (Bayley 1994; Lundman 1980). Routine "bullshit" is merely endured. Supervisors implicitly reinforce this viewpoint by pressuring officers to be in service and available to respond to serious incidents. Officers not only feel pressure from the organization and fellow officers to handle most service requests quickly and to be available for "real" police work when it arises, but in large jurisdictions, the sheer bulk of more routine calls may preclude devoting much time to them. Stereotypes about offenses and

offenders allow officers to quickly resolve the minor incidents they do not
have time for, as well as to rapidly identify the greater threats presumably
posed by "real" police work.

Scholars have long noted the tendency to stereotype citizens by the
perceived threat they pose (e.g., Skolnick 1975). Given the high priority
placed on personal safety and the perception that many citizens are potentially dangerous, entering ambiguous situations perpetually presents a
problem for patrol officers, and their first priority is to gain control over
the situation (Sykes and Brent 1980). They look, unconsciously and consciously, for cues that presage danger. They seek to "maintain their edge"
by taking and maintaining control, asserting authority, and preparing
themselves for dangerous or troublesome behavior (Van Maanen 1978a).
Officers believe that alertness and skill can protect them from the dangerous aspects of their job (see Crank 1998). Only after officers believe
they have control over the situation and have neutralized threats to their
safety do they begin to resolve the problem at hand.

Apart from the potential dangers of the job, police officers continually confront challenges to their authority. Defiant citizens are seen as at-
tacking both the institution of policing and the individual officer
(Lundman 1980; Crank 1998). Challenges to authority may involve visible irritation at police intervention, questioning an officer's right to intervene, open hostility, or failure to follow police instructions. Such
behavior impedes resolution of the problem at hand and calls into question an officer's professional competence (Skolnick 1975; Lundman
1980). It becomes not only an occupational problem but a personal affront and possible source of embarrassment (Van Maanen 1978a). In addition, challenges to authority may portend physical threats. After all,
only dangerous people would have the audacity to challenge a police officer (Skolnick 1975; Lundman 1980). Stereotypes of dangerous people
certainly encompass perceptions about defiant demeanor.

Jerome H. Skolnick's (1975) conception of the "police working personality" provides a seminal statement about how police officers organize their day-to-day duties to accommodate the exigencies of the job.
He maintains that police officers share distinct cognitive tendencies organized around the habitual issues of efficiency, authority, and danger.
Conceptions about potentially dangerous people dominate the cognitive
framework of the police officer:

> The policeman, because his work requires him to be occupied con-
> tinually with potential violence, develops a perceptual shorthand to
> identify certain kinds of people as symbolic assailants, that is, as
> persons who use gesture, language, and attire that the policeman

has come to recognize as a prelude to violence. This does not mean that violence by the symbolic assailant is necessarily predictable. On the contrary, the policeman responds to the vague indication of danger suggested by appearance. (Skolnick 1975, 45)

Minority attitudes and actions may be seen as particularly threatening (Chevigny 1969; Westley 1970; Skolnick and Fyfe 1993). No doubt this is especially true of young minority males, whose attire and attitude may indicate adherence to street values condoning violence, even when that is not at all the case (e.g., Anderson 1999). Symbolic assailants perceived as threatening an officer's well-being or as challenging an officer's authority have committed transgressions in the "police cultural statute book," thereby eliciting informal punishments deemed appropriate within the subcultural context (Skolnick and Fyfe 1993, 103). Police reward those who conform and punish those who do not.

In short, conceptions of symbolic assailants, grounded in popular stereotypes and reaffirmed continuously in selective interactions with citizens, allow the identification of routine situations and the appropriate handling of them. All residents of a neighborhood may be stereotyped based on a nonrepresentative subset of their population (Smith 1986; Anderson 1999). While most minority citizens express concern about crime problems in their neighborhoods and look to the police to address their fears, law-abiding citizens may have relatively few face-to-face encounters with the police, particularly on the streets at night, compared to the young troublemakers who catch the eye of the patrol officer. Such individuals provide the fodder for stereotypes broadly portraying racial minorities as inherently dangerous, predisposing the police to suspicion and hostility. The police may thus pejoratively characterize and differentially respond to anyone encountered in poorer minority neighborhoods (Westley 1970; Irwin 1985; Sampson 1986; Anderson 1990, 1999). Stereotypes, suspicion, cynicism, mistrust, and hostility frequently comprise their working personality in such locales.

At the same time, given their extensive contact with citizens, officers who patrol minority neighborhoods may develop relatively sophisticated, variegated stereotypes, including subtypes that combine characteristics of race, class, and gender. Such subtypes may be socially pragmatic, because they allow officers to distinguish facilely among various categories of minority citizens in a neighborhood, facilitating varied, yet still routine, responses to different types of people. No doubt young minority males are stereotyped as particularly dangerous, a view that is deeply institutionalized within the criminal justice system (Chambliss 2001). Yet all members of a minority group may still be seen as inherently different from and more dangerous than whites. For example, popular images of minority women in American culture—the welfare queen, ghetto mama, drug user, or gang-banger—highlight the presumed criminal propensity and inferiority of all members of a minority group, irrespective of their gender (see, e.g., Bender 2003). Police are hardly immune from learning those stereotypes, which are again reinforced on the job through nonrepresentative interactions with problem citizens.

Ultimately, stereotypes paint groups with a broad brush that can re-sist contradictory evidence. The use of subtypes is cognitively pragmatic insofar as they help accommodate exceptions that seem to defy a general stereotype (Fiske 1998). For example, middle-class African American and Mexican American citizens may be perceived as exceptions to popular images of their groups, despite the numerical reality that they are not, which preserves the more general stereotypes of them. Thus minority cit-izens living in more affluent neighborhoods are hardly immune from dif-ferential treatment by the police, although the constellation of social and individual characteristics found in impoverished areas is more likely to automatically trigger stereotypes that associate race and violent criminal-ity during routine encounters with citizens there.

Minority Stereotypes of Police

Racial and ethnic minorities bring their own "cultural baggage" to en-counters with police (Stretcher 1999; see also Weitzer 2000). While less attention has been afforded stereotyping *by* minorities compared to stereotyping *of* minorities (Fiske 1998), there are good reasons to think that just as the subculture of policing is replete with stereotypes about racial and ethnic minorities, minority communities embrace stereotypes about the police. After all, stereotyping is a generic human quality, and stereotype "sharedness" is a predictable outcome of communication among ingroup members (Brauer, Judd, and Jacquelin 2001; Sechrist and Sangor 2001; Lyons and Kashima 2003). People tend to communicate stereotype-consistent information in their interactions with others, a strategy that confirms prevailing stereotypes. Minority citizens may share stories of police that vicariously buttress stereotypes depicting police as dangerous representatives of a hostile larger society.

Survey research on citizens' attitudes represents a venerable tradition in research on the police. Following the riots of the late 1960s, scholarly in-terest in minority citizens' views of the police intensified. Media coverage of police practices had focused national attention on police brutality (Son and Rome 2004). The President's Commission on Law Enforcement and the Administration of Justice (1967) and the National Advisory Commis-sion on Civil Disorders (1968) further spurred scholarly interest by high-lighting the importance of police-citizen relations (Flanagan and Vaughn

1996). Unsurprisingly, early research revealed significant concerns about the police among citizens of impoverished minority neighborhoods. For example, Hahn (1971) reported widespread antagonism toward police among residents of the impoverished 12th Street minority community in Detroit, the epicenter of the 1967 riot. Hostility toward police was ubiquitous among black residents of Detroit, who commonly complained of discourteous and abusive treatment (Fine 1989).

The long history of police-minority tensions has become part of urban folklore. Stories and rumors of abusive police practices often circulate widely through minority neighborhoods (Brunson 2007). As with police "war stories," citizens' accounts help instill various beliefs regarding the police. These stories reinforce pejorative stereotypes that portray the police as dangerous people, a widely held belief among minority citizens (e.g., Feagin 1991), and educate others on special precautions to avoid problems in dealings with police officers (Weitzer 1999). In Detroit, for example, tales of the police "tac squad" of the 1960s, or the "big four," as they were known, are still told by some residents. Those units, usually staffed by four very large officers, practiced policing through intimidation (Fine 1989). They made frequent street stops of minority youth who were generally allowed to go free after a period of intimidation and humiliation, which often included the use of foul language and racial epithets. Recently an individual who had grown up in Detroit during the 1960s recounted interacting with a "big four" officer to one of the authors. As he told it, a "big four" unit pulled up next to the sidewalk where he and his friends were standing. The driver instructed him to approach the car and lean over to the window. The officer then grabbed him by the collar and pulled his head into the car to ensure he could not escape. The officer then proceeded to instruct him that he and his friends were not to loiter around the nearby businesses and that he should leave immediately, noting that the officers would be back by the intersection later. The young man was graphically informed of the unfortunate consequences that would befall him should the officers find him there again.

The use of intimidation in policing was hardly uncommon in large cities during the 1960s and 1970s. Indeed, the National Advisory Commission on Civil Disorders (1968) concluded that citizens of poor minority neighborhoods viewed the police as an occupying force. Despite years of police-community relations efforts and numerous changes in policing since then, minority citizens remain skeptical. The preponderance of research affirms the conclusion that blacks and Hispanics hold more negative views than whites about various aspects of police performance (Smith 2005; Weitzer and Tuch 2006). One body of research identifies racial/ethnic differences in perceptions of and personal experiences with police misconduct, generally reporting that minority citizens are more likely than white citizens to perceive abuses (e.g., Holmes 1998; Weitzer 1999; Son and Rome 2004;

see also Flanagan and Vaughn 1996). A recent national survey reveals that black and Hispanic citizens are more likely than whites to say that police make unwarranted street stops, use insulting language, employ excessive force, and engage in corruption (Weitzer and Tuch 2004, 2006).

Research also demonstrates neighborhood differences in citizens' perceptions of the police. One recent study reported that residents of a poor black neighborhood were more likely than residents of white and black middle-class neighborhoods to say police engage in abusive practices within their neighborhoods, including unjustified street stops, insulting citizens, and using excessive force (Weitzer 1999). Half of the respondents in the poor black neighborhood reported having seen police use excessive force, compared to 14 percent of residents in a middle-class black neighborhood and no one in a middle-class white neighborhood. Whereas black middle-class residents' perceptions of police practices within their neighborhood were more closely associated with the residents of the middle-class white neighborhood, they reported more unjustified street stops by police outside of their neighborhoods than did their white counterparts.

The veracity of citizens' reports of police misconduct remains open to question. Certainly survey data provide support for the argument that police brutality occurs most commonly in poor minority neighborhoods, yet few people have the knowledge to distinguish between force that is legitimate and that which is excessive (Holmes 2000). Clearly, however, perceptions of police abuses fuel the stereotypes and beliefs shared by minority citizens (Brunson 2007). Indeed, their stereotypes may become self-fulfilling prophecies that reinforce the mutual antagonism between them and police. In a panel survey of citizens, Steven Brandl and his colleagues (1994) discovered that citizens who held generally negative views of the police were more likely to describe later encounters with the police negatively, whereas those who held positive views of police reported later encounters more positively. They concluded that citizens' global views of the police influenced their interpretation of later specific encounters with police, suggesting "These findings are consistent with the proposition that citizens' evaluations of their personal experiences with the police are affected by stereotyping and selective perception" (Brandl, Frank, Worden, and Bynum 1994, 131).

Stereotypes and Police-Minority Relations

The real problems confronting the police and the residents of impoverished neighborhoods are amplified greatly by the derogatory stereotypes they hold of one another. Police stereotypes mirror the images linking race and crime that permeate the larger society, images reinforced by selective interactions within minority communities. Incidents of police hostility and misconduct experienced by the residents of minority neighborhoods, ranging from verbal to physical abuse, similarly become ingrained in urban folklore as minority experiences with the police are shared with others in the community. While often based on real events, the atrocity tales of police and citizens may embellish and distort what actually transpired, evolving into stereotypes that exaggerate the truths upon which they are built. The climate of mutual threat existing between police and minorities is thus amplified and reinforced by the stereotypes they embrace. The mere presence of outgroup members, irrespective of the actual danger they pose, may heighten perceptions of threat.

The information processing model sheds considerable light on these oft-noted dynamics of police-minority tensions. Research in this theoretical tradition demonstrates that people automatically and unconsciously categorize others, particularly in situations where decision making is constrained by limitations of time, information, and cognitive resources. Sometimes police officers must make decisions very quickly in complex situations that provide limited and ambiguous information about the citizens involved. Those circumstances tend to elicit stereotypic responses rather than deliberative actions; to respond slowly could jeopardize oneself or others. Such situations may occasion incidents of excessive force triggered by automatic cognitive processing of people who pose stereotypic threats. Stigmatized minorities bear visible cues that warn the perceiver of potential problems, even in the absence of any objective danger. Distinctive uniforms likewise make the occupational identity of the police officer readily visible to minority citizens who stereotypically perceive police threat. Category-based responses tend to elicit stereotype-consistent behavior from the target, and interactions may thus turn into self-fulfilling prophecies (Fiske 1998). Put simply, stereotypes may generate interactions in which the participants elicit stereotype-confirming responses from one another, intensifying their interpersonal antipathies.

Again we see that intergroup tensions may occur in the absence of realistic conflict. Stereotype activation does not require that conflicts of interest be present in a situation. Rather, it may create perceptions of threat that lead to conflict, even when no actual danger exists. Cognitive schemata simplify a complex world by categorizing familiar stimuli, which facilitate routine responses in ordinary situations. In short, category-based reasoning economizes thinking. Apart from routinizing many interpersonal interactions, visual cues associated with categories allow rapid identification of likely threats, a highly functional cognitive ability in social environments that may pose danger. Intergroup contacts in such contexts must inevitably trigger misperceptions and erroneous responses, including the excessive use of force by police officers.

Taken together, the social identity and information processing models of cognition tell us a great deal about how stereotypically perceived group differences produce intergroup conflict. Irrespective of focus, cognitive theories in social psychology assume that category-based reasoning is a universal, context-driven human phenomenon (Fiske 1998). Recall that the information processing model was built upon the insights of the social identity model—people categorize and respond to others by group membership. All humans think and act in fundamentally similar ways; however, the specific content of their cognitive maps is provided by the social environments they inhabit. Individual variations in adherence to essentialist beliefs, level of prejudice, or knowledge of cultural stereotypes may determine whether automatic biases carry over to controlled thinking. But the demands of group life—loyalty to and support of ingroup members and rapid identification of potentially hostile outgroup members—could hardly routinely require in-depth thinking. Automatic activation of cognitive processes appears to be a defining characteristic of the human mind—humans seem to be hardwired for intergroup biases (Ashburn-Nardo, Voils, and Monteith 2001).

While the insights of the information processing model have moved us closer to a complete accounting of the dynamics of police brutality, we are still left with some vexing questions. Why, for example, do the police sometimes use excessive force when they can clearly perceive that their victim poses no threat to them, even when an individual is in custody? Is activation of a racial stereotype sufficient or necessary to produce discrimination? Such issues point to a more general question surrounding stereotype activation, namely, the degree of the association between cognition and behavior. A related concern is the role of emotions. For example, does the effect of cognitions on behavior depend on the arousal of emotional memories and responses?

Certainly a link between cognitions and behaviors exists, but that nexus is not well documented by research in the tradition of cognitive social psychology (Fiske 1998). Indeed, social psychologists have paid comparatively little attention to discriminatory behavior in favor of a focus on its presumed underlying mental processes. One type of discrimination, the one of most interest to us, involves "hot prejudices," those driven by feelings such as hostility and anger. Intergroup biases are generally manifested in relatively mild ingroup favoritism, but outgroup derogation and antagonism may develop when intergroup encounters elicit powerful emotions (Brewer 2001). In particular, outgroups perceived as threatening may provoke fear and aggression. This directs our attention to "gut-level" types of affective prejudice, which may predict discrimination better than stereotypes do (Fiske 1998). This possibility has received comparatively little attention from social psychologists until recently, yet it is one that holds out considerable promise for better understanding the seemingly irrational use of excessive force by the police.

CHAPTER 5

The Emotional Roots
of Intergroup Relations

Since antiquity, Western thinking about human behavior has placed a premium on the virtues of controlled reasoning, the conscious and rational part of human thinking, and eschewed the vices of passion, the unconscious and potentially irrational basis of human action (Zajonc 1998). For example, the concepts of rationality and free will were cornerstones of the classical school of criminology, which maintained that humans balance the costs and benefits of their behavior before deciding on a course of action (Beccaria 1764/1963). But such calculations would be immeasurably complex and require an inordinate amount of time for even the simplest of decisions (Damasio 1994). Our working memory has a limited capacity, and we would soon become lost in the process. Can such a mental system handle the complexities of day-to-day life? Clearly not, but fortunately unconscious emotional markers associated with various outcomes automatically eliminate many alternative lines of action, dramatically simplifying our analyses. Seemingly rational decisions thus are heavily invested in underlying emotions. Indeed, emotional processes may take over completely in situations that demand split-second reactions and, consequently, prohibit the conscious contemplation of alternative behavioral responses.

In recent years scholars from a variety of fields, ranging from neuroanatomy to sociology, have turned their attention to the profound influence of emotions on human behavior and social life. Yet ever since the inception of intergroup relations research some fifty years ago, social psychological inquiries have stressed cognitive processes while largely overlooking the emotional bases of behavior (Zajonc 1998). The neglect of emotions in social psychology may stem from a theoretical tradition that subordinates them to a secondary role in human behavioral responses. Consider William James's (1884) pioneering statement on the psychology of emotions. He reasoned that emotional feelings follow from the perception of an existing fact. A person escaping (response) the presence of a bear (stimulus) would perceive physiological sensations (e.g., rapid heartbeat, sweaty palms) that provide the bodily feedback necessary to experience emotional feelings. That logic set the stage for a long line of theorizing that minimized the role of emotions in producing behavioral responses by conceptualizing them as outcomes rather than causes of responses to stimuli (see LeDoux 1996, 42–53). Beginning in the 1960s, cognitive approaches added the concept of appraisal to the causal sequence. Humans are said to appraise (either unconsciously or consciously) a stimulus, which results in an action tendency. Conscious access to the appraisal process occurs after the fact, which produces the emotional feeling about a stimulus. In this view, cognition is both a sufficient and a necessary condition for the production of emotion; that is, "thoughts are capable of producing emotions . . . [and] emotions cannot occur without some type of thought (Lazarus 1991, 353).

A particularly influential example of this line of reasoning is found in Albert Bandura's (1986) social learning theory, which specifies the cognitive processes involved in acquiring predictive information and the anticipatory conscious thought involved in behavioral responses. Awareness is seen as essential for learning predictive information. Emotions and behavior are not causally linked; rather, they are coeffects triggered by one's cognitive responses to environmental stimuli. The meanings of emotions depend on cognitive appraisals of visceral reactions, which then may influence subsequent responses. While emotions play a facilitative role in the production of behavioral responses, it is secondary to cognitive processes such as those involved in acquiring predictive information by observing and modeling the behavior of others.

Social learning theory remains hugely influential in social psychology and yields insights essential to developing our theoretical model of police brutality. Nonetheless, the emergence of a robust body of research on emotions has begun to alter thinking about their role in the production of behavioral responses to stimuli. Theorizing about the cognition-emotion nexus began to change with the publication of research showing that preferences, or simple emotional reactions, can develop without conscious recognition of a stimulus (LeDoux 1996). When people are exposed to some novel (previously not encountered) stimulus, they subsequently show a liking for that stimulus over ones to which they had not been preexposed (Zajonc 1980). This "mere exposure" effect may occur without any reward/reinforcement associated with or response required by the stimulus. The existence of this phenomenon appears universally among humans, and it provides compelling support for the primacy of affect and the independence of emotion and cognition (Zajonc 1998). We will have more to say about the mere exposure effect, but for the moment it suffices to note that emotions may exist before and without cognition, thus cognitions could not be necessary and sufficient conditions to form emotional responses to stimuli. Recognition of the separateness of emotion and cognition has gradually taken hold among scholars.

So what are the important differences between emotions and cognitions? In a recent review of research on emotions, Robert Zajonc (1998) suggests a number of ways in which they differ. One crucial difference is that an infinite number of possible cognitions exists, whereas the number of distinct emotions is quite circumscribed. While there are basic cognitive processes, basic cognitions (specific elements of knowledge) apparently do not exist. In contrast, various scholars have agreed on a rather short list of basic emotions that can easily be dichotomized. Cognitions vary widely across cultures, but emotions are fairly universal. Cognitions have a concrete referent, always standing for something. Even though an external standard of validity (true/false) exists for cognitions, false ones may influence behavior the same as true ones do. Emotions do not stand for anything and do not require any external referent. Each emotional category involves specific internal reactions that produce dramatically different behavioral consequences from its opposing category. Emotions may instigate action that bears drastic or dangerous consequences—for instance, fear or anger may spark aggression with potentially dire costs for the combatants. Such emotional responses may occur without activation of the cortical regions of the brain that are essential to cognition and thus need not involve any cognitive appraisal whatsoever. Cognitions, on the other hand, are incapable of activating instrumental responses without first eliciting an emotion.

As a matter of fact, different parts of the brain are implicated in emotional and cognitive processes, an observation with special significance for understanding the primacy of emotions in human behavior (LeDoux 1996). Our ability to think rationally depends upon the existence of emotions—cognitions cannot even make it past working memory without being tagged with emotional content. At the same time, we cannot ignore the fact that emotion and cognition are intricately and inextricably joined in human mental processes (e.g., Bandura 1986; Berkowitz 1993; Zajonc 1998). The evolution of the cognitive brain built on the existing foundation of the emotional brain (Turner 2000). Nor can we ignore the reality that human emotional responses are to some degree informed by cultural and social environments, although undoubtedly the contents of cognitive schemata are determined to a much larger degree by these external influences (Zajonc 1998). Basic emotions remain fundamental to specifying the human behavioral repertoire, and we shall see that they have special significance for understanding responses in situations in which threatening stimuli appear. Indeed, in light of the oppressive social conditions of impoverished minority neighborhoods, it will become apparent that interactions between police and citizens may be powerfully influenced by emotions.

The Nature of Human Emotions

The argument that emotional processes take primacy over cognitive ones is based on the evolution of the human brain and social organization (Massey 2002). The hominid line that led to modern humans (*Homo sapiens*) appeared several million years ago in the emerging ecology of savannahs and open woodlands of Africa that took hold as tropical forests retreated. Our earliest ancestors came equipped with comparatively sophisticated brains well organized for emotional responses, but the evolution of the species saw major developments in the brain that made possible the highly organized social life essential to survival in open environments. Jonathan H. Turner (2000) argues that subcortical limbic structures responsible for emotion were reorganized and elaborated, and these structures were rewired to neocortical and brain stem systems.[1] These pre-adaptations paved the way for the emergence of an expanded emotional repertoire, which allowed the forging of social bonds necessary to support stable social structures. The emotional bonds that linked our hominid ancestors into socially organized life existed long before their brains were capable of rationally calculating the potential benefits and costs of such arrangements (Massey 2002). The full expansion of the prefrontal neocortex responsible for complete rationality did not take place until *Homo sapiens* emerged about 150,000 years ago, thus the fully developed cognitive capacities of modern humans comprise but a very small part of our species' evolutionary history. Insofar as humans possess rational cognition, it is built upon pre-existing emotional structures that still profoundly influence thinking.

The modern human brain is remarkably complex, so much so that the trillions of synapses within it cannot be specified entirely by one's genetic makeup (Damasio 1994). Whereas some brain circuits are readily modifiable and may be reshaped repeatedly throughout the life span, others provide a stable backbone that is highly resistant to change. The evolutionarily modern outer layers of the brain are highly plastic. Those neocortical regions record our acquired experiences and responses to them. They produce mental images and willful actions. This complex architecture enables and coordinates the conceptualization, transmission, and processing of information, the systems of cognitive processing that were essential to the eventual emergence of complex forms of human social organization (see Massey 2005). The genome specifies only a general arrangement of those systems and circuitries, the precise arrangement of which will continue to be formed by the physical and social environment long after birth (Damasio 1994). Yet those capabilities remain intricately connected to and influenced by the archaic emotional brain. Underlying the environmentally sensitive information-processing system are evolutionarily older brain regions (e.g., the brain stem, hypothalamus, and amygdala), which the genome specifies far more precisely. These systems, central to the survival of the organism, cannot be left to chance—they regulate basic life processes, including basic emotional responses.

Ever since Charles Darwin's (1872) pioneering book *The Expression of the Emotions in Man and Animals*, considerable attention has been focused on the identification of basic human emotions (Turner 2000). Fear and anger are prominent in the emotional arsenal of animals, and scholars have uniformly recognized them as primary human emotions. Fear makes the avoidance of predation and other dangers possible, and anger may be tied to fear in defensive aggression. Activation of these emotions takes place in the amygdala, among the most ancient subcortical limbic systems. Modern humans remain highly attuned to signals of fear or anger. Happiness is another primary emotion, and it is activated in more diffuse regions of the brain, including the amygdala and septum. These emotions, along with sadness, form the foundation of the complex human emotional repertoire upon which human social solidarity developed. Derivatives of primary emotions formed the framework of intragroup and intergroup relationships that remain the backbone of human social organization.

Emotional Bonds of Ingroups

Human social structure involves complex patterns of sociality built on both positive and negative emotions (Turner 2000). The social construction of stable, cohesive, orderly local groups requires the mutual imposition of sanctions that appeal to both positive and negative emotions capable of extracting conforming behavior from group members. While humans are consciously aware of prescriptive and proscriptive moral codes and attendant sanctions, the power of those social constraints resides in their ability to arouse powerful emotional responses. The effectiveness of negative sanctions rests on the activation of humans' most primal emotions, fear and anger, which are the least associative emotions and also the ones most capable of generating antisocial counteremotions. Sanctions that elicit emotions such as fear may be essential to the maintenance of group solidarity, but stable social bonds also demand positive sanctions that elicit associative responses in people.

Positive emotional responses need not rely upon learning for activation. Simple perceptual or cognitive access to a novel stimulus produces a liking for the stimulus that grows logarithmically with repeated exposure (Zajonc 1998). This is the "mere exposure" phenomenon mentioned earlier. The term *mere* refers to the fact that the effect of exposure may occur without recognition of the stimulus, in the absence of any reward/reinforcement associated with it, and without any response required by it. The mere exposure effect has been observed for a variety of stimuli, in conditions with aversive and pleasant consequences, and across various species. Among humans, the phenomenon appears to be a cultural universal (Smith and Bond 1993). But why would this effect occur? No doubt the answer lies in its tremendous adaptive significance:

> No social bonds, or stable communities, could evolve or be maintained if nature did not equip organisms with a means of discriminating between objects that can be approached, in whose proximity the organism can remain without worry, and those to which a response must be infused with caution. (Zajonc 1998, 617)

In contrast to the dominant theoretical explanation of ingroup favoritism, the cognitive social identity model, the mere exposure argument grounds ingroup bias in emotion. According to the social identity model, cognitive processes produce the favoritism effect, with emotional and behavioral responses flowing from context-specific cognitive appraisals. Research suggests that cognitive assessments can indeed activate such emotional responses (e.g., Mackie, Devos, and Smith 2000). Yet the ingroup favoritism bias may have origins in emotional responses that take primacy over cognitive processes. The forging of social bonds essential to the survival of the species could hardly await the vagaries of far-distant evolutionary changes that ultimately produced the cognitive apparatuses that we now recognize as uniquely human qualities. Hence the mere exposure effect cannot be facilely dismissed as an emotional artifact of cognitive processes (Zajonc 1998).

Emotional Responses to Outgroup Threats

Just as ingroup responses comprise both emotional and cognitive components, so do those elicited by members of outgroups. Recall that analyses of cognitive processes show that ingroup favoritism involves milder forms of bias than found in outgroup derogation. Emotional expression involves a corresponding pattern. Fear and anger are more powerful than the prosocial emotions upon which social bonds rely so heavily (Turner 2000). These emotions are at the heart of negative sanctions essential to maintaining group life, but their expression is too costly to efficiently build and maintain intragroup solidarity. In contrast, fear and anger provide an invaluable system of protection against threats, including human outsiders. When confronting unexpected danger, whether from a consciously or an unconsciously perceived stimulus, humans may freeze in terror, flee, or physically fight back (Blanchard and Blanchard 1989). Among the ancestors of modern humans, who lived in small local bands, contact with outgroups could have carried risks that triggered fear and warranted the potential costs associated with the expression of defensive aggression.

If emotions such as fear play a vital part in the survival of an organism, then it would be expected that they can commandeer other parts of the brain when dangerous situations are encountered (LeDoux 1996). That is precisely what happens in the human brain. The amygdala is capable of influencing numerous higher-order thought processes when one confronts a potential danger, serving as part of an arousal system that directs information processing to the emotion-producing stimulus. As long as a threatening stimulus is present, the amygdala will drive the arousal system that maintains hypersensitivity in cortical networks as well as automatically activate the networks that elicit involuntary behaviors, such as fleeing or fighting. Such responses may buy time, which allows one to take conscious control and consider other strategies. Emotions may, however, produce responses to stimuli before cognitive processes can exert any influence whatsoever. A parallel processing system operates within the brain, including one path that bypasses the cortical regions and permits quicker responses than the path that runs through the cortex. A potentially threatening stimulus, such as rustling leaves that may signal the presence of a snake, demands a split-second response, even if it is unnecessary. The body unconsciously responds physiologically for evasive or aggressive action until after the threat is confronted or passes. A quick and dirty subcortical defense system that requires no cognitive input whatsoever has tremendous survival value.

How can such subconscious emotional responses be triggered? Either natural or learned triggers may elicit such emotion-based unconscious responses (LeDoux 1996). Natural triggers are innate and require no conditioning or higher mental processes for an animal to respond to a threatening stimulus. Such innate stimulus-emotional response relationships may comprise but a small part of the human behavioral repertoire, although certainly some exist. Learned or conditioned triggers no doubt play a much larger role among a species with a highly plastic capacity to acquire information from the environment. Still, only the most rudimentary form of fear conditioning is necessary. Such learning involves nothing more than a variant of the classical conditioning phenomenon observed by Ivan Pavlov, in his well-known studies of conditioned responses (anticipatory salivation) in dogs. Fear conditioning permits the efficient acquisition and storage of information about harmful stimuli and situations, thus solving a pervasive problem of survival for all species:

> Fear conditioning opens up channels of evolutionarily shaped responsivity to new environmental events, allowing novel stimuli that predict danger (like sounds made by an approaching predator or the place where a predator was seen) to gain control over tried-and-true ways of responding to danger. The danger predicted by these *learned trigger stimuli* can be real or imagined, concrete or abstract, allowing a great range of external (environmental) and internal (mental) conditions to serve as CSs [conditioned stimuli]. (LeDoux 1996, 143, emphasis in original)

Several features of fear conditioning attest to its adaptive value (LeDoux 1996). Such learning occurs very quickly. Obviously a person need encounter a mugger in a park only once to avoid that spot or approach it very cautiously in the future. Fear conditioning also is long lasting. The passage of time, even if danger is not encountered again in the same spot, is not sufficient to extinguish fully the association between the threat and the location in which it was encountered. Lastly, even among humans, conscious processes need not be involved in fear conditioning. While humans may be aware of feeling afraid, unconscious mechanisms for acquiring, storing, and retrieving emotional memories may activate both defensive responses and the consciousness of fear.

In the classical fear conditioning model, a neutral stimulus may become associated with aversive consequences when it is paired with an aversive event (Olsson, Ebert, Banaji, and Phelps 2005). Yet evolution may have "prepared" humans to learn some things more easily than others (Seligman 1970; Machalek and Martin 2004). Recurrent threats to survival may be more effectively and rapidly associated with fear because of the adaptive advantage that accrued to hominids that came with brains prewired to learn more readily when confronting naturally occurring (unconditioned) aversive stimuli. Thus fear-relevant stimuli such as snakes and spiders, compared to fear-irrelevant ones such as flowers, may more readily produce fear conditioning among humans (Öhman, Fredrikson, Hugdahl, and Rimmö 1976). Obviously prospects for survival would have improved among our ancestors, who quickly acquired an aversion to potentially poisonous creatures. The same may be true of human outsiders.

Insofar as *Homo sapiens* divided into what we now identify as races in recent evolutionary history, natural selection could not have specifically prepared humans to fear members of other races (Olsson et al. 2005). But a more general preparedness to fear those who appeared different may have evolved because those outside of one's own social group were more likely to pose threats (see, e.g., Manson and Wrangham 1991). Were humans equipped to learn fear of outsiders based on subtle distinctions between groups, more visible physical differences would clearly signify outgroup status and potential threat. That possibility finds support in a study demonstrating a robust fear-conditioning effect associated with race (Olsson et al. 2005). In the first experiment of the study, participants were presented with commonly used fear-relevant stimuli (a snake and a spider) and fear-irrelevant stimuli (a bird and a butterfly). Conditioned fear responses were elicited by pairing mildly uncomfortable electric shocks with the stimuli, and skin conductance responses were measured to determine the emotional salience of the stimuli during acquisition and extinction trials. Corresponding procedures were employed in the second experiment, in which black and white participants were presented with images of black and white male faces with neutral expressions. During the acquisition (fear conditioning) trial, electric shocks were paired with one stimulus category (face), whereas the other was presented without shock. No shocks were administered during the extinction trial. After finishing the extinction phase, the participants completed questionnaires concerning racial attitudes, stereotypes, and intergroup contact.

Consistent with previous studies, conditioned fear responses to snakes and spiders were not fully extinguished during the extinction trials in the first experiment, whereas those for birds and butterflies were. A parallel pattern of findings for ingroups and outgroups was observed in the second experiment. Conditioned fear of others was fully extinguished for the racial ingroup (fear-irrelevant) stimuli, but not for the racial outgroup (fear-relevant) stimuli. In other words, white participants' conditioned responses to black faces were not fully extinguished, and neither were black participants' conditioned responses to white faces. The only racial factor that influenced the response pattern was the participants' history of interracial dating, which attenuated a conditioned fear of outgroup members. Taken together, these findings suggest that "Millennia of natural selection and a lifetime of social learning may predispose humans to fear those who seem different from them; however, developing relationships with these different others may be one factor that weakens this otherwise strong predisposition" (Olsson et al. 2005, 787). Insofar as social learning is influenced by patterns of intergroup interaction, the spatial separation of races characteristic of American cities may exacerbate the natural tendency to fear dissimilar others.

Emotions and Rational Decision Making

Emotions not only influence learned responses to potential threats from the environment, they may also intercede in more calculated ones. Cognitions cannot make it past working memory without being tagged with an emotion—thus the elements of knowledge that form the basis of rational decision making cannot exist apart from emotion. Recall the argument that unconscious emotional markers simplify "rational" decision making by summarily eliminating many alternative lines of action from consideration. Antonio Damasio (1994) terms the gut feelings that guide cost/benefit analyses involved in rational decision making as "somatic markers." Acting as automated predictors of the likely outcomes of certain scenarios, somatic markers drastically reduce the number of behavioral options from which a decision is ultimately taken. When a likely outcome of some line of action comes to mind, no matter how fleetingly, it causes somatic (bodily) sensations that influence the course of action one takes. Negative markers serve as alarm bells, positive ones as incentives. These gut feelings or intuitions are generated from secondary emotions, the learned connections of objects and situations to primary emotions, and are shaped largely through education and socialization.

Somatic markers may act overtly or covertly. In the former instance, the individual is aware of the feelings generated during the effort to reach a decision. In the latter, approach/withdrawal attitudes are activated outside conscious awareness. Dangerous situations demanding rapid assessment and action may call upon covert somatic markers, just as stereotypical cognitions may operate unconsciously. Undoubtedly, these separate mental processes provide parallel systems for the rapid activation of negative behavioral responses in the face of threats from outgroup members.

Social Context and Emotions

While humans seem predisposed to powerful emotional responses to ingroup and outgroup members, we should remain mindful of the fact that emotions operate within social and cultural contexts, albeit less flexibly than cognitions do. Emotions comprise the internal states of individuals, but they still consist of profoundly social phenomena shaped by the individual's society and culture (Zajonc 1998). One must learn the meaning of emotions and the suitable expressions of emotions, including instrumental behaviors appropriately elicited by them. Socialization provides a framework for interpreting emotional experiences and learning to control them internally, though societies also establish external normative and institutional controls over demonstrations of emotion. Ultimately a reciprocal relationship exists between a group's characteristic expression of emotions and its normative patterns of behavior, each continually shaping the other (Markus and Kitayama 1994).

The study of social and culture influences within microcultures is an endeavor central to understanding emotional expression (Zajonc 1998), an observation with special significance for the analysis of the extra-legal violence that plagues police-minority relations. These groups are not mere microcosms of the larger society; they are, rather, microcultures that produce characteristic emotional expressions that uniquely shape intergroup relations. Police and minority citizens come equipped with the same human repertoire of emotions, yet the social and cultural framework of their day-to-day existence demands very different emotional controls and behavioral responses in interactions with one another. Vast differences in the control of emotional reactions occur any time that one group can dominate another with relative impunity. The social circumstances that shape the emotional responses characteristic of police-minority interactions seem to make certain adverse outcomes inescapable, given the structure of inequality in America.

The Emotions of the Police

America's large cities incorporate many difficult places for police officers to work. Some must patrol the impoverished, crime-ridden, disorderly areas that most citizens avoid out of fear of victimization. Their day-to-day work exposes them to the most difficult ecological and social circumstances of urban life, places where frustrated, hostile citizens challenge their authority and sometimes their personal safety. In these neighborhoods, officers perceive the greatest resistance from citizens and the greatest threats to their authority and safety (Bayley and Mendelsohn 1968). Moreover, they are called upon to deal with a wider array of problems than they must deal with elsewhere (Goldstein 1977). People call the police for all sorts of problems, including interpersonal disputes, crime, disorderly persons, medical emergencies, and accidents, and also when they just do not know where else to turn. The police handle dirty work that no one else wants to deal with, and they often see the worst of human behavior. Is it not to be expected that working under such conditions would heighten emotional bonds among officers and trigger fear and anger toward the citizens they police?

As we stressed earlier, policing is an all-encompassing occupation that cultivates deep social bonds among officers, and the literature on the subculture of policing acknowledges the importance of the emotional bonds that exist among them (e.g., Crank 1998). Those attachments undoubtedly buttress the ethnocentrism that segregates the occupational subculture from outsiders. Officers refer to others in their department not as peers, coworkers, or colleagues but as family. Many officers claim to love their work, though what they probably love most is the emotional attachments that come from being part of such a cohesive ingroup. Officers frequently socialize with their fictive police family and turn to one another for support (Skolnick and Fyfe 1993). Their loyalty to one another is plainly illustrated by the "code of secrecy." Officers may protect one another regardless of their personal beliefs about the behavior they are helping to hide, just as people with family members possessing discreditable attributes such as mental illness or alcoholism may hide them from the view of social control agents. Their emotional attachments to one another are acutely apparent when a police officer is killed on duty. The death of a police officer is felt intensely by fellow officers. Police funerals are highly ceremonial and emotional events, and even officers who did not have any personal relationship with their fallen comrade are affected by the emotional intensity of them (Crank 1998). The emotional ties that police officers feel toward one another go without question and serve as a powerful force in their lives, both on and off duty.

While the emotional bonds existing within the police subculture are well known, most scholarly work has not considered the role of emotions in explaining police behavior toward citizens, particularly the role that fear plays in officers' actions. Danger is a central and defining element of police culture and the working lives of officers (Crank 1998). Police officers often overstate the dangers of their work, sometimes comparing it to combat. At the same time, scholars often understate the dangers the police confront by focusing exclusively on deaths while ignoring the lesser injuries that befall officers. Various other comparatively minor job-related injuries may occur rather commonly, often during physical encounters with suspects.

Work-related threats may elicit fear through the processes of social learning and conditioning. Police officers are socialized to the importance of always being prepared for danger and importuned to always "maintain their edge" (Van Maanen 1978a; Kappeler, Sluder, and Alpert 1998). Formal training places a heavy emphasis on self-defense and alertness to danger. Stories of assaults and deaths while on duty allow officers to learn vicariously of dangerous people and places. They quickly learn the places where danger and threats to their authority are most likely to occur, and over time their personal experiences reinforce their knowledge of certain locales as more dangerous than others. In this way, specific areas, as well as particular types of people, become associated with danger (Crank 1998), and through this process of "ecological contamination," everyone encountered there is perceived as a potential threat (Smith 1986). Anonymous black males in disadvantaged neighborhoods arouse the utmost caution among police officers, as they are normally considered dangerous until proven otherwise (Anderson 1990).

Day-to-day police work in impoverished minority neighborhoods feeds officers' anxieties. Their personal experiences make them acutely aware of high levels of violence, particularly gun violence, in many inner-city neighborhoods. They also are highly cognizant of the hostility felt by residents of those neighborhoods.

> It seems reasonable to infer that policemen are put more on their mettle in lower-class, minority neighborhoods. . . . [They] associate patrol in disadvantaged areas with a high amount of discretionary intervention and the possibility of violence against persons. These are the kinds of situations where danger to the police officer may erupt without warning. He feels that he must be more alert to the unexpected and especially to the sudden surge of passion that precipitates an attack upon himself. By contrast, in well-to-do areas the nature of the crime is likely to be more clear and the policeman feels he is the hunter and not the hunted. (Bayley and Mendelsohn 1968, 90)

Indeed, the ecological characteristics of impoverished areas may stimulate unconscious fear arousal among officers upon entering them, even before any contact is made with threatening citizens. Officers become more alert and attuned to potential dangers, a conditioned response that requires no conscious preparation for the defensive or aggressive action that may be required at any moment. Citizens intuit the emotional responses that occur in police officers when they enter these areas. For example, participants in a qualitative study of perceptions of the police noted that officers' tension level and blood pressure must rise when patrolling poor neighborhoods (Weitzer 2000). Similarly, a respondent from another such study commented, "The cops come in and a lot of times they seem nervous, more intense than they should" (Stoutland 2001, 246). The apprehension and anxiety that police officers experience when patrolling minority neighborhoods clearly influence their actions (Bayley and Mendelsohn 1968). They avoid taking chances, demand that their authority be recognized, and act quickly to protect themselves from injury.

Apart from the threats they confront, "Police deal with the grit of social relations, the coarse, rough outcomes that accompany the collapse of human affairs" (Crank 1998, 119). They cannot turn away from people's problems; rather, they must meet the uglier side of society head on. Victims of crime, drug overdoses, child abuse and neglect, and sundry other horrific troubles are more than just television images for them. For many police officers, working depressed communities is the staple of their day-to-day job. They must deal with the grief and anger of victims and their families. The citizens involved in these situations (e.g., witnesses, victims, perpetrators) are sometimes intoxicated, injured, scared, angry, or openly hostile toward police. For many who regularly witness such events, "the thinness of the social veneer will always be too visible" (Crank 1998, 120). These emotional aspects of policing continually reinforce emotional bonds among officers and heighten their focus on danger.

The emotional strains of working in such locales may increase the likelihood of both automatic stereotypic responses and emotion-driven aggression. Stressful events spur an "allostatic" response, the triggering of physiological changes such as adrenaline and endorphin release and accelerated heart rate, which prepares the body for immediate action (McEwen and Lasley 2002). Heavy allostatic loads occasioned by the routine activation of such physiological responses, whether through immediate events or mental recollections of past events, produce a number of adverse effects on bodily systems. These include impacts on the functioning of the brain that may increase cognitive load, a condition that promotes reliance on stereotypes in responding to environmental stimuli. Moreover, as we shall see in the next chapter, aversive stimuli produce negative emotions, which may trigger expressive forms of aggression that serve no instrumental end (Berkowitz 1993).

Put simply, police officers perceive the trying situations they confront in impoverished minority neighborhoods as "the most unpleasant, complicated, discretionary, and emotional" (Bayley and Mendelsohn 1968, 164). Encounters with citizens in these areas often are seen as unpredictable and capable of erupting into danger without warning. Rote application of bureaucratic rules is not feasible within this context. Instead, "rational" decision making is deeply rooted in gut-level feelings that, hand-in-hand with unconscious stereotypic responses, allow officers to make decisions very rapidly. Ironically, the value of such intuitive responses is celebrated by some, who suggest that officers' emotion-based intuition should be nurtured (e.g., Pinizzotto, Davis, and Miller 2004). Perhaps their celebration is tempered when a videotape of officer misconduct appears on the television news. A history of both conditioned responses and social learning undoubtedly prepares officers for quick responses to situations, but not necessarily in ways envisioned by trainers or acceptable to the larger society.

The Emotions of Minority Citizens

The conditions of America's ghettos and barrios hardly promote social cohesiveness. The socially disorganized qualities of these neighborhoods are central to understanding the problems of crime and social disorder endemic to them (see, e.g., Skogan 1990; Sampson and Wilson 1995; Phillips 2002). Even so, "decent" people experience emotional bonds to family and friends and are committed to civility and conventional morality (Anderson 1999). At the same time, they are surrounded by highly alienated and embittered "street" people who victimize their neighbors and view the police as undeserving of respect. Even good citizens share serious reservations about police behavior (Stoutland 2001). Residents of impoverished minority neighborhoods are surrounded by fear-producing stimuli, not the least of which is the police who ostensibly protect them.

The recognition of criminal threats in a neighborhood increases the perceived risk of crime victimization, which causes lifestyle adjustments that constrain behavior and evoke the emotional responses of anxiety and dread that constitute fear of crime (Ferraro 1995). Neighborhood conditions may influence perceptions of crime more heavily than do individual social characteristics (e.g., Covington and Taylor 1991; Holmes 2003). Research on fear of crime has identified various environmental dimensions of the problem, specifying ecological conditions that exacerbate perceptions of risk and arouse fear among the residents of minority localities (see Covington and Taylor 1991; Ferraro 1995). Certain physical and social characteristics of poor minority areas—public drinking, drug use, graffiti, and dilapidated buildings—are signs of incivility or social disorder that highlight the possibility of victimization. Indicators of disorder are not intrinsically threatening, but they symbolize potential threats (Warr 1990). Moreover, perceptions of risk may be more widespread than the actual incidence of crime because of the experience of indirect victimization. Victimization accounts may increase as a function of the perceived frequency and seriousness of crime in an area (Bursik and Grasmick 1993), and the crime stories shared by others may elevate people's fear of crime. Persistent social disorder and perceptions of danger may cause residents to distrust their neighbors and to see them as threats. Consequently, people tend to constrain their public activities and limit outside contacts to close friends and family (Massey and Denton 1993; Ferraro 1995).

People expect the police to deal with problems of crime and social disorder, but residents of disadvantaged minority neighborhoods lack confidence in the ability of the police to perform the job effectively (Weitzer and Tuch 2006). Lack of confidence in the police may further heighten perceptions of crime risk among them (Holmes 2003). Ironically, the police charged with protecting citizens from the wrongdoers among them are yet another symbol of danger to many citizens of disadvantaged neighborhoods (Feagin 1991; Anderson 1999). Citizens living in those neighborhoods are caught in a double bind that is not of their making. While they may call upon the police to resolve the crimes and problems of disorder that engender fear, the arrival of the police may inject new threats into the situation and amplify their level of fear.

A deep-seated fear of the police is prevalent among minorities (Block 1971; Feagin 1991). It seems quite likely that many black men see white police in particular as a "major source of danger and death" (Feagin 1991,

113), and generally the police may be seen as the "biggest gang in the city" (Stoutland 2001, 246). Adverse interactions with police officers condition people to fear them, producing unconscious emotional responses whenever a patrol car or police officer appears. Thus just as the fear of crime victimization constrains public behavior, so does fear of the police (Feagin 1991; Anderson 1999). Young minority males in particular are strongly motivated to avoid them. Their public life becomes severely constrained as they strive to avoid running into the police, believing that such encounters are all too often the prelude to abuse. At least some community members believe "that young Black men should avoid any interactions with police officers" (Stoutland 2001, 242). The data on police brutality and other forms of police misconduct suggest that their fear is well grounded.

Emotion and Cognition in Police-Minority Relations

What are the implications of emotions for understanding police behavior in minority neighborhoods? The limited data on police and minority emotions generally comprise after-the-fact cognitive appraisals of unknown reliability. Still, they are highly suggestive in light of what we know about ingroup/outgroup emotions and the conditions that trigger them. Unmistakably, police and minority citizens perceive one another as alien sources of threat and become conditioned to fear one another. The related emotions of fear and anger elicited by that threat may provide the principal mechanism underlying the mutual distrust existing between them. Outgroup members may constitute unconditioned stimuli that elicit fear, even when they pose no objective threat. Encounters that associate outgroup members with real danger may produce conditioned fear responses that are readily acquired and difficult to extinguish. Armed encounters with minority citizens, even if rare, may be sufficient to summon a sense of danger and fear any time the police officer enters a minority neighborhood. Uncomfortable and frightening encounters with the police will likewise condition the citizen to respond fearfully to the presence of the police officer, perhaps amplifying the premonition of danger that puts an officer on an emotional edge. As a police monitor in Austin, Texas, described the nature of police-minority interactions, "Fear of police by blacks . . . can cause them to try to flee or act defensively when they encounter police officers. Similarly, fear of blacks by police can cause them to overreact when they encounter African Americans, especially young black men" (*Austin American-Statesman* 2006).

While we have emphasized the independent nature of emotion in this discussion, it is important to keep in mind that cognitive and emotional processes involve complementary and highly interrelated systems that produce adverse outcomes for outgroup members, especially those with great threat potential but comparatively little power. We cannot separate cognitions from emotions in a particularly important way—cognitions cannot exist apart from emotion. The meanings of cognitions are preeminently cultural in origin, yet cognitions must be tagged with some emotion to make it past working memory into long-term memory. Indeed, while stereotypes for a plethora of social groups exist, it may be the fear and hatred of particular outgroups that make bad things happen (see, e.g., Brewer 2001). Socially learned memories circulated via police war stories and citizens' police atrocity tales make people consciously aware of their fear of the dangers that surround them. Whether revealed by dark skin or a characteristic style of dress, as in the blue uniform of the police officer, early on in life people learn to associate danger with members of particular outgroups.

Merely seeing a potential adversary, even when the person clearly poses no immediate danger, may arouse emotional memories and trigger allostatic responses to the perceived threat. Whether consciously or unconsciously, recognition of a potentially threatening stimulus is sufficient to prepare one for action should it become necessary. The uncomfortable visceral states experienced by the police officer also pave the way for "rational" decisions about how to proceed in encounters with minority citizens. These gut feelings, along with automatically activated stereotypes, close the door on many potential lines of action before a more careful assessment can take place. The remaining avenue of action may leave little room for reconciliation with a perceived adversary, setting the stage for a forceful encounter.

In short, both the police and poor minority citizens continually confront threats, real and imagined, and experience attendant visceral responses. These aversive stimuli generate powerful negative emotions, which may cause them to strike out against others even when nothing is to be gained. All too often minority citizens of impoverished neighborhoods direct their violence toward fellow citizens. The police, regrettably, may unleash their emotions among the same disadvantaged population.

CHAPTER 6

═══

Translating Intergroup Biases
into Intergroup Aggression

We began this inquiry into the causes of police brutality with an argument that existing criminological explanations of the phenomenon are overly simplistic and therefore inaccurate. In our view, neither the traditional nor critical theories that have been used to explain excessive force are up to the task because they fail to address the multifaceted social-psychological dynamics of police-minority relationships. We sought to advance our understanding of the matter by considering various theories of intergroup relations. One initially promising lead was found in group-conflict theory, which implicates the realistic opposition of group interests as the primary culprit in the production of intergroup tensions. It too suffers explanatory difficulties, however. Alternative social-psychological theories allowed us to build on insights from that model to frame a more comprehensive explanation of police brutality. Those approaches, especially the ones focusing on cognitive phenomena, have come to dominate the field of social psychology, but their influence on criminology has been negligible. For example, the role of stereotyping in police behavior is widely acknowledged, but criminologists have applied the concept superficially without reference to the substantial research findings from the field of social psychology.

In addressing the problem of police-minority tensions, we discussed various theoretical models that identify cognitive and emotional processes that (1) reveal the multidimensional quality of humans' category-based responses to others, (2) operate in the absence of actual conflicts of interest, (3) function at both unconscious and conscious levels, and (4) elicit various behavioral manifestations, aggression being just one possibility. It is the last point on which we elaborate here, finishing the groundwork for the specification of a theoretical model that synthesizes the various dimensions of intergroup dynamics into a model of excessive force, a model that expressly aims to explain its differential application in impoverished minority neighborhoods. Before detailing the specific connections of cognition, emotion, and aggression, let us briefly remap the theoretical territory that we have traversed.

The Dimensions of Intergroup Relations

The group-conflict perspective has deep roots in the fields of sociology, anthropology, and social psychology, with early work appearing a century ago (e.g., Simmel 1908/1955). Surveying the various theoretical statements in the field, Donald T. Campbell (1965) synthesized their common themes into what he called "realistic-group-conflict theory." He hypothesized that intergroup conflict is a rational response when an incompatible goal or competition over scarce resources threatens groups. Perceptions of threat to ingroup interests create hostility and bias against outgroup members and strengthen ingroup identity, solidarity, and ethnocentrism.

No doubt the interests of police and minority citizens conflict in fundamental ways. Police want to handle the numerous calls from impoverished minority neighborhoods, many of which do not involve "real" police work, as quickly and efficiently as possible, whereas citizens want the police to manage effectively the problems of social disorder and crime endemic to their impoverished neighborhoods. Their different goals and expectations undeniably engender police-minority tensions, and a group-conflict approach suggests that police brutality is simply an instrument of protection for officers as police patrol dangerous neighborhoods inhabited by citizens perceived as threatening (e.g., Holmes 2000). Obviously force is very handy for controlling citizens who pose real dangers to officers or other citizens. Much of its usage reflects the police mandate, the legitimate police function of maintaining domestic order. Shooting and killing an armed suspect who refuses to relinquish a weapon and threatens the safety of others is proper police procedure under the law. It usually is acceptable to use a taser or pepper spray to subdue an unarmed suspect who is physically resisting arrest. Such force is a legitimate, instrumental form of aggression that serves a rational end. Clearly the police need not rely on excessive force to control those who pose real threats. This raises the question of whether the interests of citizens and police are sufficiently at odds to provoke police brutality, which conveys at least some potential of severe punishment for an offending officer. It is at this juncture where group-conflict theory begins to fail us. What ends could possibly make excessive force instrumental—what is to be gained by it?

Instrumentality implies that social actors reach decisions using some rational cost-benefit logic, with their chosen lines of action being the ones that provide the greatest utility. Enlightened self-interest is thus the engine that drives human behavior. Risking severe sanction for assaulting a citizen without legitimate cause defies such logic. Perhaps less vigorous uses of extra-legal force could be instrumental in certain ways, such as to psychologically protect officers' status when their authority is challenged. Protection of an officer's social status and self-esteem may warrant "waffling" a suspect on the partition in a patrol car, helping a handcuffed suspect "trip" over a curb, or even a clandestine bit of "roughing up" a citizen. Yet at times police brutality goes well beyond these injurious but usually relatively minor transgressions. Enlightened self-interest fails to provide a convincing explanation for such seemingly irrational behavior, which yields few benefits and may accrue heavy costs. By recognizing that violence also can be impulsive, we open a new avenue of inquiry based on the assumption that intergroup conflict does not always seek to protect objective group interests, at least not in the conventional sense.

The realistic-group-conflict model ultimately became less influential as social psychologists increasingly turned their attention to the various cognitive theories that emerged over the past half century. Whereas the group-conflict approach took for granted that individual phenomena were unnecessary to explain group behavior (Campbell 1965), that assumption was challenged by the new emphasis on individual psychological processes said to influence intergroup behavior (e.g., Turner 1982). Work involving one dominant perspective, a set of theories embodied in the social identity model, identified the chief failing of the group-conflict approach—numerous studies reveal that the mere perception of group membership is sufficient to produce biased judgments and gratuitous discrimination in the absence of conflicts of interest or competition (Brewer and Brown 1998).

The social identity model postulates that humans cognitively categorize themselves and others by reference to group membership and act toward others on the basis of those categorizations, even in circumstances where the group is defined in the most minimal way (Tajfel 1970; Tajfel et al. 1971). These cognitive processes operate spontaneously and seamlessly, requiring no conscious effort on the part of the individual actor. The more that social attributes such as race or occupation differentiate people from those in other social categories, the greater the perception of between-group differences and within-group similarities (Turner et al. 1987). Marked contrasts denote the existence of a high meta-contrast ratio, a condition that activates stereotypic self- and other-categorizations and increases the probability of category-based reactions to others. When social identity is salient, people see the world ethnocentrically. In this view, conflicts of interest are unnecessary for ingroup identification and favoritism to exist—competition and perceptions of threat may be consequences rather than causes of ingroup/outgroup differentiation.

The dynamics of social identity constitute one thrust of cognitive theorists' two-pronged agenda. The social identity model demonstrates the often subtle biases resulting from ingroup favoritism and lack of positive sentiments toward outgroups. It falters, however, in its inattention to the relative degree of derogation directed toward different outgroups. The second approach of cognitive theory, which encompasses various theoretical arguments that comprise an information processing model (Schaller et al. 1998), provides valuable insights into outgroup derogation. In this view, people are cognitive misers who seek to conserve mental resources in complex and demanding social environments (Fiske 1998). Cognitive categorization processes tag information about various characteristics of people and generate generalized attributions about other groups (Taylor 1981), stereotypes that simplify the world and facilitate rapid decision making when time and cognitive resources are limited (McCrae and Bodenhausen 2000). The initial activation of stereotypes may occur unconsciously, automatically eliciting behavioral responses without any forethought (Devine 1989). Subsequent deliberation, when circumstances permit, may allow for the suppression of stereotypes and a more controlled response. Yet American culture is rife with stereotypes and racial ideologies that conflate racial/ethnic group membership and criminality; hence, automatic preconscious responses, as well as more deliberate ones, may disadvantage outgroup members who in actuality pose no threat.

The two lines of cognitive theory share the assumption that cognitive categorization processes are a human universal. Both also recognize that the substantive content of cognitive schemata is learned in specific cultural and social contexts. For example, stereotyping of outgroups is a pervasive human tendency, but the targets and their alleged attributes vary from one cultural setting to another. The implications of the social identity and information processing models for understanding police-minority conflict seem readily apparent.

The deeply intertwined history of the police and minority communities in America demonstrates the salience of ingroup identity and favoritism in their relationships. The occupation of policing and the racial/ethnic identity of minorities provide readily visible and highly salient bases of social identity. Police and minority citizens also stereotype one another as threats to their respective ingroups, amplifying the anecdotal evidence upon which the stereotypes are built. Stereotypes of minority criminality are widespread in American society and are reinforced among the police by selective interactions with minority citizens. Vicarious accounts of police abuses permeate minority neighborhoods, generating stereotypic beliefs about the violent proclivities of the police.

While the cognitive approaches exemplified in these two theoretical traditions remain preeminent in the social psychology of intergroup relations, they too have difficulty with certain questions. One particularly troubling issue is the relative inattention afforded the role of emotions in human behavior (LeDoux 1996). Stereotypes may embody deep-seated prosocial and antisocial emotions, which may be implicated in the activation of discriminatory behavior, whether favoring the ingroup or injuring an outgroup. Cognitive approaches recognize that elements of knowledge stored in human memory are tagged with emotions that help create meaning and motivate behavioral responses. Yet in this perspective, emotions are seen as secondary to cognitive processes. It is commonly assumed that the presence of an environmental stimulus activates mental processes, which in turn elicits a conscious cognitive appraisal that defines one's emotional feelings.

Increasingly, scholarship on human emotions calls that assumption into question. The neocortical regions of the brain responsible for cognition were built upon lower regions of the brain and elaborated a preexisting stock of emotional responses to ingroup and outgroup members. The emergence of a complex emotional repertoire that made stable social structures possible was a central event in the evolution of modern humans, without which our distant ancestors undoubtedly would have joined the scrap heap of extinct hominid species (Turner 2000). An array of prosocial emotions supplemented the more primal emotions of fear and anger as the architecture of the brain evolved and ingroup solidarity emerged. The development of prosocial emotions overcame the solitary tendencies that existed among our early hominid ancestors, but their predispositions for weak social ties and individualism were not completely extinguished in modern humans. Consistent with the pattern observed for cognitive responses, ingroup emotions (e.g., pleasure, satisfaction) are weaker than ones commonly elicited by outgroups. Outgroups pose potential threats and activate stronger emotional responses, the upshot of natural selection advantaging those who easily learned fear of outgroup members because of the greater threat they posed (Olsson et al. 2005).

Encounters with threatening stimuli produce rapid, long-lasting effects on behavior (LeDoux 1996). An environment in which a threat has appeared in the past becomes unconsciously associated with the threat itself, later eliciting fear responses, even in the absence of the threatening stimulus. Thus encounters with threatening outgroup members may condition one to sense danger in the same locale in the future, creating a gut-level sense of foreboding that influences behavioral strategies. Human emotional responses also are influenced by cultural contexts

(Zajonc 1998), and the existence of outgroup stereotypes and vicarious learning through atrocity tales may further predispose individuals to respond to outgroup members with fear and anger. The threatening conditions of daily life and policing in impoverished minority neighborhoods may continually create and maintain feelings of frustration and fear among citizens and police, furnishing emotional fuel to the highly combustible tinder of police-minority tensions.

To this point we have established a broad theoretical framework for understanding the generally poor state of affairs between the police and citizens of impoverished minority neighborhoods. Yet many different behavioral expressions may emanate from the social psychological phenomena at work. Emotions and cognitions involve internal mental processes that translate into external actions that may vary depending upon the situation. For instance, antisocial responses to outsiders may be expressed in a variety of ways—the available options include rudeness, insults, indifference, withdrawal, avoidance, and physical aggression. While we have moved closer to understanding how it is that police brutality constitutes a normal, albeit highly unfortunate, manifestation of human psychological functioning, we still need to address the issue of why the police employ such extreme aggression rather than the less costly options in their behavioral repertoire for handling difficult citizens. In short, what elicits a specific response that conveys great potential cost to the actor? A good part of the answer lies in the reality that the emotional and cognitive mental processes producing aggression have little to do with rationality.

In addressing that issue, we first integrate insights from theories of group phenomena based on emotion and cognition with conceptually allied theories of individual aggression. As we chart these ideas, we will take a slightly different tact than the one used until now. We have presented the ideas of group-conflict, cognitive, and emotional theories in roughly the chronological order in which they arrived on the scene of intergroup relations research. That approach seemed efficacious insofar as conceptual connections can be built more easily upon a preformed foundation. Now, however, we employ a different chronology, examining the sequence in which the various processes shape aggressive behavioral responses to others. This ordering gives priority to emotion and then cognition, with group interests and other social circumstances providing the external context in which internal mental phenomena are activated. As we shall see, physiological, emotional, and cognitive responses are intricately and inextricably interwoven into the production of aggression. Once we have outlined the theoretical underpinnings of aggression, we lay out a model of police brutality that ties together the various theoretical strands of our analysis.

The Emotional and Cognitive
Foundation of Aggression

How do emotional and cognitive mental processes translate into aggressive behavior? In addressing this deceptively simple question, the first issue is defining what we mean by aggression. Social psychologists have not offered an entirely uniform definition for the term, but most would certainly agree that, at a minimum, *"aggression* [is] *any form of behavior that is intended to injure someone physically or psychologically"* (Berkowitz 1993, 3, emphasis in original). That serves as a good working definition for our purposes, pointing to the essence of police brutality, a behavior that aims to physically (and perhaps psychologically) injure another person.[1]

Another fundamental issue is the goals served by aggression. We have alluded repeatedly to the point that police brutality does not clearly reflect the enlightened self-interest of police officers. Of course much human aggression is *instrumental*, that is, it provides a means to an end. A paid assassin may kill someone in the course of her professional obligations, or a husband may assault his wife to establish and maintain social dominance. While obviously harmful to another, the injury itself is not the primary motive underlying these behaviors. They function primarily as tools to obtain some other desired goal (e.g., money or social status) and tend to be controlled consciously (Berkowitz 1993). Sometimes, however, the aggressor first and foremost seeks to injure another person, which may be called *emotional* (or sometimes hostile or angry) aggression. The act of aggression is rewarding in itself and often engaged in impulsively without any thought given to the consequences of the action. Criminologists are well aware that many homicides and assaults are instigated by unreasoned passions. Perhaps much serious police brutality is too. Generally acts of aggression entail some combination of instrumental and emotional motivations.

Two general theoretical perspectives have been especially influential in work on emotional and instrumental aggression (Geen 1998). Leonard Berkowitz's (e.g., 1983, 1988, 1989, 1993) theory of cognitive neoassociationism and Albert Bandura's (e.g., 1973, 1983, 1986) social learning theory both postulate that a complex interplay of parallel physiological, emotional, and cognitive processes organizes aggressive responses, but the theories give primacy to different processes and motivators. Cognitive neoassociationism emphasizes emotional responses to aversive instigating events, which are said to produce emotional aggression. Social learning theory stresses conscious cognitive processes, which are said to produce various functional (instrumental) forms of aggression. Taken together, the two models suggest that acts of aggression may unfold in stages—initial aggressive reactions better explained by the principles of cognitive neoassociationism, and subsequent aggressive reactions better explained by those of social learning theory (Geen 1998).

Cognitive Neoassociationism

The first prominent social-psychological theory of aggression was proposed by John Dollard and colleagues (1939) in their book *Frustration and Aggression*. They argued that aggression always requires frustration, and the occurrence of frustration always elicits some type of aggression. In other words, frustration is a necessary and sufficient condition for educing aggressive behavior. Although various definitions of frustration emerged later, the original usage of the term by Dollard and colleagues refers specifically to external circumstances that thwart goal attainment (Berkowitz 1988, 1989). The resultant act of aggression, which may be directed at the source of the thwarting or displaced unto a weaker target, was said to produce a cathartic lessening of frustration. These ideas have generated considerable controversy and criticism (e.g., Bandura 1973), with even the more favorably disposed casting doubt on the proposition that frustration is crucial to the evocation of aggression (e.g., Baron 1977). While the original frustration-aggression hypothesis holds little currency today, its resurrection in cognitive neoassociationism theory remains highly influential.

Berkowitz (1988, 1989, 1993) recast the idea of externally induced frustrations into the concept of aversive events. This line of reasoning suggests that a wide range of unpleasant events can initiate acts of aggression. It is not the event per se but the negative affect aroused by it that elicits the aggressive response. For example, the presence of someone who holds very different attitudes and values may pose an unpleasant challenge to our own attitudes and values, stimulating psychological discomfort (Berkowitz 1988). By triggering negative emotions, the presence of an aversive stimulus presumably activates biological programming that "gives rise automatically to a variety of expressive-motor reactions, feelings, thoughts, and memories" (Berkowitz 1993, 57). Some of these are said to be associated with rudimentary anger and the tendency to fight, whereas others are linked to rudimentary fear and the tendency to flee. These closely linked, primitive feelings thus initiate a response tendency, which may be further molded by more differentiated emotions that arise from subsequent thoughts and memories. Various factors, including past learning and the perception of whether the immediate situation is safe for aggression, ultimately determine whether one flees from or strikes out against the source of displeasure.

Whether a negative affect-generated instigation results in overt aggression depends upon several considerations (Berkowitz 1993). One determinant is the intensity of internal arousal. Lacking sufficient arousal, one may not openly display displeasure. The greater the intensity of internal agitation produced by a negative event, the higher the likelihood of an aggressive response. Another factor affecting the probability of an overt display of aggression is the availability of a suitable target. The pain of a headache may provoke irritability and predispose one to aggression, but it may generate nothing more than diffuse hostility in the absence of a specific target. Should a suitable target present itself, particularly one associated with the adverse event that stimulated the negative affect, the probability of aggression increases. In addition to these facilitators, two factors are correlated negatively with aggressive responses. The probability of aggression decreases as the likelihood of punishment increases and as self-regulation increases.

Berkowitz's (1993, 69) line of reasoning ties aggression specifically to "negative affect-generated internal stimulation." Whereas internal stimulation plays a crucial role in pushing out aggressive responses, impulsive aggression also involves reactions to various external cues. External cues evoke stronger reactions when they convey an aggressive meaning or are associated with earlier unpleasant events. An important example of stimuli that signify aggressive meaning is weapons. Several studies indicate that the presence of a weapon, even if not directly associated with the aversive stimulus, heightens aggressive responses (Geen 1998). Situations related to unpleasant events in the past may generate negative feelings when encountered again, because they remind one of the suffering experienced before. Certainly a police officer must feel some measure of apprehension and fear when patrolling neighborhoods in which dangerous encounters with citizens occurred in the past. The mere presence of a weapon, even if not under the target's control, could enhance the probability of an aggressive response to a citizen in such a neighborhood.

In a nutshell, Berkowitz's logic maintains that acts of aggression involve a sequential process. An instigating event produces a rudimentary affective response, which in turn gives rise to expressive motor reactions, memories, and cognitions. Memories are located in both emotional and cognitive schemata, which operate in parallel to focus attention very rapidly on specific stimulus features and generate expectations about what may take place later. Flight and fight tendencies occur simultaneously, with factors such as prior learning influencing the initiation of the immediate response. Purely emotional aggression would occur at this point. The impulsive stage is followed by a period during which the aggressive tendency may come under some degree of cognitive control. Cognitive appraisals, attempts to interpret and make sense of one's emotions,

occur after emotional arousal has already taken place. Such interpretations of one's emotions may influence subsequent behavioral responses
(Berkowitz 1993). Thinking about the instigating event that generated the
emotional response may either amplify angry feelings and aggressive tendencies or reduce them, depending on individual values, situational circumstances, and target characteristics.

Social Learning Theory

The cognitive dimensions of aggression provide the analytical focus of Albert Bandura's (1973, 1983, 1986) social learning theory. In contrast to
the approach of cognitive neoassociationism, Bandura embraces the primacy of cognition and relegates emotion to a secondary role. In this view,
environmental events may arouse conditioned physiological and emotional reactions, but those with psychological significance exert a
stronger influence on those reactions. Humans do not just react to stimuli—they interpret them and organize that information into predictive expectations and beliefs. Consider, for example, symbolic and vicarious
forms of affective learning that require no firsthand experience with an
external stimulus. People can acquire strong emotional reactions to other
people or places in the absence of any personal contact with them, with
emotion-laden symbols, such as words or pictures, creating new fears and
hatreds or arousing existing feelings of dread. Likes and attractions can
be acquired similarly through such associative symbolic experiences. Affective learning also may occur through vicarious experience, as people
observe the emotional reactions of others to what were previously neutral
stimuli. In short, the direct experience required for conditioned emotional
responses is but one avenue, arguably one less traveled, to the learning of
emotional reactions to environmental stimuli.

Social cognitive mechanisms are said to perform a seminal role in fear
arousal and defensive behavior, such as aggression. The argument of social learning theory acknowledges that cognition, emotion, and behavior
interact in complex ways, but it is assumed that emotional arousal and behavioral responses coexist rather than share a causal connection (Bandura
1986). In contrast to the position that fear may be an unconsciously conditioned response to an environmental stimulus, this line of reasoning
maintains that people learn little unless they recognize the connection between a stimulus and a painful event. Awareness is critical. Often both
human emotion and behavior are activated by threatening events, about
which one learns through direct or symbolic association with painful experiences. But the aversive quality of the threatening cue is not what triggers the behavioral response. Rather, it evokes a defensive response
because of its predictive qualities with respect to the avoidance of a painful

outcome. Anticipatory thought may influence behavior without the activating effect of emotional arousal.

The nonoccurrence of a painful outcome following a defensive act provides evidence that danger was averted and confirms the utility of the behavioral response, which makes it difficult to eliminate an established defensive behavior (Bandura 1986). Even fallacious beliefs (such as stereotypes) about potential threats may be sustained; the lack of painful experience provides evidence about the efficacy of whatever behavioral response was employed to ward off the threat. When painful outcomes occur irregularly and unpredictably, beliefs about potential dangers and the effectiveness of defensive strategies cannot be altered easily. Just as conditioning is said to unconsciously elicit a sense of fear in an environment where danger has been encountered, the recognition that dangers may lurk there sustains conscious awareness of potential threats, even when their occurrence is empirically improbable, and elicits both fear and defensive behavior.

The maintenance of aggressive behavior depends in no small part upon its positive consequences, whether in fact it is instrumental in achieving desired goals (Bandura 1983). Aggression can effectively obtain tangible or psychological rewards, as well as reduce aversive treatment by others. Rather than unthinking emotional motivation to injurious behavior, people aggress against others to obtain some reward or to reduce pain. Likewise, constraints over aggressive behavior operate through the costs associated with its enactment. Punishing consequences are rooted in threats of external punishment (fear) and anticipatory self-condemnation (guilt). Aggressive behavior bearing a high risk of punishment will be abandoned in favor of more socially acceptable strategies, assuming such alternatives are available and effective. The lack of acceptable alternatives requires severe punishment to outweigh the benefits accruing to aggression. Just as aggression can be learned vicariously, so too can its consequences.

In short, the social cognitive approach sees aggression largely as functional, a means of avoiding painful experiences or acquiring desirable outcomes (Bandura 1986).[2] Acquisition of aggressive modes of behavior typically takes place via observation and modeling of others and then is refined through direct experience and reinforcement. Modeling allows one to observe the consequences of behavior, whether accurately or inaccurately (e.g., in many media portrayals of violence). The forms, frequency, situations, and targets of aggression are determined largely by the mechanisms of social learning. The motivation to aggress, although sometimes involving aversive stimulation, far more commonly involves learned provocations. Events that instigate aggressive responses, such as verbal and physical challenges, acquire their meaning socially (Bandura 1983). Appropriate targets of aggression also are defined socially. People learn to dislike and attack certain types of other people. While aggressive propensities toward others may be acquired through direct experience, they can be learned symbolically and vicariously. Cultural context plays a crucial part—societies that are warlike and reward aggression inevitably reproduce conflict, whereas those that are peaceful and devalue aggression foster nonviolent relations.

An important intersection between cognitive neoassociationism and social learning theories concerns the effects of dehumanizing others (cf. Bandura 1986; Berkowitz 1993). When members of other groups, such as racial/ethnic minorities, are divested of their human qualities through the mechanisms of victim blaming, pejorative stereotyping, and sectarian ideology, self-regulating mechanisms lose their grip. The belief that a target is inhuman and somehow deserving of punishment thus disinhibits the aggressor and even justifies the aggression as an admirable act. The conditions of modern life spawn dehumanization:

> Bureaucratization, automation, urbanization, and high social mobility lead people to relate to each other in anonymous, impersonal ways. In addition, social practices that divide people into in-group and out-group members produce human estrangement that fosters dehumanization. Strangers can be more easily cast as unfeeling beings than can personal acquaintances. (Bandura 1983, 32)

Moreover, the nature of certain jobs further contributes to the dehumanization of others. Those who confront recurrent human problems become prone to routinization and the depersonalization of others, even coming to see them as subhuman (Bandura 1986, 384). Many of the contributing factors read like a laundry list of police work: protracted, intense interaction with those in distress; limited breaks from impersonal work; unvaried job routines; lack of control over work-related policies; the inability to leave the job behind during off hours; and exposure to the cynical and dehumanizing beliefs of coworkers regarding people in distress. Surely the geographic isolation of impoverished minorities in America's cities and the job of policing their neighborhoods cultivate a predisposition among police officers to dehumanize those who live there.

The Inseparability of
Emotional and Cognitive Responses

Despite their differences on certain matters, cognitive neoassociationism and social learning theory complement one another in important ways.

Clearly the key difference between them concerns what initiates acts of aggression. Is aggression driven by emotion, a response to an aversive event? Or is it the predictive qualities of an event that drive it, allowing one to avoid pain or gain reward? In many respects, these questions pose an artificial dichotomy—aggression may serve both emotional and instrumental ends. It is apparent that the arguments presented in the previous chapter on emotion make a compelling case that humans' basic emotional responses to threats can operate without cognitive intervention. Moreover, memories, cognitions, and conscious thinking all depend heavily on input from the complex human emotional repertoire. Rational decision making, the tour de force of cognitive development, cannot be separated from emotion. At the same time, the evolution of cognitive processes profoundly enhanced humans' ability to recognize and respond differentially to ingroup and outgroup members.

While social psychologists continue to wrestle with the nuances of the complex interplay of emotion and cognition in the production of behavioral responses, it is clear that the brain relies on these inseparably linked mental systems to demarcate ingroups from outgroups and to shape intergroup relations. Consistent with current thinking about the causes of aggression (Geen 1998), in the next chapter we propose a model of police brutality that gives primacy to emotions and automatic cognitive processes in the early stages of behavioral responses to threatening stimuli, with conscious appraisals of emotional feelings, personal beliefs, and potential consequences of alternative lines of behavior kicking in during later stages of the behavioral response sequence. The social context of police-minority interactions in disadvantaged neighborhoods provides a backdrop that increases the likelihood of untoward aggression taking place there.

CHAPTER 7

———

A Social, Emotional, and
Cognitive Theory of Excessive Force

The fundamental premise of our work is that category-based psychological processes are at the heart of intergroup relations between the police and various minority groups. Category-based phenomena include emotions and stereotypes regarding ingroup and outgroup members, as well as discriminatory responses that favor or disadvantage the members of the respective groups (Fiske 1998). A complex interplay exists among the various category-based reactions. Threatening stimuli (i.e., members of certain outgroups) may quickly trigger emotional and cognitive processes, both working to activate a behavioral response before any conscious attention is given to the matter. In the absence of immediate danger demanding a rapid response, one has more time to think through things. Yet the passage of time hardly offers any assurance of a "rationally" calculated decision. Often even conscious decisions must be reached quickly, and gut feelings and stereotypes provide convenient avenues to behavioral responses. Past memories, heavily infused with emotional content, may fuel hostile responses to threatening outgroup members, people often seen as less than human and thus more deserving of harsh treatment.

Figure 7.1 presents a schematic outline summarizing how such category-based processes may operate to produce police brutality, laying out the causal relationships between various social and psychological factors implicated in occurrences of excessive force. The model identifies several factors as key to the production of police brutality. First, it specifies social and cultural background conditions that increase the likelihood of police brutality taking place via the engagement of emotional and cognitive preconditions to aggressive behavior. Second, a stimulus, the potential target of a specific act of police brutality, is necessary to trigger aggression, the likelihood of which

111

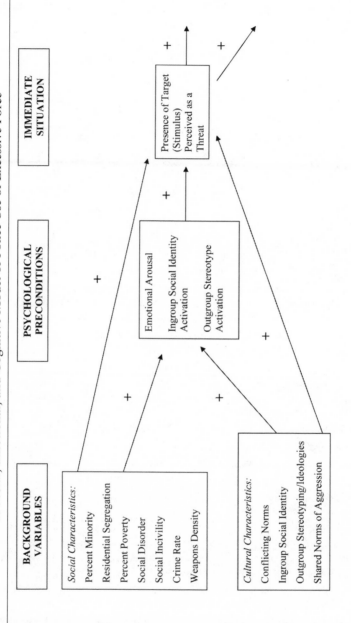

FIGURE 7.1
A Social, Emotional, and Cognitive Model of Police Use of Excessive Force

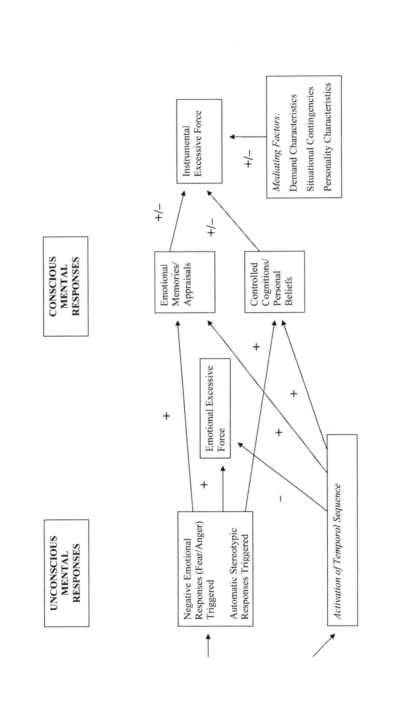

depends upon whether the target's personal characteristics and demeanor signify threat. Third, the presence of the target automatically activates unconscious emotional and cognitive processes, as well as beginning the temporal sequence of events. The temporal sequence is critical in determining the motivation for and the likelihood of police brutality occurring. Rudimentary emotions and automatic cognitions may predispose officers to an impulsive act of emotional aggression. Fourth, should that impulse be held in check, the passage of time may either amplify or diminish the likelihood of police brutality occurring. Conscious mental processes become engaged, including appraisals of emotions and assessments of the situation vis-à-vis personal beliefs. The motive for police brutality changes from primarily emotional, seeking simply to injure the victim, to largely instrumental, providing some reward, albeit one that may not appear rational in any conventional sense. Finally, various mediating factors may influence whether police brutality takes place. We devote the remainder of this chapter to fleshing out the substance of the model.

Background Variables and Psychological Preconditions

Not everyone shares full candidacy for the role of victim at the hands of the police. Affluent citizens in comfortable neighborhoods rarely qualify. Their suburban communities generally see only minor tensions between police and citizens. Crime rates are low, citizens are usually polite, and whatever social problems exist are swept under the carpet of private practitioners. Personal problems are generally kept secret from the police. Parents who abuse alcohol, children who use drugs, the mentally ill, and others who violate norms of the middle class are more likely to come to the attention of private medical counselors than the state's agents of social control. Weapons are kept for sport, usually out of sight, and rarely employed against fellow humans. Police work is comparatively comfortable, entailing relatively little street-level stress and few real dangers.

Impoverished African American and Mexican-origin neighborhoods in urban America present a very different set of circumstances. Crime rates are high, and many citizens are generally distrustful of and at times overtly hostile toward the police. Poverty exacts a heavy toll on people, creating a constant stream of social problems. Lacking knowledge of alternative ways out, citizens frequently look to the police for solutions to their problems, most of which fall outside of the professional purview and competence of the police (see Goldstein 1977). Day-to-day exposure to people's troubles inures police officers to the miseries surrounding them, a form of psychological self-preservation. Violence is taken for granted; weapons are commonly used against fellow citizens. Challenges to authority and physical threats become staples of police work.

In short, the lives of more affluent citizens and impoverished minorities are tragically different. Percent minority correlates with a host of challenging social circumstances—residential segregation, poverty, high crime rates, weapon availability, and social disorder/incivilities (see, e.g., Skogan 1990; Massey and Denton 1993; Anderson 1999). Unsurprisingly, percent minority in cities is a key predictor of the use of coercive crime control strategies by the police. Empirical tests of the threat hypothesis, which stipulates that percent minority is related positively to the use of such strategies, provide consistent support for the proposition that racial/ethnic minorities are singled out for both legal and extra-legal force (e.g., Liska and Yu 1992; Jacobs and O'Brien 1998; Holmes 2000; Smith and Holmes 2003). As we have seen, the traditional explanation of these findings—police violence serves the interests of elites and/or police officers—pays little heed to some difficult issues. Poor minority neighborhoods pose potential threats to the officers who patrol there, but acts of police brutality may bear tremendous costs to perpetrators and no clear benefits, defying self-interest. Social-psychological phenomena other than calculated self-interest must play a larger role in triggering police violence.

The presence of people who not only appear different but who live in worlds apart from the larger society, activates several category-based emotional and cognitive processes. Merely entering their neighborhoods heightens emotional arousal among police officers, an unconscious, conditioned response to a history of dangerous encounters. Conscious apprehension arises from emotion-laced memories of personal experiences and the war stories of other officers. Often physically and socially different, notably in the hue of their skin and their demeanor, the residents of minority neighborhoods lose their humanity, becoming dangerous "predators" in the eyes of the police (Chambliss 2001). Each dark street, each dark face, signifies potential danger. The dehumanizing conditions of urban life provide a context in which apprehension and fear are always close to the surface, ready to take hold of officers' conduct as they confront threats both real and imagined.

Apart from the physical conditions of minority neighborhoods, cultural rifts set citizens and police apart from one another. Here we can see the influence of rational conflicts of group interests. Citizens want the police to solve endemic problems of crime and social disorder, whereas the police seek to dispense quickly with the menial calls that are the staple of their day-to-day work. And the police demand respect for their authority and status, expecting citizens to obey their commands. Many citizens hold the police in contempt, seeing them as mere handmaidens of an oppressive white power structure. Competing expectations about police duties and authority undoubtedly lead to raucous exchanges (see Chambliss 2001), continually amplifying emotional arousal and reinforcing pejorative stereotypes among all involved. Alone, however, these inevitable violations of competing norms would probably not instigate much unwarranted physical aggression. Conflicts over such matters are just a customary part of the larger backdrop of social circumstances that, in totality, will set the stage on which periodic outbreaks of extra-legal violence take place.

Police officers and minority citizens see one another as members of entirely different worlds, clearly delineated by the police officer's distinctive uniform and the citizen's physical characteristics. The perception of occupational identity and social separateness is strongly held by police officers. Among some minority citizens, a sense of collective identity emerges in opposition to the dominant group, based on values that challenge the dominant society and its agents of social control. Police and citizens readily identify with their own group and perceive little similarity, indeed stark contrast, to outgroup members. Put in terms of social identity theory, a high meta-contrast ratio exists—people's perceptions highlight ingroup similarities and outgroup dissimilarities, as well as the homogeneity of both groups. When it comes to taking sides, one does not have to make a conscious decision about who should be favored. Except for the most egregious of transgressions, citizens tend to side with fellow citizens and officers with fellow officers.

Pejorative outgroup stereotypes pervade the subcultures of the police and minority citizens and exacerbate invidious distinctions. Consistent with popular imagery, selectively reinforced by personal experience, the police stereotype minorities as criminally inclined and prone to violence. Many minority citizens stereotype the police as authoritarian thugs. Vicarious tales circulated among police and minorities amplify the real threats posed by outgroup members. Continually reinforced by personal experience and folklore, stereotypes offer constant reminders of the threats posed by outsiders. The mere presence of an outgroup member symbolizes threat, always signifying the potential for an imminent eruption of conflict. Ingroup identification and outgroup stereotyping heighten intergroup tensions, further augmenting the psychological backdrop of police brutality.

Apart from specific stereotypes, more general ideologies fuel intergroup tensions. Some white police officers avow racist dogma that justifies existing inequalities on the premise of innate differences between whites and racial minorities (see Bolton and Feagin 2004). The belief that minorities are less intelligent and less civilized than whites buttresses existing social arrangements and racial privileges by implication of inevitability.

Stereotypes of criminality are just one element of a larger ideology that sees the often bleak conditions of minority life as natural in the overall scheme of things. Even while rejecting such racist dogma, minority police officers may still see their poor counterparts in dangerous neighborhoods as threats to their personal well-being and authority (Alex 1969). Ideology also permeates minority communities, where the police are seen as the "man," a figure of power who is avoided out of fear, especially by young males (Anderson 1990). Tales of police abuse circulate within minority neighborhoods, reinforcing citizens' stereotypes and personal beliefs.

A cultural chasm separates police officers and minority citizens in urban America. Ironically, the one solid bridge between the two worlds is built upon norms about the appropriateness of violence. One well-established theme of criminological explanations for high rates of personal crime is the existence of subcultures of violence that define aggression as an acceptable means to maintain honor in the face of interpersonal challenges. Subcultures do not necessarily promote aggressive behavior, but they may define the various circumstances in which it is appropriate (Baumiester and Heatherton 1996). In some subcultures, physical aggression is acceptable in situations that call for restraint in others. Permissive norms about the range of situations appropriate for aggression make violent resolutions to intergroup conflict more likely. Police officers and minority citizens have ample opportunity to learn a great deal about violent solutions to life's problems.

The ability to use force defines the police. It is their "special competence"; it is why we have police (Klockars 1993). It is hardly surprising, then, that the use of force is a central element of police culture (Crank 1998). Both formally and informally, police culture encourages the use of violence to resolve problematic situations, ways that would often constitute criminal behavior if employed by citizens. For example, a police officer may legally use handcuffs to restrain someone who does not comply with legitimate orders, but citizens generally cannot. Indeed, learning the appropriate situations and means of violence permeates virtually every dimension of police training. Through a combination of formal instruction and informal "war stories," academy training highlights the dangers of policing and focuses heavily on self-defense. The use of weapons, in particular, consumes a large portion of formal training, with firearms at the center of much of it. In-service training often continues the focus on the use of firearms as well as other nonlethal weapons and techniques. Fledgling police officers quickly learn the importance of being prepared and willing to use violence to resolve problems. Officers perceived as unwilling to use force in situations where it is deemed necessary or appropriate are seen as a liability by other officers (Hunt 1985). Adding to the formal emphasis on the use of force training, the informal culture stresses the necessity of force in police work. Rookie police officers quickly learn through observation and informal instruction from experienced peers that they must be willing to use it. They also learn the circumstances in which force, including excessive force, is considered appropriate, as well as established subcultural excuses and justifications to account for its extra-legal use.

Just as the police learn to use violence at times and in ways prohibited for civilians, life in minority neighborhoods socializes citizens to call upon violence in situations in which it would be eschewed in more affluent ones (Anderson 1999). Although the "decent" families in black neighborhoods do not subscribe to violence as a means of protecting their self-respect,

> for children from decent homes, the immediate and present reality of the street situation can overcome the compunctions against tough behavior that their parents taught them. . . . The child is confronted with the local hierarchy based on toughness and the premium placed on being a good fighter. As a means of survival, one often learns the value of having a "name," a reputation for being willing and able to fight. (Anderson 1999, 67)

Specific occasions for violence, however, are determined by the nature of the situation and the way it is interpreted by participants. Staging areas for violence, such as multiplex theatres and concerts, attract crowds of youth who campaign for respect and "represent" their neighborhoods, places where signs of disrespect cannot go unchallenged. Fights in public places frequently involve knives or guns, and young people often keep their "shit" or "equalizers" in close proximity for protection when attending public events, their taken-for-granted presence providing a cue that elicits aggression and an effective means of performing it.

The material, psychological, and cultural conditions of minority neighborhoods provide a background against which day-to-day violence plays out. These background features set the stage for violent interactions. While the setting virtually guarantees their enactment, it does not directly produce the acts of aggression that take place there. Rather, it primes people by constantly eliciting the emotional and cognitive precursors to interpersonal aggression and defining certain types of people as threats. The physical conditions of ghetto life and the dangerous interactions between police and citizens occurring there arouse fear. Perceived dissimilarities between police and citizens, made apparent by physical characteristics and attire, activate social identity and stereotyping processes. Any time the police and minority citizens interact, all involved are emotionally and cognitively on edge, ready to respond automatically to any sign of danger.

Threatening Situations and Mental Responses

Aggression generally does not take place randomly. The distal backdrop against which police brutality commonly occurs helps explain the higher overall *incidence* of police brutality in cities with large minority populations. Still, it does not fully clarify what motivates individual police officers to take the personal risk of breaking the law by assaulting a citizen. The cases making up aggregate rates are triggered by the personal characteristics of specific targets within minority areas, those whose status attributes, attire, and demeanor portend the immediate threat that provides the proximate instigation for aggression. Emotionally and cognitively primed by the challenging conditions of minority communities, police officers may unconsciously respond with aggression any time a threatening citizen, often a young male, is encountered. Most of the time that aggression can be justified legally, but sometimes it cannot. Many times the violence serves a purpose, but sometimes it does not. The nuances of law and departmental policy may ultimately provide a basis for a determination about the appropriateness of police violence, but such subtleties have appreciably less influence over what transpires on the street.

Danger, whether real or imagined, may suddenly confront police officers at any moment. They become attuned to the possibility that relative tranquility can be shattered by a potentially life-threatening situation that demands immediate action. A threat may present itself during a routine interaction with a citizen. Does a glint of light indicate a set of car keys, or perhaps a weapon? Too quick of a response may be unduly injurious; too slow of one may portend serious injury or even death for an officer. This is not an occasion for careful, deliberate decision making. Fortunately, the human brain can initiate behavioral responses without the intervention of any conscious deliberation. Unfortunately, such responses may run afoul of modern laws that aim to constrain untoward behavior.

Humans can be easily conditioned to fear threatening stimuli. They rapidly acquire fear of outgroup members, a response difficult to extinguish once established (Olsson et al. 2005). Information stored in cognitive schemata further prepares humans to react automatically and rapidly to outgroup members (Correll et al. 2002). The experiences of urban police officers almost assure such emotional and cognitive responses. Inevitably, they confront hostile, sometimes dangerous, citizens who pose real threats. Such encounters engender conditioned fear responses in officers. Day-to-day experiences also reinforce stereotypes and typifications of minority criminality and danger. Even those who are not actually dangerous may wear clothes or evince a demeanor that signifies threat (Anderson 1990, 1999). When a minority citizen symbolically displays a threat to police authority or safety, the programming of an officer's emotional and cognitive schemata may automatically stimulate emotional aggression against the threatening stimulus without any conscious consideration of possible consequences. Although instantaneous responses are not routinely demanded, they are always a possibility, and officers become predisposed to quick responses in situations demanding them. Indeed, formal police training and culture strongly reinforce the necessity of responding rapidly and decisively to perceived danger (Crank 1998; see also Hunt 1985).

Perhaps the most critical factor in the threatening stimulus-response relationship is time. As the temporal sequence of a police-citizen encounter extends, conscious deliberation exerts greater influence. As conscious mental processes kick in, one is able to assess the potential outcomes of a line of behavior. The punishment occasioned from time to time by acts of police brutality may influence officers' decisions about employing excessive force. Recognition that potential witnesses are present or other situational contingencies may weigh into conscious decisions about an appropriate response to a troublesome citizen.

Several mental processes interact in complex ways as the temporal sequence of a behavioral response unfolds. The activation of emotion-laden memories may unconsciously eliminate many prospective lines of action, making decisions far less rational than commonly believed (Damasio 1994). Conscious memories are tagged with emotional content also, and past anger and hostility associated with similar citizens and encounters may elicit those feelings again (Berkowitz 1993). But thinking about a citizen's alleged transgression does not necessarily amplify feelings of anger. Awareness of mitigating circumstances or lack of personal responsibility surrounding the citizen's behavior has the potential to assuage one's wrath. For example, the police consider mitigating circumstances in classifying citizens and determining appropriate responses to affronts (Van Maanen 1978a). Those who know what they are doing and could have acted differently are labeled "assholes" and punished accordingly, whereas those who could not have acted differently under the circumstances or who do not know any better (e.g., mentally disordered persons) may be ignored or isolated. Of course, officers' recollections may include punishments awarded to others for meting out excessive force, fear-producing images that can deter aggression. Yet awareness of that possibility may simply delay a beating until the sanctuary of a secluded part of the police station has been reached.

Controlled cognitions also can intervene in determining an officer's line of action, potentially contravening the effects of automatic stereotype activation. Whereas unconsciously activated stereotypes weigh heavily into behavioral responses, subsequent deliberation about egalitarian or other humanitarian beliefs may alter the course of discriminatory action (Devine

1989). Such values are hardly commonplace among the police, however. Consider, for instance, mobile data terminal (in-car computer terminal) transmissions from LAPD officers, reported by the Christopher Commission, that so clearly reveal some officers' belief that African Americans are less than human. Lawrence Powell and Timothy Wind, two officers involved in the Rodney King beating, once referred to a domestic disturbance call at an African American family's home as "right out of 'Gorillas in the Mist'" (Independent Commission on the Los Angeles Police Department 1991, 71). Other communications revealed by the commission (pp. 72–73) included various derogatory references to blacks and Mexicans, such as:

"Well . . . I'm back over here in the projects, pissing off the natives."

"Sounds like monkey slapping time."

"I almost got me a Mexican last nite but he dropped the dam gun to quick, lots of wit."

In addition, the commission reported the findings of a survey of LAPD officers that show that about a quarter of them acknowledged that racial prejudice toward minority citizens exists among officers and contributes to tensions with the minority community. About the same percentage reported that officers' racial prejudice is a factor in the use of excessive force.

Clearly the belief system and work conditions of policing interact to dehumanize those seen as innately different, enhancing the prospects of excessive force more often than reducing them (see Bandura 1983, 1986). After all, force is prized in the police subculture as an expedient for controlling the disreputable and disrespectful elements of society (Hunt 1985). While the passage of time may alter a police officer's course of action, obviously it provides little assurance that police brutality will not happen. The passage of time, however, clearly amends the motivation for aggression.

The aim of emotional aggression elicited automatically and rapidly against a threatening stimulus is primarily injurious; when an aggressive act unfolds over time and entails some degree of conscious deliberation, instrumental ends become involved. Police officers may resort to police brutality to reestablish their authority or to defend their social status. It also is a means of dispensing "justice" that is seen as deserved but that may not be forthcoming in formal legal proceedings for reasons such as lack of evidence. Moreover, it may send a deterrent message not just to the victim but to the minority community as a whole. Force that is unnecessary and unjustified from a legal standpoint can still serve many useful purposes for handling the difficult challenges posed by day-to-day police work in impoverished minority neighborhoods. Indeed, police rely upon the idea of instrumentality to justify instances of excessive force as deserved by the victim's actions (Hunt 1985). Emotions also may be called upon to excuse it as being beyond the officer's control. Officers' rationalizations of their untoward behavior thus parallel the motivations for aggression identified by scholars.

The cases of Rodney King and Abner Louima, recounted in the introduction to this book, provide anecdotal evidence regarding these psychological dynamics. In the first instance, we saw a severe beating dispensed immediately in the aftermath of a high-speed pursuit. There is little question that a high-speed chase through a densely populated urban area would arouse strong emotional responses—fear for one's safety and anger at the cause of the fear (see Hunt 1985; Alpert, Kenney, and Dunham 1997). Perhaps the officers had time to contemplate the situation cursorily as they pursued their suspect, certainly comprehending that some "asshole" had produced a serious problem for them. Once the chase had ended, the culprit proving to be a substantial black man, powerful unconscious mental processes undoubtedly took control as the officers set upon their target, their violence likely expressing little more than a desire to injure the man who had provoked them. Ironically, their ad hoc justifications for the beating focused on the threat King allegedly posed while the police took him into custody. No doubt his actions had presented a threat to police authority and safety, but the violence employed against him was grossly unnecessary to make the arrest. It was far more likely an expression of powerful emotions and pejorative stereotypes automatically and unconsciously activated by a black man's willful disobedience to police authority.

The sodomizing of Abner Louima presents a notoriously egregious case of police misconduct. Arrested outside of a nightclub, Louima was mistakenly thought to have punched Officer Justin Volpe. Although questions about the case remain unanswered, one thing is certain about the events that later transpired at the precinct station—Volpe had ample opportunity to contemplate his response to Louima's alleged transgression. Clearly the violence that played out served some instrumental purpose, perhaps intended to reestablish the authority and respect "rightfully" owed a police officer. Yet powerful emotion-laced memories, perhaps the product of unremitting experience with a difficult work world, eliminated more levelheaded alternatives from his deliberations.

Mediators of Police Brutality

Whether aggression takes place depends partly on various contingencies surrounding the actors and the situation. These may have comparatively little impact on spontaneous expressions of emotional aggression, but their influence on instrumentally motivated acts of aggression is appreciably stronger. These mediating factors include various demand characteristics, situational contingencies, and personality factors that shape encounters between the police officer and the citizen.

The demands of police work certainly promote the use of aggression. We have seen that aversive stimuli, such as dangerous or hostile others, arouse fear that activates either a fight or a flight response (Berkowitz 1993). Police officers rarely have the luxury of fleeing danger. Their job requires them to confront society's dangerous citizens, irrespective of the personal risks they assume in doing so. Failure to perform one's duties would discredit and stigmatize the officer within the police subculture and may lead to formal sanctions for dereliction of duty. Moreover, officers must demonstrate their willingness to use force in questionable circumstances; to do otherwise would risk their standing within the police subculture (Hunt 1985). It is better to use too much force than not enough.

Just as the presence of a threatening citizen arouses emotions in the police officer, the officer's presence activates fear in citizens who have been conditioned by experience and vicarious accounts. A history of hostile encounters between minority citizens and police officers, whether experienced directly or indirectly through others' stories, undoubtedly elicits strong aggressive tendencies among citizens. Their thoughts are laced with emotional and cognitive memories of the police and the conviction that their people suffer unjust treatment at the hands of the criminal justice system. They too may become aroused to aggression, fueling angry exchanges with the police. Though generally outmanned and outgunned, on occasion minority citizens may become sufficiently aroused to physically assault an officer. Unencumbered by occupational demands to face threats square on, however, citizens may choose other options. Far more commonly, they either acquiesce to officers' orders or flee, fearing the consequences that might otherwise be forthcoming.

The nature of police work creates other demands. Officers patrolling impoverished neighborhoods are under pressure to deal with routine calls for service quickly without much deliberation about the nuances of the situation (Bayley 1994). In addition to time constraints, they typically arrive at the scene of a problem armed with limited information and find themselves forced to resolve complex legal and moral dilemmas perfunctorily. Formal bureaucratic and informal subcultural constraints call for them to simplify citizens and their complaints, encouraging officers to dispense summarily with most problems. Not being required to reflect deeply on matters, officers may give little thought to employing excessive force in problematic minority neighborhoods because it is a normal procedure learned through socialization into the informal culture of policing.

Situational characteristics surrounding encounters between police officers and citizens also have the potential to alter the course of events. One
such situational contingency is the presence of credible witnesses. Needless
to say, on occasion, the police employ excessive force irrespective of who is
observing the event. Recent police beatings leading to allegations of brutality in Los Angeles and New Orleans occurred in full view of the media. In
New Orleans, a film crew, openly standing close by, became secondary targets of the police. These incidents appeared to involve emotional aggression, acts motivated by a pursuit in the Los Angeles case (Madigan 2004)
and possibly a perceived affront in the New Orleans episode (Associated
Press 2005). While anecdotal, such evidence makes a compelling case that
emotions can easily override reason in police decision making. At the same
time, credible witnesses may generally deter officers from employing excessive force, at least in the immediate setting, for fear of punishment.

Another consequential situational characteristic is the presence of a
weapon, a cue that symbolizes threat and engages emotional and cognitive schemata in ways that heighten the likelihood of aggressive responses
to minority citizens, even when they pose no actual threat to police officers. The weapon need not be associated directly with an aversive event
for an instigating effect to occur (Berkowitz 1993). For instance, a
weapon found in a hostile or disrespectful young black male's car trunk
during a search may not pose a direct threat from the suspect in custody,
but his demeanor may have already aroused negative emotions, and the
weapon may amplify an officer's feelings of anger and fear. Moreover,
stereotypes of criminality associate weapons with minority citizens. Experimental studies indicate that participants, including actual police officers, make video game shoot/don't shoot decisions more rapidly for
stereotype-congruent targets—armed blacks and unarmed whites—and
more slowly for stereotype-incongruent ones—unarmed blacks and
armed whites (Correll et al. 2002, 2007). In the face of the challenging
conditions of minority neighborhoods, these response tendencies may
further predispose police to use aggression gratuitously against citizens
encountered there.

A thread woven throughout our argument is the suggestion that police
brutality, albeit reprehensible, is a product of normal social-psychological
functioning rather than individual personality characteristics. Insofar as
individual differences affect the propensity for aggression, they serve to
mediate aggressive responses to provocations (Geen 1998). For example,
habitual aggression by some individuals may represent maladaptive behavior caused by deficient information processing. The deficiency affects the
encoding and interpretation of cues perceived in social interactions, leading
to inappropriate responses that, in turn, lead to rejection by others. The

hostile attribution bias, in which attributions of hostility by others are incorrectly inferred from what are actually benign intentions (e.g., Nasby, Hayden, and DePaulo 1980), may be explained by these social processing deficiencies. Flawed cognitive skills may be exacerbated by personal experience or highly arousing conditions, such as when biased attributions become automatic responses acquired through a history of defending oneself against mistreatment by others (e.g., Dodge and Coie 1987). Given that policing in minority neighborhoods perpetually presents threats and stresses, it certainly seems plausible that hostile attribution biases might appear even among those who come to the job with rather ordinary cognitive skills. That possibility directs attention to the issue of whether police officer candidates can be sorted by psychological characteristics that influence behavior on the job, or whether the job molds the personality of police officers. Such questions are central to the question of how the problem of police brutality might be ameliorated.

Is Police Brutality Inevitable?

The difficult conditions of life in impoverished minority neighborhoods are alien to many Americans, who rely on the police to maintain the geographic and social boundaries that divide the haves from the have-nots. A separate world exists for those with little opportunity, those who subsist in the socially disorganized conditions of urban life. The day-to-day lives of police officers who patrol there immerse them in that world, one where they often are viewed not as authority figures deserving of respect but as alien invaders seeking to dictate citizens' lives. There police work involves routine confrontations with hostile citizens who challenge authority and sometimes pose real threats of physical harm. The all-too-frequent tragedies and misdeeds that take place in impoverished minority neighborhoods numb the senses, making the citizens there seem dangerously less than human and thus deserving of harsh treatment to defend the authority and safety of officers. The suspicions and hostilities of police officers and minority citizens provide a volatile cocktail, one that provokes interpersonal confrontations that reinforce and amplify their reciprocal perceptions of threat.

Above all, our analysis reveals that police brutality is a tragic yet profoundly normal by-product of intergroup relations. We chose it as our analytical focus for good reason. Recall that physical aggression by the police, when unjustified, legally constitutes police brutality. It strikes at the heart of the most cherished principles of democratic societies. At the same time, our theoretical model has broader implications than just police brutality, speaking more generally to police-minority relations. Less directly injurious forms of aggression, such as verbal insults, also undermine the legitimacy of democratic arrangements and dehumanize society's most unfortunate citizens. Shaped by the same intergroup dynamics that produce more egregious physical assaults, lesser expressions of aggression are commonplace in policing. Conveying far less potential cost to police officers, such behavior can impulsively express negative emotions or instrumentally serve to control threatening others, thereby buttressing the power and status differentials that separate police officers from poor minority citizens.

We have seen that the conditions of minority life in American society provide a veritable recipe for police brutality as well as many lesser forms of police misconduct against citizens. Can the recipe be altered? That is the question to which we now turn our attention. Paradoxically, far more has been written about how to reduce the incidence of police brutality than about the causes of it. As we have seen, previous theories of police brutality condense the problem into relatively simplistic formulae that do not capture its intricacies. If we are uncertain about the cause of an ailment, then can we hope to craft an effective cure for it?

CHAPTER 8

Can Popular Policies
Reduce Police Brutality?

We have identified a related set of social, emotional, and cognitive processes that seems to suggest the inevitability of police brutality in the context of impoverished minority neighborhoods. An important question of theory and policy concerns whether these dynamics can be significantly altered by currently popular proposals to reduce the incidence of excessive force. Deeply rooted in the history of American policing, organizational reforms have been widely touted by police administrators and scholars alike. These recommendations aim to alter the organizational structure or culture of police departments. In so doing, it is thought that the behavior of police officers will change. It is said that the formal and informal characteristics of police organizations determine the street-level behavior of police officers, behaviors that foster police-minority tensions and promote police brutality.

Clearly the work responsibilities of policing serve to separate officers from citizens and help produce an occupational culture characterized by an "us-versus-them" worldview (Crank 1998). Informal norms of the subculture exacerbate the solidarity and isolation of the police and concomitantly decrease police accountability to citizens (Kappeler, Sluder, and Alpert 1998). The subculture also provides normative parameters that define the "acceptable" uses of extra-legal force by officers, providing excuses and justifications to account for its occurrence (Hunt 1985). But are such organizational characteristics of policing amenable to change? Would those changes actually address the underlying social-psychological dynamics of police brutality? Could any such changes alter the background conditions that breed police brutality?

We concur with reformers that the organization of policing is conducive to the production of police violence, but making meaningful changes in

127

police behavior by changing organizations is an endeavor fraught with difficulties. An implicit assumption of reform proposals, as well as much of social science, is the malleability of human behavior. Put simply, many believe people's behavior can be modified for the better with relative ease. Indubitably, the social-psychological dynamics outlined earlier exert greater influence than organizational characteristics over police-citizen interactions in impoverished minority neighborhoods, and those psychological forces may be far more intractable than envisioned by many police reformers. Moreover, it remains unclear how organizational change in police organizations could affect the social conditions that trigger the social-psychological processes implicated in police brutality.

Changing Police Organizations to Change Police Behavior

Judged against the present, it appears likely that police brutality was rampant during the nineteenth and early twentieth centuries, a period in which the police subculture and bureaucratic controls were minimal in comparison to what exists in large police departments today. Policing did not offer civil service positions with job security, there was limited training, and police relied heavily on personal authority. At the same time, ethnic and racial tensions were more acerbic than today. America's large cities were "boiling cauldrons" of preexisting ethnic enmities imported by immigrants from Europe (Walker 1998, 51). Arguably, significant improvements have taken place in policing and racial/ethnic relations since then, yet police brutality remains endemic, and reformers diligently persist in their endeavor to devise new organizational policies to alleviate that problem as well as to improve police-minority relations generally. Perennially popular policy proposals focus on improving police professionalism, increasing bureaucratic control over police officers, and increasing police accountability to the community.

Police Professionalism

Notions of police professionalism originated in the reform efforts of the late nineteenth to mid-twentieth centuries (Uchida 2001). Professionalism seeks to restructure policing by selecting and molding police recruits into efficient and effective bureaucratic workers. These efforts rest on the presumption that individuals with good moral character, higher education, and stable personalities provide the cloth from which professional police officers are woven, those who carry out the police function according to law and policy without prejudice or malice. The philosophy of professionalism focuses on individual "problem" officers, bad apples in an otherwise good barrel, as the root cause of police brutality. Some officers are thought to invite interpersonal conflict because they are violence prone or lack certain interpersonal skills (Grant and Grant 1996; Toch 1996). An investigation commissioned by the NAACP in the aftermath of the Rodney King incident echoed the views of many reformers, urging that "a special effort should be made to recruit candidates who are less potentially violent" (NAACP 1995, 122).

One long-standing professionalism proposal calls for increasing the educational qualifications of police officers, a recommendation that has become part of the conventional wisdom of police reform (Worden 1990; Hawley 1998) Underlying such proposals is the belief that individuals with higher education will bring different values and attitudes to the job (Worden 1990). In the case of brutality, it is argued that police officers will act less aggressively toward citizens because they possess better communication skills, have more tolerance of people with different backgrounds and lifestyles, and are more likely to appreciate the importance of acting lawfully. The validity of those claims remains open to debate as studies about the link between education and police behavior suffer from serious methodological flaws, leading the National Research Council (2004, 141) to conclude that the available evidence is "inadequate to make recommendations regarding the desirability of higher education for improving police practice." It seems likely, however, that police officers with higher levels of education may act much the same as less educated ones on the street, particularly in volatile situations that do not allow for careful reflection. There is no reason to believe that education would suppress one's visceral emotional responses to dangerous situations. Nor do the better educated avoid learning stereotypes that are automatically activated by the presence of outgroup members, although their personal beliefs might alter the course of their responses in situations that allow more careful deliberation (see Devine 1989). That assumes, of course, a liberalizing educational experience that promotes critical thinking and acceptance of diversity. This may be a dubious assumption about many criminology and criminal justice programs, which may begin the process of occupational socialization in the classroom (see Crank 1998). Moreover, it assumes that socialization into the subculture of policing, replete with invidious racial ideology, and experience on the street in poor minority neighborhoods will not overwhelm the abstract lessons of earlier classroom education. Even if higher education does prepare officers to communicate better with citizens and solve problems more effectively, the value of those skills may be limited by the time constraints and organizational demands placed on officers, which often preclude handling citizens' problems conscientiously.

Another line of reasoning related to hiring practices suggests that preexisting personality traits explain police brutality, and that such proclivities can be identified in prospective officers. This makes some sense. Certain individuals may have aggression-prone personalities cultivated by socialization experiences from early childhood on (Berkowitz 1993). Such personality characteristics may not directly cause aggression, but they may serve as mediating variables in the production of the behavior (Geen 1998). Various techniques used to select police officers are based on the assumption that these personality traits are readily detectable (Worden and Catlin 2002). Arguably, the most popular screening proposal, and the only one with sufficient research from which to draw conclusions, is the use of psychological testing. Psychological screening has become very common in policing, and its use is still on the rise (Travis 1994; Fyfe, Greene, Walsh, Wilson, and McLaren 1997). Indeed, such testing is so common that an industry devoted to it has emerged. Yet research on psychological screening for aggression-prone candidates reveals that the instruments lack scientific validity and do not predict police brutality (see Travis 1994; Grant and Grant 1996). This type of screening is probably best limited to its original intent, identifying the relatively rare candidates who have extreme personality problems (Fyfe et al. 1997).

A third component of professionalism involves in-service training for officers. A common response from police agencies to a scandalous incident is some form of training (Buerger 1998; National Research Council 2004). As with psychological screening, the growth of such training programs has spawned an industry (see Mastrofski 1990). Two closely related varieties of training include programs to alter officers' beliefs (e.g., diversity training) or to teach them to control their tempers (see Fyfe 1996; Flynn 2002). It is said that trainers need to impart an understanding that citizens' behavior must not be judged simply as good or evil, and that officers should not take insults and attacks personally (Fyfe 1996). The untenable assumption of even the most theoretically informed analyses is that officers can learn to consciously control cognitive and emotional processes through training (e.g., Griffin and Bernard 2003).

Diversity training programs take for granted that by providing complete and accurate information about minority groups, attitudes based on incorrect or insufficient information can be changed (Buerger 1998). In fact, police officers' day-to-day experiences may run directly counter to what they are taught in such curricula. Their stereotypes of racial and ethnic minorities often are reinforced by selective interactions with citizens in poor neighborhoods, and all too frequently the content of cultural diversity training programs inadvertently fortifies officers' stereotypes of racial and ethnic minorities (Blakemore, Barlow, and Padgett 1995). Ironically, attempts to suppress stereotypic thinking may backfire in various ways that may actually exacerbate the effects of racial stereotyping when people are not strongly motivated to overcome stereotypes of others (see

McCrae and Bodenhausen 2000). Diversity training is generally disliked by officers, often viewed as an illegitimate attempt to change their worldview by imposing what they see as a "special-interest political agenda that is at odds with their street experiences" (Buerger 1998, 35). Officers generally prefer training that imparts practical skills about subjects such as use of force strategies (Buerger 1998), a focus that may actually increase their paranoia about potential threats (Fyfe 1996).

Bureaucratic Controls

Despite the widely espoused rhetoric of professionalism, many reformers and police administrators appear to distrust officers, advocating stricter controls over behavior rather than the autonomy traditionally associated with professional status. In this view, stopping police brutality is a matter of monitoring officers and punishing those who break the rules—officers will be deterred from brutality and serious violators banished from policing. Such methods include written policies designed to guide officer behavior, reporting requirements to allow review of officer decisions, and oversight by supervisors to ensure compliance with rules (National Research Council 2004).

Departmental rules set the boundaries of acceptable officer behavior and provide guidance in decision making. Large agencies have a plethora of rules that officers must follow. Notably, they often require officers to self-report their activities, particularly those relating to the use of force, so the behavior may be reviewed by supervisors to determine whether departmental rules were followed (National Research Council 2004). Criminal statutes and departmental policies clearly forbid the use of excessive force. Still other policies aim to help officers avoid circumstances likely to produce unjustified violence. For instance, some departments discourage the primary officer in a high-speed pursuit from making the arrest of suspects upon completion of a chase (Alpert, Kenney, and Dunham 1997). This policy is premised on the belief that the intensity of a car chase at high speeds will arouse strong emotions and thereby encourage aggressive behavior by the primary officer. That makes sense in light of what we know about emotional arousal, but it remains unclear why other closely pursuing officers would experience appreciably less emotional provocation.

The discretion afforded officers in most situations allows them to disregard rules and avoid reporting requirements. The low visibility of much police work precludes direct supervision or verification of reporting (Goldstein 1960). In the case of brutality, it seems unlikely that officers would honestly report violations of departmental regulations or laws. The tenets of the police subculture deter officers from reporting the transgressions of fellow officers or cooperating with internal investigations

(Skolnick and Fyfe 1993). Thus these control mechanisms may be of limited value for egregious rule violations that may carry severe penalties.

A related problem with bureaucratic controls involves first-line supervisors. Bureaucratic controls designed to reduce police brutality rest on the willingness of first-line supervisors to hold officers accountable for their actions. Some, however, may hold the same views of minority neighborhoods and citizens as the patrol officers they are supervising. Given the structure of police organizations, wherein supervisors are recruited from the ranks of patrol officers, it seems unlikely that they will want to punish subordinates for attitudes and actions they support. In fact, research suggests that some first-line police managers' styles of supervision may be more aligned with police culture than with administrators' views of appropriate behavior (see Engel 2001). Some supervisors view their role as protecting patrol officers from management; others spend considerably more time engaged in patrol work than in supervisory duties.

A more recent innovation and expansion of the bureaucratic control model is the use of early intervention (EI) systems. These data-based management tools are used to identify officers who exhibit potentially problematic behavior (Walker, Alpert, and Kenney 2000). They provide a means of centralizing and tracking a wide variety of readily available information on supposed risk indicators, such as citizen and departmental complaints, accidents (vehicular and otherwise), and use of force incidents. Some proponents also argue that EI systems can alter line-level supervisors' behavior by providing systematic data on officer performance that can be reviewed by higher-level administrators (Walker 2005). In short, police agencies can force supervisors to address problems rather than to ignore them or protect officers.

Early intervention systems are based on the premise, supported by some research (Brandl, Stroshine, and Frank 2001; Independent Commission on the Los Angeles Police Department 1991), that a small percentage of officers is responsible for a disproportionate share of misconduct. Yet it is unclear whether this pattern exists in the case of brutality, as the majority of cases may not involve frequent offenders (Toch 1996). Furthermore, EI systems suffer from many of the same limitations as traditional methods of bureaucratic control, depending on official records of behavior that officers may actively seek to hide from supervisors. They also are dependent on effective citizen complaint mechanisms (Walker 2005). Agencies where officers underreport use of force and citizens are discouraged from filing complaints will be unable to operate effective EI systems. Moreover, the choice of indicators is based largely on anecdotal information or guesswork. While the indicators may make intuitive sense to many police administrators and scholars, no research has adequately assessed their predictive validity. Like many reform proposals, these assumptions seem to be part of commonsense thinking about policing—they seem so obvious that they must be valid.

A more sophisticated and broadly conceptualized version of the bureaucratic control model involves adherence to clear guidelines combined with training and messages from supervisors designed to create and reinforce a culture of rule following. It is said that the formal organization can mold its informal culture through the use of mutually reinforcing rules, training, supervision, and discipline (Skolnick and Fyfe 1993). Clear messages from police administrators, combined with proper implementation of bureaucratic controls (i.e., investigation and punishment), can influence the climate of an organization and officer behavior. The basic elements of the bureaucratic control model are sound and simply in need of more effective implementation; police agencies have failed to use effectively what has always been at their disposal. Proponents of this viewpoint see a failure of leadership in some police agencies, a position clearly articulated by Skolnick and Fyfe (1993, 136–37, emphasis in original):

> To be sure, the routine of policing is governed in large measure by peer pressures and . . . peer approval, but, whether through act or omission, the chief is the main architect of police officers' street behavior. This is so because the strength and direction of street-level police peer pressures ultimately are determined by administrative definitions of *good* and *bad* policing and by the general tone that comes from the top. When administrations are weak or too far out of touch with the reality of the streets— as when police chiefs pretend that hard and fast rules govern officers' behavior—they are rejected by officers. Then . . . [officers] develop their own *sub rosa* codes of behavior, their own loyalties, their own systems for defining and dealing with good police work and bad police work, their own methods of telling headquarters what it wants to hear.

The most recent recasting of this view incorporates elements of bureaucratic control and community accountability, envisioning a more effective implementation of rules, reporting procedures, citizen complaint procedures, and EI systems as methods to transform the formal and informal culture of a police organization toward accountability (Walker 2005).

Ultimately even the most sophisticated models of bureaucratic control rest on a flimsy foundation. The approach assumes that officers will gravitate toward aggressiveness and brutality if not tightly controlled. Paradoxically, increased oversight may encourage ingroup solidarity and heighten resistance to rule enforcement (Crank 1998; Reuss-Ianni 1983).

Moreover, the nature of police work and police culture will make the supervision of officers and the investigation of misbehavior inherently difficult. We agree that close supervision, vigorous investigation, and appropriately severe punishment of infractions may influence officer behavior to a degree, particularly in places with relatively few threats to officer safety. Sufficiently severe punishments may deter some instrumental aggressive behavior if effective alternative lines of action are available (Bandura 1983). Prospects for the punishment of police brutality are highly uncertain, however. In all likelihood, nearly all incidents of excessive force go undetected, and those that are detected often go unpunished for lack of credible witnesses or other evidence. It seems unlikely that any threat of punishment could completely overcome the powerful emotional forces at work among officers who confront the immediate threats, real and perceived, of poor minority neighborhoods. Indeed, James Q. Wilson's (1968) influential work on policing acknowledged the importance of emotions in encounters between police and citizens and pointed out that administrative controls are limited in their ability to influence emotionally charged behavior (see also Crank 1998).

Community Accountability

Policies advocating professionalism and bureaucratic control have deep roots in the history of modern policing, going back to the Progressive Era of American politics. While these proposals remain in vogue, a new approach has surfaced since the urban unrest of the1960s. It emphasizes making police more accountable to the communities they serve. This viewpoint holds considerable sway, because it underlies leading policy recommendations intended specifically to improve police-minority relations and to reduce the use of excessive force (e.g., National Advisory Commission on Civil Disorders 1968; NAACP 1995; U.S. Department of Justice 2001). The premise of police accountability is simple: By making officers interact with and answer to citizens, social barriers between them will break down, and police-minority tensions will subside. Central policy proposals in this tradition include changing the composition of police personnel (i.e., greater representation of minority and female officers), citizen oversight, and community policing.

Diversifying the agencies of municipal government has been the most prominent proposal until the recent popularity of community policing. Many researchers, reformers, and commissions continue to call for agencies that reflect the populations they serve as a means to improve relations between the police and minority communities (Fyfe 1988; Skolnick and Fyfe 1993; NAACP 1995; U.S. Department of Justice 2001). Citizens also tend to see a racially and an ethnically representative police force as a useful means of improving street-level interactions between police and citizens (Weitzer and Tuch 2006). Indeed, minority officers may be more knowledgeable about minority communities and cultures and may be more empathetic to minority concerns (Goldstein 1977; Decker and Smith 1980). In addition, minority and female police officers may hold different attitudes regarding citizens and the job of policing and may rely on different approaches to their work. The inclusion of more minority and women officers in police agencies also may influence white male police officers and thus alter the police subculture (Walker, Alpert, and Kenney 2000).

Despite the enthusiasm among reformers and scholars for diversifying police departments, limited empirical evidence regarding the effects of minority and female representation on police brutality exists. Our work on the effects of community accountability and racial/ethnic threat provides the most comprehensive examination of the issue to date (Smith and Holmes 2003). We used city-level data for U.S. cities with 150,000 or more residents to examine the effects of community accountability and minority threat variables on the average annual number of federal civil rights criminal complaints alleging police brutality during the period 1985–1990. The percent of black and percent of Hispanic (in the Southwest) population proved powerful predictors of civil rights complaints. Both were related positively to the average number of complaints, consistent with an earlier study using these data to test the threat hypothesis (Holmes 2000). Findings for minority and female representation in police departments were a different matter. The ratio of black citizens to black officers did not have a statistically significant relationship to complaints, although the ratio of Hispanic citizens to Hispanic officers had a positive relationship to complaints (the larger the underrepresentation of Hispanics, the greater the number of complaints). The percent of female officers had no effect on the number of complaints.

While advocates of minority representation argue that increasing diversity should create police departments that are more sensitive to and less threatened by the conditions of minority neighborhoods, simply increasing ethnic and racial diversity in police agencies may not dramatically alter the culture and practice of policing. This proposal presupposes homogeneity within racial and ethnic minority populations. Race/ethnicity, however, represents only one dimension of social identity—social groups defined by occupation and social class also comprise salient elements. Minority candidates chosen to become police officers may not be representative of the residents of impoverished inner-city neighborhoods. Black police officers are more likely to come from working-class and middle-class backgrounds than from the impoverished neighborhoods where residents are generally less qualified to become police officers (Williams and Murphy 1990), and they may perceive citizens of impoverished minority neighborhoods as a threat to their personal safety and authority, much the same as white officers do (Alex 1969; Smith and Holmes 2003). As we have seen, policing is characterized by a uniquely powerful subculture. Conceivably, minority police officers may be co-opted by this subculture and experience pressures to accept pejorative stereotypes about minority neighborhoods and their residents (Alex 1969; Locke 1996).

More than anything, the ameliorative effect of Hispanic representation in police departments may reflect the unique social background of this group. Residents of Hispanic barrios experience social and economic disadvantages, yet conditions fostering social organization also exist (Martinez 2002). They have a fairly high rate of both formal and informal labor force participation and share a common cultural legacy, such as Spanish-language usage and Catholicism, and they may experience a higher degree of social integration than found among poor blacks in inner cities. Hispanic police officers may be better integrated into the barrio community than black officers are into the ghetto, producing greater empathy toward and lesser perceived threat from Hispanic citizens.

The lack of an effect of percent of female officers on police brutality complaints flies in the face of the common belief that women are less aggressive than men, but the relationship between sex and aggression is far from simple (see Geen 1998). Many of the proposed benefits attributed to women's representation in policing are based on gender stereotypes about their innate empathy and superior communication skills rather than on empirical evidence of actual differences between male and female police officers (Smith 2003). Consider that sex differences in aggressive responses may be attenuated in certain situations where individuals are provoked (Bettencourt and Miller 1996). Notably, insults or physical attacks increase females' level of aggression and significantly reduce the difference in aggression level between them and males in such circumstances. In addition, the arguments for female representation overlook the powerful socialization pressures of policing, pressures that may be intensified for women. New female police officers may face gender biases that create unique demands to conform and display physical abilities (Hunt 1985).

Around the same time that diversity proposals became prominent, reformers began recommending citizen review of complaints against police officers. Citizen review is strongly supported by citizens (Weitzer and Tuch 2006), as well as endorsed by a variety of investigative commissions and researchers (see Walker 2001). Its popularity continues to grow, and citizen review of complaints is becoming increasingly common in large cities (Walker and Bumphus 1992; Walker 2001). Citizen review is designed to overcome the self-protective isolation of the police by including citizens in the process of investigating complaints about police conduct (Walker 2001). Police agencies have traditionally responded defensively to citizen complaints, attempting to reject or discredit them (Walker 2005). Citizen review processes are based on the inability of police departments to fairly investigate and discipline officers accused of misconduct. Advocates argue that even honest internal investigations of police misconduct lack the transparency and legitimacy of impartial external inquiries. Furthermore, citizens may be more willing to come forward to an independent agency. Indeed, we found that cities with citizen review mechanisms have higher rates of police brutality criminal complaints, which supports the assumption that these processes may increase citizens' willingness to come forward (Smith and Holmes 2003). If so, eventually greater scrutiny of police behavior may help deter the use of excessive force. Still, these review processes suffer from many of the same limitations as bureaucratic controls. The low visibility of police work and the blue wall of silence mean that details of many incidents of police brutality are known only to the police officers and citizens involved. As a result, excessive force complaints often are determined to be unfounded for lack of credible evidence.

Evolving from the police-minority relations programs advocated after the urban unrest of the 1960s, community policing has become the fashionable proposal to improve police-community relations and reduce police brutality. These widely touted programs encompass a somewhat amorphous set of ideas (National Research Council 2004). Partly because of this ambiguity, community policing involves an array of tactics that vary considerably across agencies. Still, the various expositions of its merits generally subscribe to a philosophy that revolves around the goal of developing a consultative partnership with citizens to address a broad range of problems. Presumably this partnership will allow police to draw on the resources of the community and is purported to have a variety of interrelated benefits, including better quality of service, decreased tensions with citizens, and increased accountability to the community (Goldstein 1987). For instance, one popular tactic of community policing is foot patrol. Officers given permanent walking-patrol assignments in neighborhoods must interact with members of the public they usually would not encounter (Wilson and Kelling 1982). They would interact regularly with residents in nonconfrontational situations and might develop a greater stake in the neighborhoods they patrol. This is just one illustration of the wide variety of initiatives suggested by the proponents of community policing to increase officers' engagement with citizens and to improve rapport.

Unlike many of the reforms designed to improve police-community relations, community policing is not simply a new program or tactic but a new model of policing that redefines the role of the police and the relationship between the police and citizens. Such fundamental changes in policing face a variety of challenges. In impoverished minority communities, a number of problems will undermine the implementation of community policing.

A critical underlying assumption is that a wide range of citizens will work with police to build a consensus about problems and the appropriate responses to them. Unfortunately, police quickly discover that getting citizens involved and building relationships in impoverished minority communities is extremely difficult (Sadd and Grinc 1996; Bohm, Reynolds, and Holmes 2000). Of course, many citizens living in disadvantaged neighborhoods distrust the police and do not desire a close working relationship with them, even though many would like greater police protection (see Weitzer and Tuch 2006). Police may find themselves consulting with an unrepresentative group of concerned and involved residents (see Bohm et al. 2000). Improving relationships with "upstanding" adult citizens who already support the police seems unlikely to override officers' apprehension during contacts with young neighborhood men, those who fit criminal stereotypes and are thus perceived as threatening by police officers. Those young men, in turn, often see the police as dangerous and assiduously avoid them.

In short, the impoverished neighborhoods most in need of community policing programs are exactly where these programs may be least effective (National Research Council 2004; Williams and Murphy 1990). The "community" envisioned in community policing does not exist in America's most crime-ridden and socially disorganized urban neighborhoods, and more basic economic improvements may be needed before any meaningful partnership can take place (Buerger 1994). After all, the police must still address the problems of crime and disorder that bring them into normative conflicts with citizens.

Prospects for Organizational Reforms

More than a century of reform initiatives has increased the educational levels of police officers, improved the screening processes of police agencies, and enhanced the training of officers. Police bureaucracies around the country have implemented clearer rules to guide officer behavior, improved internal oversight mechanisms, and moved toward stricter enforcement of rules. Since the 1960s, many agencies have implemented various mechanisms to increase police accountability to the public. Increasing diversity, implementing citizen oversight processes, and establishing community policing are immensely popular reform initiatives. Undoubtedly those reforms have improved the practice of policing and helped open historically closed police agencies, possibly even working to dilute the insularity of the police subculture. If nothing else, efforts to diversify police departments achieve one laudable goal, namely, offering greater employment opportunities to those traditionally excluded from the relatively good jobs offered by policing. Moreover, a representative police force may produce symbolic benefits and thereby build trust in police (Weitzer and Tuch 2006).

Despite such apparent benefits, the evidence on organizational reforms indicates that they hardly provide a panacea for the problem of police brutality. Indeed, the unintended consequences of some policies include the production of contexts reinforcing the intergroup dynamics that create the problem. Rigid bureaucratic controls may have increased officers' isolation from citizens, and the long-term careers associated with professional policing may have fostered a police subculture that heightens ingroup/outgroup distinctions. In fact, the movement toward professionalism helped establish the police as a distinct interest group. An even more problematic issue is that the social-psychological processes underlying the conflicts between groups of unequal power and status are not readily amenable to manipulation via organizational changes. Whereas the ingroup/outgroup dynamics of police minority relations are rooted in a social structure characterized by the unequal distribution of resources and power, improvements in intergroup relations depend heavily on *equal-status contact* between groups (e.g., Allport 1954; Fiske 2003). Positive changes also require contact that is extended, constructive, and cooperative (Fiske 2003), as well as allowing opportunities for friendships to develop (Pettigrew 1998). Police professionalism and bureaucratic controls obviously cannot address those issues, as such policies do not change the underlying social-psychological dynamics or social inequalities.

Policies to make the police more accountable to the communities they serve presumably have greater potential to create interactions that break down intergroup barriers and improve relationships—or so it would seem. In reality, these policies may create a veneer of improved contact and relations without any underlying substance to actually effect meaningful change. Consider the residency requirements for police officers that exist in some cities. Officers may be required to live inside city limits for various reasons (e.g., rapid response if called in emergencies), and proponents of the policy suggest that it also may improve police-minority relations (e.g., NAACP 1995). Officers may develop a greater rapport with citizens, a better knowledge of community problems, and a greater stake in the community (Murphy and Worrall 1999). Yet such residency requirements have no effect on civil rights criminal complaints of police brutality (Smith and Holmes 2003). Why? Middle-class police officers are hardly likely to choose to live in the most blighted, dangerous neighborhoods of the inner city, favoring instead the safer climate, better schools, and more pleasant surroundings of neighborhoods far removed, both socially and geographically, from the ones they police (see, e.g., Wilson and Taub 2006).

Community policing seems to provide a more nuanced and potentially effective solution to improving relationships in impoverished neighborhoods. But police officers should not be mistaken for social workers. The community policing movement may, indeed, represent little more than a circumlocution obfuscating the fundamental reality that the police are the social mechanism for the distribution and control of nonnegotiable coercive authority (Klockars 1988). The special role of the police is to maintain domestic order and protect citizens from the usurpations of others. Even the most sweeping proposals for organizational change (e.g., Chambliss 2001) cannot alter this fundamental reality of policing. Selective social control by the police inevitably alienates minorities who see them as a mechanism of oppression rather than of protection, whereas the attitudes of minority citizens, along with the conditions of their impoverished neighborhoods, may intensify the perception of an immediate and ongoing threat among the police. Dominant group members also perceive minorities as criminal threats and tacitly approve of even extra-legal strategies of crime control, as long as they remain hidden from view and do not overtly challenge the widely espoused political tenet of equal justice.

While sharing the commitment of organizational reformers to improving relationships between police and citizens, we remain less than sanguine about the efficacy of popular proposals because of the intractable qualities of the intergroup dynamics involved. Perhaps organizational structures and policies can influence the incidence of police brutality to some degree, yet even a modest reduction would require a much greater commitment to reform than presently exists. A deeper understanding of the problem and its causes will be necessary. This will certainly involve rethinking some popular though poorly developed strategies. For example, diversity training programs will require a much more careful consideration of the psychological processes we have identified—it may be much easier to inadvertently reinforce stereotypes than to change them (see Blakemore, Barlow, and Padgett 1995; McCrae and Bodenhausen 2000). Agencies need well developed, ongoing programs designed to do more than simply provide information regarding specific populations. Other reform proposals will require a similar reexamination and a sustained commitment to have even minimal prospects of alleviating police brutality. Put simply, an appreciation for the immense complexity of the problem and the inherent limits of organizational reform is needed.

Most proposals rely on a popular social psychology that oversimplifies the deeply rooted mental processes underlying intergroup conflict. The complex mental apparatus implicated in group fealty and hostility undoubtedly evolved among our distant ancestors (e.g., Turner 2000; Massey 2002, 2005). In the environments they confronted, preconscious automatic emotional and cognitive responses helped secure survival by facilitating ingroup bonds and protecting against outgroup threats. Responses to potentially threatening outgroup members were unfettered by the niceties of modern legal constraints—the continued existence of our species depended on behavior that now, ironically, appears less than human to many. These psychological processes still bestow tremendous advantages in the complicated social environments of the modern world, even though they may trigger unseemly behavior toward outgroup members.

Cognitive and emotional schemata facilitate rapid decisions and preserve mental resources in the face of the multitudinous complexities of day-to-day life in urban environments. We have seen that stereotyping is a universal characteristic of humans that influences automatic responses to others, particularly those perceived as potential threats in situations that do not permit deliberate decision making. The activation of outgroup stereotypes can trigger unnecessarily injurious behavioral responses, no matter one's personal beliefs or intentions to the contrary. Likewise, propensities for biased learning affect the acquisition and maintenance of fear-based responses to outsiders. Even when circumstances permit more careful deliberation, invidious ideologies of racial difference embedded in American culture and reinforced by the street-level experiences of policing provide no impediment to the use of excessive force. On the contrary, the dehumanization of others facilitates acts of aggression. Yet avenues for meaningful change exist insofar as culture and social structure provide the contexts for specific outgroup biases. By breaking down the barriers that separate racial/ethnic and social class groupings, stereotypes and fears of each other may become less salient in interactions between the police and minorities as the kinds of contacts that improve intergroup relations are made possible.

CHAPTER 9

Roots of an Urban Dilemma

A widely espoused ideology of equal justice exists in American society, yet a double standard exists in the practice of policing. Socially and economically disadvantaged minority citizens suffer various forms of police misconduct. Police brutality is an especially pernicious problem. While black and Hispanic citizens are well aware of police misconduct, whites seem quite oblivious to it (Weitzer and Tuch 2006). Perhaps it is difficult for many whites to imagine that the police officer, a heroic icon of popular culture who is sometimes seen as intimidating but nearly always as entirely decent, could somehow symbolize oppression and danger among the less advantaged. Moreover, popular ideology holds that blacks and Hispanics are inherently violent and pose a criminal threat to the dominant group (e.g., Chambliss 2001; Bender 2003). The police may not overtly pander to the fears and political interests of whites, but whites' concerns give them ample latitude in the treatment of minority citizens. Surely they are no exception when it comes to learning cultural stereotypes conflating race/ethnicity and crime, which are reinforced on the streets in selective interactions with citizens who pose real and symbolic threats and thus provide anecdotal support for the stereotypes. The police subculture embraces the use of extra-legal violence and other abuses to accomplish the goals of the police role, and officers may easily justify misconduct as richly deserved by minority citizens perceived as threatening personal safety or challenging authority.

Various nuances of this argument exist, but it is at the heart of many conflict-based theories that seek to explain police behavior that disadvantages minorities (e.g., Jacobs and O'Brien 1998; Chambliss 2001). Such an approach has much to recommend it, particularly if we are interested in the full range of misconduct popularly assumed to comprise police brutality. Many lesser abuses, such as racial epithets and unjustified searches, may convey considerable advantage to the police by widening their arsenal of coercive control while carrying little risk of negative sanction. Yet excessive force, the behavior that legally constitutes police brutality, presents a paradox when analyzed in this framework. What do the police gain from such action, which carries appreciably greater risks? After all, the police are empowered to use necessary force, including lethal force, to accomplish a legitimate duty—but they cannot use force gratuitously. Although excessive force often can be concealed, neither white citizens nor police administrators may be able to turn a blind eye when credible allegations surface. Perpetrators may face the criminal justice system themselves; sometimes harsh dispositions are meted out. It is not at all clear whether any significant advantages accrue to the use of excessive force. Recognition of its paradoxical nature has forced us to rethink the causes of police brutality. We have shown that it is far more deeply rooted in complex human mental processes than existing theories realize.

The vast majority of human experience played out in societies that were very different from our own. The brain evolved fully while our ancestors still lived in simple foraging societies, long before the advent of even the smallest cities (Massey 2005). Members of such societies remained relatively isolated from groups other than their own. Free of the constraints of modern legal codes, individuals behaved in ways that helped ensure their survival. Fealty to the ingroup and aversion to outgroups served that end, and such responses developed into fundamental emotional and cognitive processes. Although the growth of humans' sophisticated cognitive abilities ultimately paved the way to the emergence of the complex societies that exist today, basic human mental processes operate the same as they did in far simpler social environments. Even in large urban areas, where secondary role relationships have become paramount, people's lives remain enmeshed in smaller, more isolated networks that create durable connections to others. Subcultural groups within cities provide an integrative force grounded in the emotional and cognitive processes that forged intergroup dynamics among modern humans' distant ancestors. They also are a divisive force as racial/ethnic and social class divisions grow. Whereas ingroups are the source of lasting emotional attachments, people remain wary of outsiders. They rely on socially learned cognitive schemata that commonly elicit superficial responses in interactions with outgroup members. Sustaining effective social interaction does not require personal knowledge of the other people involved in the situation—various markers, such as characteristic forms of attire and visible physical characteristics, provide cues that prompt rapid assessments about others and facilitate social interactions. Intergroup competition and conflict are greater within large cities, which strengthen subcultural boundaries and heighten ingroup identity in the face of perceived outgroup challenges.

Social inequality and the geographic concentration of people within cities exacerbate these propensities and are keys to understanding the differential use of excessive force, as well as the effective means of ameliorating the problem. Some four decades ago, David H. Bayley and Harold Mendelsohn (1968, 203) argued that meaningful prospects for improving police-minority relations must address "the deprivation and inequality of minority groups." Unfortunately, as was the case then, the concentration of disadvantage among certain minorities in urban localities continues to weigh heavily against prospects for improved police-minority relationships. Social change has, indeed, taken us in the wrong direction, increasingly consolidating poverty geographically within urban areas, a trend that inflicts the greatest disadvantages on groups segregated by race or ethnicity (Massey 2005). Among other adverse outcomes, the racial and ethnic concentration of poverty reinforces negative stereotypes held by the more affluent and the sense of relative deprivation and injustice felt by minority populations.

These observations call attention to a central point of our analysis— that the conditions of concentrated disadvantage experienced by blacks and those of Mexican origin elicit characteristic emotional and cognitive responses in police officers who patrol their neighborhoods, mental processes that may culminate in the use of excessive force. But we must remain mindful of the complexities of the urban landscape. Multitudinous locales exist in between the extremes of concentrated white affluence and concentrated minority poverty. Obviously there are relatively affluent African American and Mexican American neighborhoods (see, e.g., Wilson and Taub 2006), and concentrations of poor whites exist as well (Massey 2005). Moreover, new waves of immigrants from several countries have fueled urban diversity in recent years (Alba and Nee 2003). What are the implications of social class and racial/ethnic diversity for our analysis?

Here we have focused on African Americans and those of Mexican origin in the Southwest, because previous research indicates that these populations are disproportionately victimized by excessive force. But police brutality is a difficult issue to study, and even the most rigorous analyses suffer limitations. For example, our research on civil rights criminal complaints alleging police brutality compared only blacks, Hispanics, and non-Hispanic whites, not just because blacks and Hispanics have long experienced discrimination at the hands of police but also because the total population of big cities contained in the data set was not large enough to allow for analyses containing more numerous racial/ethnic categories. Other systematic studies have used observational data that contain so few incidents of excessive force that even the simplest (i.e., black-white) comparisons are rendered problematic. While such research has yielded valuable insights, much remains to be learned.

The question of race/ethnicity versus social class has special significance, because white poverty is increasingly becoming concentrated in
American cities (Massey 2005). Spatial concentrations of poverty may produce a constellation of structural disadvantages and subcultural adaptations, irrespective of the racial or ethnic identity of the inhabitants of such
localities. Impoverished environments engender joblessness, crime, violence,
and family instability. In these areas, endemic violence becomes structurally
embedded, and it develops into an adaptive strategy. Survival may demand
adopting the "code of the street," which requires cultivating a reputation for
the willingness to use force, a reputation that serves as a deterrent to victimization (Anderson 1999). Over time, "a self-perpetuating upward spiral
of violence" may build as more people adopt violent attitudes and behaviors
in response to the ever increasing threat of victimization (Massey 2005,
284). Moreover, deeply disadvantaged neighborhoods lack the mechanisms
of social control and noncriminal role models that help deter crime (Krivo
and Peterson 1996; Anderson 1999). The various structural disadvantages
and subcultural adaptations that produce violence among blacks and
Hispanics may have the same effects among whites concentrated in impoverished areas (Krivo and Peterson 1996; Phillips 2002). For example,
Columbus, Ohio, has numerous extremely disadvantaged, racially homoge-
neous black and white neighborhoods with high levels of violent crime, and
the effects of structural disadvantage indicators on violent crime are similar
for blacks and whites (Krivo and Peterson 1996). The overall difference in
black-white rates of violent crime in that city is attributable largely to differences in the structural characteristics of neighborhoods.

We have demonstrated that the conditions of disadvantaged minority
neighborhoods, especially the ever-present threat of violence, are likely to
produce fear and to activate stereotypes among the police officers who patrol them. Yet social distinctions other than race may activate the psychological mechanisms involved in categorizing and responding to others:

> At the same time that the concentration of poverty and violence
> produces distinct subcultures of poverty and affluence, their jux-
> taposition within a single urban ecology also heightens class
> awareness and promotes social stereotyping. High rates of crime,
> delinquency, and social disorder within poor neighborhoods are
> all too evident to the affluent, reinforcing their negative stereo-
> types about the poor while inculcating a deep sense of fear of peo-
> ple who exhibit visible markers associated with poverty, which
> may be physical (e.g., height, skin color, hair texture) or cultural
> (e.g., speech, clothing, bearing). (Massey 2005, 287)

Conversely, social inequality and isolation may engender hostility toward the larger society among the poor, irrespective of their racial or ethnic identity. Given that the structural conditions and subcultural adaptations of extremely disadvantaged neighborhoods may affect black, whites, and Hispanics similarly, is it not also possible that the police perceive all who live in such areas as threatening? This line of reasoning suggests that the conditions of impoverished neighborhoods more than racial/ethnic identity trigger the emotional and cognitive processes underlying excessive force (see Correll et al. 2007). Certainly the mere presence of indicators of concentrated disadvantage (e.g., dilapidated buildings) may alert police to prospective threats and arouse aggressive tendencies, but we also must keep in mind that virulent racial stereotypes of blacks and those of Mexican origin existed long before they became geographically concentrated in impoverished urban neighborhoods.

The history of race and ethnic relations reveals that ideologies and stereotypes of race routinely become part of public discourse regarding the social disadvantages confronted by various groups. Some dissipate relatively quickly, whereas others endure tenaciously. For example, stereotypes depicting white European immigrants as racially inferior to native-born whites served as useful justifications for the rampant discrimination experienced by many immigrant groups during the nineteenth century. Consider the Catholic Irish. Relegated to low-paying jobs, they lived in dilapidated neighborhoods and suffered severe social ills, including crime (Ignatiev 1995). Often living in close proximity to blacks, they were viewed as racially inferior to native-born whites. They became objects of scorn, stereotyped as belligerent and drunken. Nativist sentiment was at the heart of political movements that aimed to halt immigration and keep the Irish, along with other Catholic immigrants, from acquiring political power. For example, the anti-immigrant Know Nothing Party and the anti-drinking American Temperance Movement held somewhat different philosophies regarding nativist hostility and moral benevolence, but they were clearly allied with respect to curtailing the assault on the American way of life allegedly mounted by Catholic immigrants (Gusfield 1963). The early movement to reform city police was, in part, an attempt to wrest control of city politics from urban immigrants (Walker 1977). Despite a history of hostile treatment and racist ideology, by the 1950s the various Catholic immigrant groups, once seen as racially inferior and consigned to conditions of abject poverty, were largely assimilated into mainstream American society (Alba and Nee 2003). Although vestiges of their various ethnic identities and past stereotypes no doubt still exist (e.g., popular images of the Mafia), beliefs about racial inferiority and criminality have largely faded away. Now various white ethnic groups are not normally cast as violent or criminal by nature, and those whites who commit crimes often are seen as suffering some individual anomaly that produced the behavior (Miller, Like, and Levin 2002). Generally, group-level biological differences are not said to distinguish criminal whites from noncriminal whites.

In sharp contrast, popular stereotypes portraying people of African and Mexican descent as racially inferior and innately inclined to violence have remained relatively invariable. That imagery is an extension of racial ideologies that existed at the time of the conquest of the indigenous people of Africa and the Americas several centuries ago, people who were seen as animallike and reduced to chattel by their European conquerors (Winant 2001). During the twentieth century, such nefarious practices as lynching were still being justified by the extraordinary threat that blacks ostensibly posed as they reverted to their naturally primitive and brutish ways in the absence of slavery's coercive control (Kennedy 1997). While overt racist ideology is not so openly called on today, it still implicitly underlies various themes of popular and political rhetoric (Winant 2001). Certainly invidious stereotypes and racist beliefs remain deeply embedded in the police subculture, where they may be expressed more freely than they are in politically demure circles of the dominant society (see NAACP 1995; Bolton and Feagin 2004).

The social dynamics that produced the divergent outcomes of Europeans, Africans, and Hispanics have long been a topic of academic discourse (see, e.g., Gordon 1964; Blauner 1972; Barrera 1979; Alba and Nee 2003). What is important here is that many immigrants who entered America voluntarily faced racist ideology and profound discrimination but ultimately assimilated, even if somewhat unevenly, into the larger society. Yet many people of African and Mexican descent, whose ancestors originally entered not by choice but by conquest, remain segregated spatially, socially, and economically. Stereotypes about their allegedly inherent violent nature remain entrenched in American culture. Numerous studies of emotional and cognitive processes show that racial identity activates these psychological mechanisms, potentially producing discriminatory responses. Even affluent black and Mexican Americans may encounter police suspicion and hostility, whereas economically marginal whites may be relatively isolated from police misconduct. Poor whites may experience differential treatment at the hands of the police, but the presence of a white target would not automatically trigger fear or activate stereotypes in a police officer in the same way the presence of a black or Mexican-origin person would. In short, while they provide a key facilitative social context, more than impoverished neighborhood conditions are at work in cases of police brutality—a citizen's racial/ethnic identity is a crucial contributor. Put simply, the combination of contextual factors and ordinary intergroup dynamics produces the behavior. In substantive terms, the interaction of structural disadvantage and racial/ethnic identity accounts for the exceptionally high incidence of police brutality in poor minority neighborhoods.

None of this is intended to suggest that black and Mexican-origin citizens have a monopoly on victimization at the hands of police today. Certainly it is likely that a range of police reactions to different racial/ethnic groups exists within a city at any given time. For example, the long-established Puerto Rican population of East Harlem experiences similar disadvantages as blacks in the area (Bourgois 1995). Unremitting poverty, dilapidated housing, drugs, and violence are staple conditions of their neighborhoods. Police are said to be hostile to the area's residents and prone to brutality and corruption. In addition, new immigration to the United States has taken place over the last half century, bringing diverse people from Asia, the Caribbean, South America, Central America, and especially Mexico (Portes and Rumbaut 2001; Alba and Nee 2003). Certainly these immigrants may experience hostility from the police as well as from the larger society, as did the European immigrants of the nineteenth century. In the late 1970s, Vietnamese fishermen fleeing postwar Vietnam began settling on the Gulf Coast to ply their trade (Alba and Nee 2003). They were perceived as competitive threats by locals, creating acute intergroup tension and violence. Undoubtedly, local police shared some measure of hostility toward the Vietnamese. Yet tensions have subsided, and now Vietnamese immigrants generally appear to be on the track of assimilation (Zhou and Bankston 1996; Portes and Rumbaut 2001).

Despite their ethnic and racial differences, many of the new immigrant groups have relatively high levels of human (education and skills) capital and social (family and community ties) capital, and they show clear evidence of assimilation among the second generation, despite the societal prejudices they confront (Portes and Rumbaut 2001; Alba and Nee 2003). Many are able to avoid the impoverished ethnic enclaves that spawn police-minority tensions. But other immigrant groups, notably Afro-Carribeans and Mexicans, appear to be merging with the existing underclass of the central city. Thus a model of segmented assimilation may describe immigrant trajectories better than traditional conceptualizations that hypothesize a more uniform pattern (Portes and Rumbaut 2001; Alba and Nee 2003). The process of "downward" assimilation, incorporation as a disadvantaged minority because of "rigid racial/ethnic boundaries and economic segmentation" (Alba and Nee 2003, 161), is nowhere more apparent than with Mexican immigrants.

Those arriving from Mexico comprise by manyfold the largest immigrant stream and provide the largest supply of low-wage workers entering the country (Portes and Rumbaut 2001; Alba and Nee 2003). They are overwhelmingly manual laborers originating from rural areas and possessing minimal human capital. Their greatest asset is social capital, the network of ties providing informal assistance in crossing the border and finding jobs. While an invaluable resource, reliance on social capital also creates dependence on one's ethnic community and embeds the newcomer into an immigrant enclave. Proximity to the border and bilingualism bolster cultural traditions within the barrio, and profound hostility and relentless discrimination by the larger society bolster ethnic boundaries and spatial separation. A lack of human capital and a segmented labor market relegate Mexican immigrants to low-paying jobs that offer few benefits. Downward assimilation fosters an oppositional identity, and students of Mexican origin perform poorly in school and have high dropout rates. Even as later generations move away from the barrio, the ongoing stream of newcomers replenishes it. In a nutshell, the impoverished barrios of the Southwest continually foster a context ripe for police-minority tensions.

To be sure, however, the theory of police brutality developed here is not limited to specific racial/ethnic groups. The intergroup dynamics involved in police-minority tensions are generic to all humans rather than being the characteristic of specific subgroups. The underlying psychological processes are triggered by contextual factors, and certain racial/ethnic groups share social and economic characteristics that make them targets of the police. Socioeconomic inequality and residential segregation comprise the structural mainstays that shape the lives of various racial/ethnic groups (see, e.g., Massey 2005). Many immigrant groups experience spatial segregation and concentrated poverty for a period of time, but most enter mainstream American life within a few generations (Alba and Nee 2003). Undoubtedly, the intergroup dynamics described here produce tensions with and abuses of power by the police during immigrant groups' early experiences in the United States.

At the same time, African Americans and the Mexican-origin people of the Southwest share certain social and economic experiences manifestly different from those of other minority groups. They appear to be the primary victims of excessive force, and the tensions that exist between them and the police have persisted virtually since the inception of modern policing (e.g., Escobar 1999; Williams and Murphy 1990). The intractability of the problem is rooted in persistent patterns of urban spatial isolation and economic inequality that have endured since their forced incorporation into the United States. The relative invariance of these structural conditions has nurtured the fears and stereotypes that have become deeply embedded in the subcultures of both white citizens and police. Of course, many African American and Mexican-origin citizens are not part of the underclass so at odds with the police, but even the more affluent are not immune from police hostility and misconduct (e.g., Feagin 1991). They cannot shed the physical and cultural characteristics thought by many to signify inherent racial differences, the popular ideology that they are prone to violence, or the belief that they are perhaps lesser humans than whites. Widely publicized images of violent crime, along with the existence of an oppositional culture that overtly defies the larger society, reinforce public stereotypes and fears of victimization. All of this becomes magnified for the police officer, who confronts on a daily basis the injurious manifestations of concentrated disadvantage and perceived threats to authority and safety.

So what is to be done? Police brutality seems inevitable in America's current social milieu. Its roots are deeply embedded in fundamental psychological processes and in a social structure that deeply divides America along racial and ethnic lines. Human emotional and cognitive processes are not readily amenable to change. These mental mechanisms make humans acutely aware of and responsive to intergroup differences, psychological processes not easily overcome when huge sociocultural differences separate people. Social and cultural contexts, particularly the concentration of certain minorities into impoverished neighborhoods, provide the substance for the operation of these processes. Thus to meaningfully combat the problem of police brutality, as well as to alleviate the many other afflictions of poverty, America must commit itself to reversing the inexorable social trends certain to further erode police-minority relations. As Douglass S. Massey and Nancy A. Denton (1993, 235–36) conclude in their seminal work *American Apartheid*,

> If segregation is permitted to continue, poverty will inevitably deepen and become more persistent within a large share of the black community, crime and drugs will become more firmly rooted, and social institutions will fragment further under the weight of deteriorating conditions. As racial inequality sharpens, white fears will grow, racial prejudices will be reinforced, and hostilities towards blacks will increase, making the problems of racial justice and equal opportunity even more insoluble.

We see no reason to be any more sanguine about the prospects of the impoverished barrios of the Southwest given the overtly hostile reception of the larger society to the stream of poor immigrants flowing into the United States from Mexico (see, e.g., Bender 2003).

Perhaps at this juncture some may claim that we are taking the road of *most* resistance, implicitly suggesting that nothing really can be done. Not so. Large-scale social changes face immense structural inertia and profound political ambivalence, and even after equal-status contact between races became commonplace, it undoubtedly would take many more years before deeply embedded stereotypes and hostilities began to fade. But meaningful changes can take place if the political will dictates. Certainly a key to that change involves breaking down the spatial barriers that separate people residentially, a major piece of unfinished business on the civil rights agenda (Massey and Denton 1993). Many promising mechanisms for reforming discrimination in housing markets already exist in law but are often willfully circumvented in practice. Yet many whites remain skeptical about the existence of discrimination in housing and other social spheres, such as education and employment (Hochschild 1995; Schuman, Steeh, Bobo, and Krysan 1997), and most steadfastly support the police (Weitzer and Tuch 2006). Can we really expect meaningful reform initiatives to emerge from the community of economically affluent and politically influential whites?

Historians of race and ethnic relations tell us that past advances in the lives of African Americans (Franklin and Moss 1988) and Mexican Americans (Acuña 1988) have stemmed largely from grassroot movements originating from within their communities. Nonviolent protests such as the marches and boycotts of the civil rights movement and farm workers movement made considerable strides. Further inroads against discriminatory practices have been made through legal actions initiated by various organizations dedicated to minority concerns, such as the NAACP and the Mexican American Legal Defense and Educational Fund (MALDEF). Increasingly, African Americans and Mexican Americans are becoming elected to city, state, and national offices and may use the political arena to further the cause of racial and ethnic equality. Perhaps their leadership can help spur organizational changes in police departments that could produce some modest interim improvements in police-minority tensions, even if those policies are incapable of addressing the real problems underlying the friction.

Minority initiatives to further the cause of racial and ethnic equality have drawn support from the larger society—there also has been bitter resistance to the perceived erosion of white opportunity through mechanisms such as affirmative action policies. But we should remain mindful that minority political expression has sometimes taken a violent turn, such as seen in the devastating urban unrest of the 1960s and the sporadic outbreaks that have occurred in our cities since then. If the political will of white America continues to resist the sorely needed transformation of the ghetto and barrio, then the sense of injustice felt by the disadvantaged will undoubtedly erupt into large-scale social disorder again. Inevitably the police, the visible symbols of inequality and oppression in minority neighborhoods, will be implicated in the unrest. Once more the public eye will turn to the police, and new calls for organizational reform will be heard. But little is likely to change until we acknowledge that police brutality is just one small sign of the deep currents of intergroup enmity that internally threaten our nation's long-term stability.

NOTES

Chapter 1

1. Although the finding of an individual race and neighborhood racial composition is important, a caveat must be attached to it, as the measure of coercive authority used by Smith (1986) included both excessive force incidents and those involving lesser abuses. More generally, while observational studies provide a rich source of information about police practices, caution must be attached to findings reported from such data. Even these large-scale observational data sets include only a few jurisdictions and a very limited number of excessive force incidents. Combined, the two data sets discussed here include over 10,000 observations of police-citizen encounters, but only about sixty-five involve force judged excessive. Such a small number of excessive force cases renders reliable generalization problematic, particularly when complex multivariate statistical models are employed.

2. Percent black did not have an effect on civil rights criminal complaints in the cities in the original DOJ data set, which included only those with two-plus complaints annually, but it had a strong positive effect in the data for all cities of 150,000-plus population. The different findings resulted from the inclusion of a nonrepresentative sample of cities in the original DOJ data set. More than half (56%) of cities with populations of 150,000-plus were not included because they averaged less than two complaints annually. On average, 150,000-plus cities with two-plus complaints annually had appreciably larger percent black populations than did those with fewer than two complaints. Thus the effect of percent black was suppressed in the two-plus complaints cities because of sample-selection bias.

Chapter 2

1. Hispanic is an umbrella term for those individuals who trace their ancestry primarily to Mexico or other Latin American countries. Where appropriate, we employ Hispanic for consistency with the U.S. Census racial/ethnic categorizations, although disagreement exists about the most suitable designation for the group. We variously employ terms such as *Mexican, Mexican origin, Mexican immigrant,* or *Mexican American* to describe the subsets of the Hispanic population that are the focus of this analysis. We strive to use the terms to be consistent with the usage and/or intent of the authors we cite, as well as to make clear the population to which we are referring. Where appropriate, we use the term *Anglo* to denote non-Hispanic individuals of primarily European ancestry. Many scholars use the more general term *white*, which is not a good descriptor because it conflates racial and ethnic designations (those who identify themselves as Hispanic in the U.S. Census also choose a racial designation, and many select white).

2. Although the land ceded to the United States by Mexico in the Treaty of Guadalupe Hidalgo included parts of other contemporary states, the historical and current concentration of Mexican settlement is located principally in five states—California, Arizona, New Mexico, Colorado, and Texas—that are generally considered to constitute the Southwest (see, e.g., McWilliams 1948/1968). The territory constituting Nevada and Utah was included in the lands ceded to the United States, but no established Mexican settlements existed in those areas. Even today there are few Hispanics in those states compared to the other southwestern states (see Guzmán 2001). Thus we define the Southwest as roughly comprising the five aforementioned states, in which the majority of America's Mexican-origin population still resides.

Chapter 3

1. Two issues surrounding police culture arise here. First, an important feature of policing is the division between street-level patrol officers and administrative officers, two distinct but related components of the culture of policing that sometimes come into conflict (Reuss-Ianni 1983). Our focus is on the street-level culture of patrol officers, because they comprise the majority of police and engage in the everyday street-level work where police brutality takes place. The second issue is that some scholars question the salience and unity of police culture, arguing that its monolithic nature is overstated (see Paoline 2004). They point to a variety of changes in policing that may have fragmented police culture

(e.g., increased diversity among personnel, community policing) and created a number of subcultures. Evidence of different officer types or multiple clusters of officer attitudes provides support for the argument. At the same time, the fact that micro-level variations among officers exist in no way negates the existence of an overarching macro-level police culture that pervades policing, albeit with various degrees of commitment exhibited by members. Here we use the idea of a subculture to identify overall commonalities that clearly distinguish the world of police officers from other segments of society, and we do not suggest that all officers hold identical worldviews (see, e.g., Skolnick 1975, 42–44).

2. Today, academies range from the traditional quasi-military, stress academy to a more college-like, non-stress academy (see Lundman 1980). The latter rely on role-playing, more varied curricula, and fewer rules. The preceding discussion focuses on the former, more traditional model of police training. Although the non-stress approach is now used in some departments, most still operate in the traditional format or retain significant components of that style. Some argue that a focus on danger may have replaced extensive rules and their arbitrary enforcement as a means of promoting solidarity among recruits in non-stress academies (e.g., Crank 1998). Such academies still heavily emphasize crime fighting and the physical aspects of policing, including weapons training, and some suggest that police training really has not changed much in recent years (Bradford and Pynes 1999).

Chapter 4

1. Much of the literature on policing is cast in terms of symbolic interaction theory, which shares certain commonalities with the approach employed here. *Typification* is a term employed in that literature to describe the cognitive shortcuts that develop through direct experience with the social environment. The typification concept involves fundamentally the same ideas as stereotyping, except stereotypes include mental images acquired vicariously as well as those derived directly from personal experience. Stereotype is thus the more general concept, and it is far better developed in contemporary social psychology.

Chapter 5

1. The "triune" brain of modern humans contains three major sectors that developed over the course of human evolution (MacClean 1990). These include the reptilian brain (brain stem and cerebellum), the mammalian

brain (the limbic system), and the neomammalian brain (the neocortex). This model maintains that the neomammalian region of the triune brain was superimposed onto the preexisting limbic (mammalian) region, which was an earlier overlay onto the archaic autonomic (reptilian) region. While this model of the brain somewhat oversimplifies the complex mental processes of emotion and cognition (LeDoux 1996), it provides a useful heuristic. A more detailed exposition on the architecture of the human brain would go well beyond the scope of our analysis; however, LeDoux's (1996) work provides an accessible introduction to the neuroanatomy of emotions, as does that of Damasio (1994) and Turner (2000).

Chapter 6

1. Recall that we are not directly concerned with such matters as verbal abuse, which will generally fall outside of the legal definition of police brutality. Such behavior, however, clearly falls within the definition of aggression, and the social-psychological dynamics described here also are implicated in such lesser forms of police abuse.

2. The concept of instrumental aggression is used by Berkowitz (1993), but Bandura (1983) eschews that term in favor of functional aggression. He maintains that all aggression is instrumental and is more meaningfully differentiated in terms of its functional value to the actor. Insofar as we posit that police brutality frequently involves spontaneous behavior instigated by powerful emotions and bestows few rewards relative to costs, we follow Berkowitz and treat emotional and instrumental aggression as conceptually separable phenomena distinguishable by the actor's motivation.

REFERENCES

Acuña, R. 1988. *Occupied America: A history of Chicanos*. 3rd ed. New York: HarperCollins.

Ahern, J. F. 1972. *Police in trouble: Our frightening crisis in law enforcement*. NewYork: Hawthorn Books.

Alba, R., and V. Nee. 2003. *Remaking the American mainstream: Assimilation and contemporary immigration*. Cambridge, MA: Harvard University Press.

Alex, N. 1969. *Black in blue: A study of the Negro policeman*. New York: Appleton-Century-Crofts.

Alfieri, A. V. 1999. Prosecuting race. *Duke Law Journal* 48:1157–1264.

Allport, G. W. 1954. *The nature of prejudice*. Reading, MA: Addison-Wesley.

Alpert, G. P., D. J. Kenney, and R. Dunham. 1997. Police pursuits and the use of force: Recognizing and managing "the pucker factor"—A research note. *Justice Quarterly* 14:371–85.

Anderson, E. 1990. *Streetwise: Race, class, and change in an urban community*. Chicago: University of Chicago Press.

———. 1999. *Code of the street: Decency, violence, and the moral life of the inner city*. New York: W. W. Norton.

Archibold, R. C. 2007. Los Angeles police chief notes failures of command at rally. *New York Times*, May 30, 2007. http://www.nytimes.com/2007/05/30/us/30LAPD.html (accessed July 30, 2007).

Ashburn-Nardo, L., C. I. Voils, and M. J. Monteith. 2001. Implicit associations as the seeds of intergroup bias: How easily do they take root? *Journal of Personality and Social Psychology* 81:789–99.

Associated Press. 2005. Victim of police beating says he was sober: Retired teacher, 64, struck by New Orleans officers; Cops plead not guilty. *MSNBC.com*, October 10, 2005.http://www.msnbc.com/id/9645260/ (accessed August 21, 2006).

———. 2006. 3 New Orleans cops indicted in beating: Incident caught on videotape by news crew covering Katrina. *CBS News. com*, May 29, 2006. http://www.cbsnews.com/stories/2006/03/29/national/main1454076.shtml (accessed August 21, 2006).

Austin American-Statesman. 2006. Get to the bottom of police force reports. *Austin American-Statesman*, September 17, 2006. http://www.statesman.com/opinion/content/editorial/stories/09/17/17police_edit.html (accessed September 29, 2006).

Bamshad, M. J., and S. E. Olson. 2003. Does race exist? *Scientific American* 289:78–85.

Bamshad, M. J., S. Wooding, W. S. Watkins, C. T. Ostler, M. A. Batzer, and L. B. Jorde. 2003. Human population genetic structure and inference of group membership. *American Journal of Human Genetics* 72:578–89.

Bandura, A. 1973. *Aggression: A social learning analysis*. Englewoods Cliffs, NJ: Prentice Hall.

———. 1983. Psychological mechanisms of aggression. In *Aggression: Theoretical and empirical reviews*, vol. 1, ed. R. G. Geen and E. I. Donnerstein, 1–40. New York: Academic Press.

———. 1986. *Social foundations of thought and action: A social cognitive theory*. Englewoods Cliffs, NJ: Prentice Hall.

Barlow, D. E., and M. H. Barlow. 2000. *Police in a multicultural society: An American story*. Long Grove, IL: Waveland Press.

———. 2002. Racial profiling: A survey of African American police officers. *Police Quarterly* 5:334–58.

Baro, A. L., and D. Burlingame. 1999. Law enforcement and higher education: Is there an impasse? *Journal of Criminal Justice Education* 10:57–73.

Baron, R. A. 1977. *Human aggression*. New York: Plenum.

Barrera, M. 1979. *Race and class in the Southwest: A theory of racial inequality*. Notre Dame, IN: University of Notre Dame Press.

Baumiester, R. F., and T. F. Heatherton. 1996. Self-regulation failure: An overview. *Psychological Inquiry* 7:1–15.

Bayley, D. H. 1994. *Police for the future*. New York: Oxford University Press.

Bayley, D. H., and H. Mendelsohn. 1968. *Minorities and the police: Confrontation in America*. New York: The Free Press.

Beccaria, B. 1764/1963. *On crimes and punishments*. Trans. H. Paolucci. Indianapolis, IN: Bobbs-Merrill.

Bender, S. W. 2003. *Greasers and gringos: Latinos, law, and the American imagination*. New York: New York University Press.

Berkowitz, L. 1983. The experience of anger as a parallel process in the display of impulsive aggression. In *Aggression: Theoretical and empirical reviews*, vol. 1, ed. R. G. Geen and E. I. Donnerstein, 103–33. New York: Academic Press.

———. 1988. Frustrations, appraisals, and aversively stimulated aggression. *Aggressive Behavior* 14:3–11.

———. 1989. Frustration-aggression hypothesis: Examination and reformulation. *Psychological Bulletin* 106:59–73.

———. 1993. *Aggression: Its causes, consequence, and control*. Philadelphia: Temple University Press.

Bettencourt, B. A., and N. Miller. 1996. Sex difference in aggression as a function of provocation: A meta-analysis. *Psychological Bulletin* 119:422–47.

Bittner, E. 1967. The police on skid-row: A study of peace keeping. *American Sociological Review* 32:699–715.

———. 1970. *The functions of police in modern society*. Washington, DC: U.S. Government Printing Office.

Black, D., and A. J. Reiss. 1967. *Patterns of behaviors in police and citizen transactions, Vol. 2 of Studies of crime and law enforcement in major metropolitan areas*. Washington, DC: U.S. Government Printing Office.

Blakemore, J. L., D. Barlow, and D. L. Padgett. 1995. From the classroom to the community: Introducing process in police diversity training. *Police Studies* 28:71–83.

Blanchard, D. C., and R. J. Blanchard. 1989. Experimental animal models of aggression: What do they say about human behaviour? In *Human aggression: Naturalistic approaches*, ed. J. Archer and K. Brown, 94–121. New York: Routledge.

Blauner, R. 1972. *Racial oppression in America*. New York: Harper and Row.

Block, R. L. 1971. Fear of crime and fear of police. *Social Problems* 19:91–101.

Blumer, H. 1958. Race prejudice as a sense of group position. *Pacific Sociological Review* 1:3–7.

Bodenhausen, G. V. 1988. Stereotyping biases in social decision making and memory: Testing process models of stereotype use. *Journal of Personality and Social Psychology* 55:726–37.

Bodenhausen, G. V., and M. Lichtenstein. 1987. Social stereotypes and information-processing strategies: The impact of task complexity. *Journal of Personality and Social Psychology* 52:871–80.

Bogomolny, R. 1976. Street patrol: The decision to stop a citizen. *Criminal Law Bulletin* 12:544–82.

Bohm, R. M., K. M. Reynolds, and S. T. Holmes. 2000. Perceptions of neighborhood problems and their solutions: Implications for community policing. *Policing: An International Journal of Police Strategies and Management* 23:439–65.

Bolton Jr., K., and J. R. Feagin. 2004. *Black in blue: African-American police officers and racism*. New York: Routledge.

Bonifacio, P. 1991. *The psychological effects of police work: A psychodynamic approach*. New York: Plenum Press.

Bouhris, R. Y. 1994. Power, gender, and intergroup discrimination: Some minimal group experiments. In The psychology of prejudice: *The Ontario Symposium*, ed. M. P. Zanna and J. M. Olsen, 204–32. Hillsdale, NJ: L. Erlbaum Associates.

Bourgois, P. 1995. *In search of respect: Selling crack in El Barrio*. Cambridge: Cambridge University Press.

Bradford, D., and J. E. Pynes. 1999. Police academy training: Why hasn't it kept up with practice? *Police Quarterly* 2:283–301.

Brandl, S. G., J. Frank, R. E. Worden, and T. S. Bynum. 1994. Global and specific attitudes toward the police: Disentangling the relationship. *Justice Quarterly* 11:119–34.

Brandl, S. G., M. S. Stroshine, and J. Frank. 2001. Who are the complaint-prone officers? An examination of the relationship between police officers' attributes, arrest activity, assignment, and citizens' complaints about excessive force. *Journal of Criminal Justice* 29:521–29.

Brauer, M., C. M. Judd, and V. Jacquelin. 2001. The communication of social stereotypes: The effects of group discussion and information distribution on stereotypic appraisals. *Journal of Personality and Social Psychology* 81:463–75.

Brewer, M. B. 1988. A dual process model of impression formation. In *Advances in social cognition*, vol. 1, ed. R. S. Wyer and T. K. Srull, 1–36. Hillsdale, NJ: L. Erlbaum Associates.

———. 1999. The psychology of prejudice: Ingroup love or outgroup hate? *Journal of Social Issues* 55:429–44.

———. 2001. Ingroup indentification and intergroup conflict: When does ingroup love become outgroup hate? In *Social identity, intergroup conflict, and conflict reduction*, ed. R. D., Ashmore, L. Jussim, and D. Wilder, 17–41. New York: Oxford University Press.

Brewer, M. B., and R. J. Brown. 1998. Intergroup relations. In *The handbook of social psychology*, 4th ed., vol. 2, ed. D. T. Gilbert, S. T. Fiske, and G. Lindzey, 554–94. Boston, MA: McGraw-Hill.

Brown, J. A., and P. A. Langan. 2001. *Policing and homicide, 1976–98: Justifiable homicide by police, police officers murdered by felons*. Washington, DC: Bureau of Justice Statistics.

Brunson, R. K. 2007. "Police don't like black people": African-American young men's accumulated police experiences. *Criminology & Public Policy* 6:71–102.

Buerger, M. E. 1994. The limits of community. In *The challenge of community policing: Testing the promises*, ed. D. P. Rosembaum, 270–273. Thousand Oaks, CA: Sage Publications.

———. 1998. Police training as a pentecost: Using tools singularly ill-suited to the purpose of reform. *Police Quarterly* 1:27–63.

Bursik, R. J., and H. G. Grasmick. 1993. *Neighborhoods and crime: Dimensions of effective community control*. New York: Lexington Books.

Campbell, D. T. 1965. Ethnocentric and other altruistic motives. In *Nebraska Symposium on Motivation*, ed. D. Levine, 283–311. Lincoln: University of Nebraska Press.

Chambliss, W. J. 1994. Policing the ghetto underclass: The politics of law and law enforcement. *Social Problems* 41:177–94.

———. 2001. *Power, politics, and crime*. Boulder, CO: Westview Press.

Chambliss, W. J., and R. B. Seidman. 1971. *Law, order, and power*. Reading, MA: Addison-Wesley.

Chamlin, M. B. 1989. Conflict theory and police killings. *Deviant Behavior* 10:353–68.

Chevigny, P. 1969. *Police powers: Police abuses in New York City*. New York: Vintage.

Chiricos, T., M. Hogan, and M. Gertz. 1997. Racial composition of neighborhood and fear of crime. *Criminology* 35:107–31.

Chiricos, T., K. Welch, and M. Gertz. 2004. Racial typification of crime and support for punitive measures. *Criminology* 42:359–89.

Correll, J., B. Park, C. M. Judd, and B. Wettenbrink. 2002. The police officer's dilemma: Using ethnicity to disambiguate potentially threatening individuals. *Journal of Personality and Social Psychology* 83:1314–29.

Correll, J., B. Park, C. M. Judd, B. Wittenbrenk, M. S. Sadler, and T. Keesee. 2007. Across the thin blue line: Police officers and racial bias in the decision to shoot. *Journal of Personality and Social Psychology* 92:1006–23.

Coser, L. 1956. *The functions of social conflict*. New York: Free Press.

Covington, J., and R. B. Taylor. 1991. Fear of crime in urban residential neighborhoods: Implication of between- and within-neighborhood sources for current models. *Sociological Quarterly* 32:231–49.

Crank, J. P. 1998. *Understanding police culture*. Cincinnati, OH: Anderson.

Crocker, J., B. Major, and C. Steele. 1998. Social stigma. In *The handbook of social psychology*, 4th ed., vol. 2, ed. D. T. Gilbert, S. T. Fiske, and G. Lindzey, 504–53. New York: McGraw Hill.

Curry, B. 1978. Hispanics protest in Houston. *Washington Post*, April 3, 1978. http://www.lexisnexis.com/us/lnacademic/search/homesubmit Form.do (accessed August 21, 2007).

Damasio, A. 1994. *Descartes' error: Emotion, reason, and the human brain*. New York: Penguin.

Darwin, C. 1872. *The expression of the emotions in man and animals*. London: Watts.

Daudistel, H. D., H. M. Hosch, M. D. Holmes, and J. B. Graves. 1999. Effects of defendant ethnicity on juries' dispositions of felony cases. *Journal of Applied Social Psychology* 29:317–36.

Decker, S. H., and R. L. Smith. 1980. Police minority recruitment: A note on its effectiveness in improving black evaluations of the police. *Journal of Criminal Justice* 8:387–93.

Devine, P. G. 1989. Stereotypes and prejudice: Their automatic and controlled components. *Journal of Personality and Social Psychology* 56:5–18.

Dodge, K. A., and J. D. Coie. 1987. Social information processing factors in proactiveand reactive aggression in children's peer groups. *Journal of Personality and Social Psychology* 53:1146–58.

Dollard, J., L. W. Doob, N. E. Miller, O. H. Mowrer, and R. R. Sears. 1939. *Frustration and aggression.* New Haven, CT: Yale University Press.

Dorfman, L., and V. Schiraldi. 2001. *Off balance: Youth, race, and crime in the news: Executive summary and final report.* Washington, DC: Justice Policy Institute.

Duncan, B. L. 1976. Differential social perception and attribution of intergroup violence: Testing the lower limits of stereotyping of blacks. *Journal of Personality and Social Psychology* 34:590–98.

Ehrlich, H. J. 1973. *The social psychology of prejudice.* New York: Wiley.

Ellemers, N. H., R. Spears, and B. Doosjie. 2002. Self and social identity. *Annual Review of Psychology* 53:161–86.

Ellemers, N., H. Wilke, and A. Van Knippenberg. 1993. Effects of the legitimacy of low group or individual status on individual and collective status-enhancement strategies. *Journal of Personality and Social Psychology* 64:766–78.

Engel, R. S. 2001. Supervisory styles of patrol sergeants and lieutenants. *Journal of Criminal Justice* 29:341–55.

Escobar, E. J. 1999. *Race, police, and the making of a political identity: Mexican Americans and the Los Angeles Police Department, 1900–1945.* Berkeley: University of California Press.

Farrell, R. A., and M. D. Holmes. 1991. The social and cognitive structure of legal decision-making. *The Sociological Quarterly* 32:529–42.

Feagin, J. R. 1991. The continuing significance of race: Antiblack discrimination in public places. *American Sociological Review* 56:101–16.

Ferraro, K. F. 1995. *Fear of crime: Interpreting victimization risk.* Albany: State University of New York Press.

Fine, S. 1989. *Violence in the model city: The Cavanagh administration, race relations, and the Detroit riot of 1967.* Ann Arbor: University of Michigan Press.

Fiske, S. T. 1998. Stereotyping, prejudice, and discrimination. In *The handbook of social psychology,* 4th ed., vol. 2, ed. D. T. Gilbert, S. T. Fiske, and G. Lindzey, 357–411. Boston, MA: McGraw-Hill.

———. 2003. *Social beings: A core motives approach to social psychology.* New York: Wiley.

Fiske, S. T., and S. E. Taylor. 1991. *Social cognition.* 2nd ed. New York: McGraw-Hill.

Flanagan, T. J., and M. S. Vaughn. 1996. Public opinion about the police abuse of force. In *Police violence: Understanding and controlling police abuse of force,* ed. W. A. Geller and H. Toch, 113–28. New Haven, CT: Yale University Press.

Flynn, K. W. 2002. Training and police violence. In *Policing and violence,* ed. R. G. Burns and C. E. Crawford, 127–46. Upper Saddle River, NJ: Prentice Hall.

Fogelson, R. M. 1977. *Big-city police.* Cambridge, MA: Harvard University Press.

Foster, M. 2005. New Orleans officers taped beating man: Journalist who recorded incident also assaulted. *Washington Post,* October 10, 2005. http://www.lexisnexis.com/us/lnacademic/search/homesubmit Form.do (accessed August 21, 2006).

Franklin, J. H., and A. A. Moss Jr. 1988. *From slavery to freedom: A history of Negro Americans.* New York: Alfred A. Knopf.

Freidrich, R. J. 1980. Police use of force: Individuals, situations, and organizations. *Annals of the American Academy of Political and Social Science* 452:82–97.

Fyfe, J. J. 1980. *Philadelphia police shootings, 1975–78: A systems model analysis.* Report to the U.S. Department of Justice, Civil Rights Division. Washington, DC.

———. 1988. Police use of deadly force: Research and reform. *Justice Quarterly* 5:165–205.

———. 1996. Training to reduce police-civilian violence. In *Police violence: Understanding and controlling police abuse of force,* ed. W. A. Geller and H. Toch, 165–79. New Haven, CT: Yale University Press.

Fyfe, J. J., J. R. Greene, W. F. Walsh, O. W. Wilson, and R. C. McLaren. 1997. *Police administration.* 5th ed. Boston, MA: McGraw-Hill.

Fyock, J., and C. Stanger. 1994. The role of memory biases in stereotype maintenance. *British Journal of Social Psychology* 33:331–43.

Geen, R. G. 1998. Aggression and antisocial behavior. In *The Handbook of social psychology,* 4th ed., vol. 2, ed. D. T. Gilbert, S. T. Fiske, and G. Lindzey, 317–56. Boston, MA: McGraw-Hill.

Goffman, E. 1963. *Stigma: Notes on the management of spoiled identity.* Englewood Cliffs, NJ: Prentice Hall.

Goldstein, H. 1977. *Policing a free society.* Cambridge, MA: Ballinger.

———. 1987. Toward community oriented policing: Potential, basic requirements, and threshold questions. *Crime and Delinquency* 33:6–30.

Goldstein, J. 1960. Police discretion not to invoke the criminal process: Low-visibility decisions in the administration of justice. *Yale Law Journal* 69:543–94.

Gordon, M. M. 1964. *Assimilation in American life: The role of race, religion, and national origins.* New York: Oxford University Press.

Gould, J. B., and S. D. Mastrofski. 2004. Suspect searches: Assessing police behavior under the U.S. Constitution. *Criminology & Public Policy* 3:315–62.

Grant, D., and J. Grant. 1996. Officer selection and the prevention of abuse of force. In *Police violence: Understanding and controlling police abuse of force,* ed. W. A. Geller and H. Toch, 150–64. New Haven, CT: Yale University Press.

Griffin, S. P., and T. J. Bernard. 2003. Angry aggression among police officers. *Police Quarterly* 6:3–21.

Gusfield, J. R. 1963. *Symbolic crusade: Status politics and the American temperance movement.* Urbana: University of Illinois Press.

Guzmán, B. 2001. *The Hispanic population.* Census Brief 2000: C2KBr/01-3. Washington, DC: U.S. Census Bureau.

Haberman, C. 2005. NYC; 41 shots, then 6 years of healing. *New York Times,* February 4, 2005. http://www.nytimes.com/2005/02/04/ny region/04nyc.html?_r=1&oref=slogin (accessed September 6, 2006).

Hahn, H. 1971. Ghetto assessments of police protection and authority. *Law and Society Review* 6:183–94.

Hahn, H., and J. L. Jefferies. 2003. *Urban America and its police: From the postcolonial era through the turbulent 1960s.* Boulder: University Press of Colorado.

Haller, M. 1976. Historical roots of police behavior: Chicago 1890–1925. *Law and Society Review* 10:303–23.

Hamilton, D. L., ed. 1981a. *Cognitive processes in stereotyping and intergroup behavior.* Hillsdale, NJ: L. Erlbaum Associates.

———. 1981b. Illusory correlation as a basis for stereotyping. In *Cognitive processes*, ed. D. L. Hamilton, 115–44.

———. 1981c. Stereotyping and intergroup behavior: Some thoughts on the cognitive approach. In *Cognitive processes*, ed. D. L. Hamilton, 333–53.

Hawley, T. J. 1998. The collegiate shield: Was the movement purely academic? *Police Quarterly* 3:35–59.

Hays, T. 2001. Haitian immigrant emerges as symbol of police brutality. Associated Press, LexisNexis, July 13, 2001. http://www.lexisnexis.com/us/lnacademic/search/homesubmitForm.do (accessed November 4, 2004).

Herbert, S. 1998. Police subculture reconsidered. *Criminology* 36:343–69.

Hewstone, M., M. Rubin, and H. Willis. 2002. Intergroup bias. *Annual Review of Psychology* 53:575–604.

Hochschild, J. 1995. *Facing up to the American dream: Race, class, and the soul of the nation*. Princeton, NJ: Princeton University Press.

Holmes, M. D. 1998. Perceptions of abusive police practices in a U.S.-Mexico border community. *Social Science Journal* 35:107–18.

———. 2000. Minority threat and police brutality: Determinants of civil rights criminal complaints in U.S. municipalities. *Criminology* 38:343–67.

———. 2003. Ethnicity, concentrated minority disadvantage, and perceived risk of victimization. *Journal of Ethnicity in Criminal Justice* 1(3–4):1–20.

Holmes, M. D., B. W. Smith, A. B. Freng, and E. A. Muñoz. 2008. Minority threat, crime control, and police resource allocation in the southwestern United States. *Crime and Delinquency* 54:128–52.

Horn, D. G. 2003. *The criminal body: Lombroso and the anatomy of deviance*. New York: Routledge.

Hughes, E. C. 1964. Good people and dirty work. In *The other side*, ed. H. Becker, 23–36. New York: Free Press.

Hunt, J. 1985. Police accounts of normal force. *Urban Life* 13:315–41.

Ignatiev, N. 1995. *How the Irish became white*. New York: Routledge.

Independent Commission on the Los Angeles Police Department. 1991. *Report of the Independent Commission on the Los Angeles Police Department*. Los Angeles: Unpublished report.

Irwin, J. 1985. *The jail: Managing the underclass in American society.* Berkeley: University of California Press.

Jackson, P. I., and L. Carroll. 1981. Race and the war on crime: The sociopolitical determinants of municipal police expenditures in 90 nonsouthern U.S. cities. *American Sociological Review* 46:290–305.

Jacobs, D., and R. M. O'Brien. 1998. The determinants of deadly force: A structural analysis of police violence. *American Journal of Sociology* 103:837–862.

James, W. 1884. What is an emotion? *Mind* 9:188–205.

Jetten, J., R. Spears, and T. Postmes. 2004. Intergroup distinctiveness and differentiation: A meta-analytic integration. *Journal of Personality and Social Psychology* 86:862–879.

Johnson, M. S. 2003. *Street justice: A history of police violence in New York City.* Boston, MA: Beacon Press.

Johnston, W. A., and K. J. Hawley. 1994. Perceptual inhibition of expected inputs: The key that opens closed minds. *Psychonomec Bulletin & Review* 1:56–72.

Jost, J. T., and M. R. Banaji. 1994. The role of stereotyping in system justification and the production of false consciousness. *British Journal of Social Psychology* 33:1–27.

Kania, R. R. E., and W. C. Mackey. 1977. Police violence as a function of community characteristics. *Criminology* 15:27–48.

Kappeler, V. E., R. D. Sluder, and G. P. Alpert. 1998. *Forces of deviance: Understanding the dark side of policing.* 2nd ed. Prospect Heights, IL: Waveland Press.

Katz, P. A. 1976. The acquisition of racial attitudes in children. In *Towards the elimination of racism*, ed. P. A. Katz, 125–34. New York: Pergamon Press.

Kennedy, R. 1997. *Race, crime, and the law.* New York: Vintage Books.

Kent, S. L., and D. Jacobs. 2005. Minority threat and police strength from 1980 to 2000: A fixed-effects analysis of nonlinear and interactive effects in large U.S. cities. *Criminology* 43:731–60.

Klockars, C. B. 1988. The rhetoric of community policing. In *Community policing: Rhetoric or reality*, ed. J. R. Greene and S. D. Mastrofski, 239–58. New York: Praeger.

———. 1993. The legacy of conservative ideology and police. *Police Forum* 3:1–6.

Krivo, L. J., and R. D. Peterson. 1996. Extremely disadvantaged neighborhoods and urban crime. *Social Forces* 75:619–48.

Langworthy, R. H., and L. F. Travis III. 2003. *Policing in America: A balance of forces*. 3rd ed. Englewood Cliffs, NJ: Prentice Hall.

Lazarus, R. S. 1991. Cognition and motivation in emotion. *American Psychologist* 46:352–67.

LeDoux, J. 1996. *The emotional brain: The mysterious underpinnings of emotional life*. New York: Simon and Schuster Paperbacks.

Lee, M. T., R. Martinez Jr., and R. Rosenfeld. 2001. Does immigration increase homicide rates? Negative evidence from three border cities. *Sociological Quarterly* 42: 559–80.

Levy, S. R., S. J. Stroessner, and C. S. Dweck. 1998. Stereotype formation and endorsement: The role of implicit theories. *Journal of Personality and Social Psychology* 74:1421–37.

Liska, A. E. 1992. Introduction to the study of social control. In *Social threat and social control*, ed. A. E. Liska, 1–29. Albany: State University of New York Press.

Liska, A. E., and M. B. Chamlin. 1984. Social structure and crime control among macrosocial units. *American Journal of Sociology* 90:383–95.

Liska, A. E., M. B. Chamlin, and M. D. Reed. 1985. Testing the economic production and conflict models of crime control. *Social Forces* 64:119–38.

Liska, A. E., J. J. Lawrence, and A. Sanchirico. 1982. Fear of crime as a social fact. *Social Forces* 60:760–70.

Liska, A. E., and J. Yu. 1992. Specifying and testing the threat hypothesis: Police use of deadly force. In *Social threat and social control*, ed. A. E. Liska, 53–68. Albany: State University of New York Press.

Locke, H. G. 1996. The color of law and the issue of color: Race and the abuse of police power. In *Police violence: Understanding and controlling police abuse of force*, ed. W. A. Geller and H. Toch, 129–49. New Haven, CT: Yale University Press.

Lundman, R. J. 1980. *Police and policing: An introduction*. New York: Holt, Rinehart & Winston.

Lyons, A., and Y. Kashima. 2003. How are stereotypes maintained through communication? The influence of stereotype sharedness. *Journal of Personality and Social Psychology* 85:989–1005.

MacClean, P. D. 1990. *The triune brain in evolution: Role in paleocerebral functions*. New York: Plenum.

Machalek, R. M., and M. W. Martin. 2004. Sociology and the second Darwinian revolution: A metatheoretical analysis. *Sociological Theory* 22:455–76.

Mackie, D. M., T. Devos, and E. R. Smith. 2000. Intergroup emotions: Explaining offensive action tendencies in an intergroup context. *Journal of Personality and Social Psychology* 79:602–16.

Madigan, N. 2004. Los Angeles moves to ease tensions after tape captures police beating of black suspect. *New York Times*, June 25, 2004. http://www.query.nytimes.com/gst/fullpage.html?res=9D02E 2D91F39F936A15755C0A9629C8B63 (accessed August 8, 2006).

Malone, N., K. F. Baluja, J. M. Costanzo, and C. D. Davis. 2003. The foreign-born population: 2000. Census Brief 2000:C2KBR-34. Washington, DC: U.S. Census Bureau.

Manson, J. H., and R. W. Wrangham. 1991. Intergroup aggression in chimpanzees and humans. *Current Anthropology* 32:369–90.

Markus, H., and R. B. Zajonc. 1985. The cognitive perspective in social psychology. In *The handbook of social psychology*, 3rd ed., vol. 1, ed. G. Lindzey and E. Aronson, 137–230. New York: Random House.

Markus, H. R., and S. Kitayama. 1994. The cultural construction of self and emotion: Implications for social behavior. In *Emotion and culture: Empirical studies of mutual influence*, ed. S. Kitayama and H. R. Markus, 89–130. Washington, DC: American Psychological Association.

Martin, C. L., and S. Parker. 1995. Folk theories about sex and race differences. *Personality and Social Psychology Bulletin* 21:45–57.

Martinez Jr., R. 2002. *Latino homicide: Immigration, violence, and community*. New York: Routledge.

Massey, D. S. 1993. Latinos, poverty, and the underclass: A new agenda for research. *Hispanic Journal of Behavioral Sciences* 15:449–75.

———. 2002. A brief history of human society: The origin and role of emotion in social life. *American Sociological Review* 67:1–29.

———. 2005. *Strangers in a strange land: Humans in an urbanizing world*. New York: W. W. Norton.

Massey, D. S., and N. A. Denton. 1989. Residential segregation of Mexicans, Puerto Ricans, and Cubans in U.S. metropolitan areas. *Sociology and Social Research* 73:73–83.

———. 1993. *American apartheid: Segregation and the making of the underclass*. Cambridge, MA: Harvard University Press.

Mastrofski, S. D. 1990. The prospects of change in police patrol: A decade in review. *American Journal of Police* 9: 1–79.

McClelland, J. L., B. L. McNaughton, and R. C. O'Reilly. 1995. Why there are complementary learning systems in the hippocampus and neocortex: Insights from the success and the failures of connectionist models of learning and memory. *Psychology Review* 102:419–57.

McCrae, C. N., and G. V. Bodenhausen. 2000. Social cognition: Thinking categorically about others. *Annual Review of Psychology* 51:93–120.

McCrae, C. N, A. B. Milne, and G. V. Bodenhausen. 1994. Stereotypes as energy-saving devices: A peek inside the cognitive toolbox. *Journal of Personality and Social Psychology* 66:37–47.

McCrae, C. N., C. Stangor, and A. B. Milne. 1994. Activating social stereotypes: A functional analysis. *Journal of Experimental Social Psychology* 30:370–89.

McEwen, B. S., and E. N. Lasley. 2002. *The end of stress as we know it.* Washington, DC: Joseph Henry Press.

McGreevy, P., and R. Winton. 2007. Bratton issues report on melee: He blames police use of force at May 1 rally on "command and control breakdown." *New York Times*, May 30, 2007.http://www.latimes.com/news/local/crime/la-me-lapd30may30,1,4473797.story?coll=la-util-news-local-crime&ctrack=1&cset=true (accessed July 30, 2007).

McWilliams, C. 1948/1968. *North from Mexico*. New York: Greenwood Press.

Miller, J., T. Z. Like, and P. Levin. 2002. The Caucasian evasion: Victims, exceptions, and defenders of the faith. In *Images of color, images of crime: Readings*, 2nd ed., ed. C. R. Mann and M. S. Zatz, 100–14. Los Angeles: Roxbury.

Mirandé, A. 1987. *Gringo justice*. South Bend, IN: University of Notre Dame Press.

Monkkonen, E. H. 2002. *Crime, justice, history*. Columbus: Ohio State University Press.

Montejano, D. 1987. *Anglos and Mexicans in the making of Texas: 1836–1886*. Austin: University of Texas Press.

Moore, J. 1989. Is there an Hispanic underclass? *Social Science Quarterly* 70:265–284.

Morales, A. 1972. *Ando sangrando (I am bleeding): A study of Mexican-American police conflict*. La Puente, CA: Perspectiva.

Mullen, B., R. Brown, and C. Smith. 1992. Intergroup bias as a function of salience, relevance, and status: An integration. *European Journal of Social Psychology* 22:103–22.

Murphy, D. W., and J. L. Worrall. 1999. Residency requirements and public perceptions of the police in large municipalities. *Policing: An International Journal of Police Strategies and Management* 22:327–42.

Myrdal. G. 1944. *An American dilemma*. Vol. 2. New York: Harper Brothers.

Nagel, J., and S. Olzak. 1982. Ethnic mobilization in old and new states: An extension of the competition model. *Social Problems* 30:127–43.

Nasby, W., B. Hayden, and B. M. DePaulo. 1980. Attributional bias among aggressive boys to interpret unambiguous social stimuli as displays of hostility. *Journal of Abnormal Psychology* 89:459–68.

National Advisory Commission on Civil Disorders. 1968. *Report of the National Advisory Commission on Civil Disorders*. New York: Bantam Books.

National Association for the Advancement of Colored People (NAACP) and the Criminal Justice Institution at Harvard Law School. 1995. *Beyond the Rodney King story: An investigation of police conduct in minority communities*. Boston, MA: Northeastern University Press.

National Research Council. 2004. *Fairness and effectiveness in policing: The evidence, Committee to review research on police policy and practices*, ed. W. Skogan and K. Frydl. Washington, DC: National Academies Press.

Noble, P. 1970. *The Negro in films*. New York: Arno Press.

Öhman, A., M. Fredrikson, K. Hugdahl, and P.-A. Rimmö. 1976. The premise of equipotentiality in human classical conditioning: Conditioned electrodermal responses to potentially phobic stimuli. *Journal of Experimental Psychology: General* 105:313–37.

Olsson, A., J. P. Ebert, M. R. Banaji, and E. A. Phelps. 2005. The role of social groups in the persistence of learned fear. *Science* 309:785–87.

Paoline, E. A. 2004. Shedding light on police culture: An examination of officers' occupational attitudes. *Police Quarterly* 7:205–36.

Payne, B. K. 2001. Prejudice and perception: The role of automatic and controlled processes in misperceiving a weapon. *Journal of Personality and Social Psychology* 81:181–92.

Peterson, R. D., and L. J. Krivo. 2005. Macrostructural analyses of race, ethnicity, and violent crime: Recent lessons and new directions for research. *Annual Review of Sociology* 31:331–56.

Pettigrew, T. F. 1979. The ultimate attribution error: Extending Allport's cognitive analysis of prejudice. *Personality and Social Psychology Bulletin* 5:461–76.

———. 1998. Intergroup contact theory. *Annual Review of Psychology* 49:65–85.

Phillips, J. A. 2002. White, black, and Latino homicide rates: Why the difference? *Social Problems* 49:349–73.

Phinney, J. S. 1990. Ethnic identity in adolescents and adults: A review of research. *Psychology Bulletin* 108:499–514.

Piliavin, I., and S. Briar. 1964. Police encounters with juveniles. *American Journal of Sociology* 70:206–214.

Pinizzotto, A. J., E. F. Davis, and C. E. Miller. 2004. Intuitive policing: Emotional/rational decision making in law enforcement. *FBI Law Enforcement Bulletin* (February): 1–6.

Portes, A., and R. G. Rumbaut. 2001. *Legacies: The story of the immigrant second generation.* Berkeley: University of California Press.

President's Commission on Law Enforcement and the Administration of Justice. 1967. *The challenge of crime in a free society.* Washington, DC: U.S. Government Printing Office.

Quillian, L., and D. Pager. 2001. Black neighbors, higher crime? The role of racial stereotypes in evaluations of neighborhood crime. *American Journal of Sociology* 107:717–67.

Rampart Independent Review Panel. 2000. *Report of the Rampart Independent Review Panel.* Los Angeles: Los Angeles Board of Police Commissioners.

Reiss, A. J. 1968. Police brutality-answers to key questions. *Transaction* 5:10–19.

Reuss-Ianni, E. 1983. *Two cultures of policing: Street cops and management cops.* New Brunswick, NJ: Transaction Books.

Rome, D. M. 2000. *Stereotyping by the media: Murderers, rapists, and drug addicts. In Images of color, images of crime,* 2nd ed., ed. C. R. Mann and M. S. Zatz, 71–81. Los Angeles: Roxbury.

Rosales, F. A. 1999. *¡Pobre raza!: Violence, justice, and mobilization among Mexico lindo immigrants, 1900–1936.* Austin: University of Texas Press.

Rushton, J. P. 1997. *Race, evolution, and behavior: A life history perspective.* New Brunswick, NJ: Transaction Books.

Sachdev, I., and R. Y. Bourhis. 1991. Power and status differentials in minority and majority group relations. *European Journal of Social Psychology* 21:1–24.

Sadd, S., and R. M. Grinc. 1996. *Implementation challenges in community policing: Innovataive neighborhood-oriented policing in eight cities*. Washington, DC: National Institute of Justice.

Sagar, H. A., and J. W. Schofield. 1980. Racial and behavioral cues in black and white children's perceptions of ambiguously aggressive acts. *Journal of Personality and Social Psychology* 39:590–98.

Sampson, R. J. 1986. Effects of socioeconomic context on official reaction to juvenile delinquency. *American Sociological Review* 51:876–85.

Sampson, R. J., and W. J. Wilson. 1995. Toward a theory of race, crime, and urban inequality. In *Crime and inequality*, ed. J. Hagan and R. D. Peterson, 37–54. Stanford, CA: Stanford University Press.

Schaller, M., M. C. Rosell, and C. H. Asp. 1998. Parsimony and pluralism in the psychological study of intergroup processes. In *Intergroup cognition and intergroup behavior*, ed. C. Sekides, J. Schopler, and C. A. Inkos, 3–25. Mahwah, NJ: L. Erlbaum Associates.

Schuman, H., C. Steeh, L. Bobo, and M. Krysan. 1997. *Racial attitudes in America: Trends and interpretations*. Cambridge, MA: Harvard University Press.

Sechrist, G. B., and C. Sangor. 2001. Perceived consensus influences intergroup behavior and stereotype accessibility. *Journal of Personality and Social Psychology*. 80:645–54.

Seligman, M. E. P. 1970. On the generality of the laws of learning. *Psychological Review* 77:406–18.

Sellin, T. 1930. The Negro and the problem of law observance and administration in the light of social research. In *The Negro in American civilization*, ed. C. S. Johnson, 443–52. New York: Holt.

Shallice, T. 1988. *From neuropsychology to mental structure*. New York: Cambridge University Press.

Sherif, M. 1967. *Group conflict and cooperation: Their social psychology*. London: Routledge & Keegan Paul.

Silver, A. 1967. The demand for order in civil society: A review of some themes in the history of urban crime, police, and riot. In *The police: Six sociological essays*, ed. D. J. Bordura, 1–24.. New York: John Wiley & Sons.

Simmel, G. 1908/1955. *Conflict and the web of group affiliations*. Trans. K. H. Wolf and R. Bendix. New York: Free Press.

Skogan, W. G. 1990. *Disorder and decline: Crime and the spiral of decay in American neighborhoods*. New York: Free Press.

Skolnick, J. H. 1975. *Justice without trial: Law enforcement in a democratic society*. 2nd ed. New York: Wiley.

Skolnick, J. H., and D. H. Bayley. 1986. *The new blue line: Police innovation in six American cities*. New York: Free Press.

Skolnick, J. H., and J. J. Fyfe. 1993. *Above the law: Police and the excessive use of force*. New York: Free Press.

Smith, B. W. 2003. The impact of police officer diversity on police-caused homicides. *The Policy Studies Journal* 31:147–62.

———. 2005. Ethno-racial political transition and citizen satisfaction with police. *Policing: An International Journal of Police Strategies and Management* 28:242–254.

Smith, B. W., and M. D. Holmes. 2003. Community accountability, minority threat, and police brutality: An examination of civil rights criminal complaints. *Criminology* 41:1035–63.

Smith, B. W., K. J. Novak, and J. Frank. 2001. Community policing and the work routines of street-level officers. *Criminal Justice Review* 26:17–37.

Smith, D. A. 1986. The neighborhood context of police behavior. In *Crime and justice: A review of research*, vol. 8, ed. A. J. Reiss Jr. and M. Tonry, 313–41. Chicago: University of Chicago Press.

Smith, D. A., and C. A. Visher. 1981. Street level justice: Situational determinants of police arrest decisions. *Social Problems* 29:167–77.

Smith, P. B., and M. H. Bond. 1993. *Social psychology across cultures*. New York: Harvester Wheatsheaf.

Son, I. S., and D. M. Rome. 2004. The prevalence and visibility of police misconduct: A survey of citizens and police officers. *Police Quarterly* 7:179–204.

Sorensen, J. R., J. W. Marquart, and D. E. Brock. 1993. Factors related to killings of felons by police officers: A test of the community violence and conflict hypotheses. *Justice Quarterly* 10:417–40.

Steen, S., R. L. Engen, and R. R. Gainey. 2005. Images of danger and culpability: Racial stereotyping, case processing, and criminal sentencing. *Criminology* 43:435–68.

Stoutland, S. E. 2001. The multiple dimensions of trust in resident/police relations in Boston. *Journal of Research in Crime and Delinquency* 38:226–56.

Stretcher, V. G. 1999. People who don't even know you. In *The police and society: Touchstone readings*, 2nd ed., ed., V. E. Kappeler, 203–19. Prospect Heights, IL: Waveland Press.

Sumner, W. G. 1906. *Folkways*. New York: Ginn.

Swigert, V. L., and R. A. Farrell. 1977. Normal homicides and the law. *American Sociological Review* 42:16–32.

Sykes, R. E., and E. E. Brent. 1980. The regulation of interaction by police: A system view of taking charge. *Criminology* 18:182–197.

Tajfel, H. 1969. Cognitive aspects of prejudice. *Journal of Social Issues* 25:79–97.

———. 1970. Experiments in intergroup discrimination. *Scientific American* 223:96–102

———. 1981. *Human groups and social categories*. Cambridge: Cambridge University Press.

Tajfel, H., M. G. Billig, R. P. Bundy, and C. Flament. 1971. Social categorization and intergroup behaviour. *European Journal of Social Psychology* 1:149–75.

Tajfel, H., and J. C. Turner. 1979. An integrative theory of intergroup conflict. In *The social psychology of intergroup relations*, ed. W. G. Austin and S. Worchel, 33–47. Monterey, CA: Brooks/Cole.

Taylor, S. E. 1981. A categorization approach to stereotyping. In *Cognitive processes*, ed. D. L Hamilton, 83–114. Hillsdale, NJ: L. Erlbaum Associates.

Time Magazine. 1978. End of the rope. *Time*, April 17. http://www.time.com/time/printout/0,8816,916056,00.html (accessed July 20, 2007).

Toch, H. 1996. The violence-prone police officer. In *Police violence: Understanding and controlling police abuse of force*, ed. W. A. Geller and H. Toch, 94–112. New Haven, CT: Yale University Press.

Tooby J., and L. Cosmides. 1992. The psychological foundations of culture. In *The adapted mind: Evolutionary psychology and the generation of culture*, ed. J. H. Barkow, L. Cosmides, and J. Tooby, 19–136. New York: Oxford University Press.

Travis, M. A. 1994. Psychological health tests for violence-prone police officers: Objectives, shortcomings, and alternatives. *Stanford Law Review* 46:1717–70.

Turk, A. 1969. *Criminality and the legal order*. Chicago: Rand McNally.

Turner, J. C. 1982. Towards a cognitive redefinition of the social group. In *Social identity and intergroup relations*, ed. H. Tajfel, 15–40. Cambridge: Cambridge University Press.

———, with M. A. Hogg, P. J. Oakes, S. D. Reicher, and M. S. Wetherell. 1987. *Rediscovering the social group: A self-categorization theory*. Oxford: Basil Blackwell.

Turner, J. H. 2000. *On the origins of human emotions: A sociological inquiry into the evolution of human affect*. Stanford, CA: Stanford University Press.

Uchida, C. D. 2001. *The development of the American police: An historical overview*. In *Critical issues in policing: Contemporary readings*, 4th ed., ed. R. G. Dunham and G. P. Alpert, 18–35. Prospect Heights, IL: Waveland Press.

U.S. Commission on Civil Rights. 1970. *Mexican Americans and the administration of justice in the Southwest*. Washington, DC: U.S. Government Printing Office.

———. 2000. *Police practices and civil rights in New York City*. Washington, DC: U.S. Government Printing Office.

U. S. Department of Justice. 2001. *Principles for promoting police integrity: Examples of promising police practices and policies*. Washington, DC: U.S. Department of Justice.

U.S. Department of Justice, Civil Rights Division, Criminal Section. 1991. *Police brutality study FY 1985–FY 1990*. Unpublished report.

Useem, B. 1997. The state and collective disorders: The Los Angeles riot/protest April, 1992. *Social Forces* 76:357–77.

Valdez, A. 2006. Drug markets in minority communities: Consequences for Mexican American youth gangs. In *The many colors of crime: Inequalities of race, ethnicity, and crime in America*, ed. R. D. Peterson, L. J. Krivo and J. Hagan, 223–36. New York: New York University Press.

Van Knippenberg, A. D., A. P. Dijksterhuis, and D. Vermeulen. 1999. Judgement and memory of a criminal act: The effects of stereotypes and cognitive load. *European Journal of Social Psychology* 29:191–201.

Van Maanen, J. 1973. Observations on the making of policemen. *Human Organization* 32:407–18.

———. 1974. Working the street: A developmental view of police behavior. In *The potential for reform of criminal justice*, ed. H. Jacob, 83–130. Beverly Hills, CA: Sage Publications.

———. 1978a. The asshole. In *Policing: A view from the street*, ed. P. K. Manning and J. Van Maanen, 221–38. Pacific Palisades, CA: Goodyear.

———. 1978b. Kinsmen in repose: Occupational perspectives of patrolmen. In *Policing: A view from the street*, ed. P. K. Manning and J. Van Maanen, 115–28. Pacific Palisades, CA: Goodyear.

Vold, G. B. 1958. *Theoretical criminology*. New York: Oxford University Press.

Waegel, W. B. 1981. Case routinization in investigative police work. *Social Problems* 28:263–75.

Walker, S. 1977. *A critical history of police reform: The emergence of professionalism*. Lexington, MA: Lexington Books.

———. 1998. *Popular justice: A history of American criminal justice*. 2nd ed. New York: Oxford University Press.

———. 1999. *The police in America: An introduction*. 3rd ed. Boston, MA: McGraw-Hill.

———. 2001. *Police accountability: The role of citizen oversight*. Belmont, CA: Wadsworth.

———. 2005. *The new world of police accountability*. Thousand Oaks, CA: Sage Publications.

Walker, S., G. P. Alpert, and D. J. Kenney. 2000. Early warning systems for police: Concept, history, and issues. *Police Quarterly* 3:132–52.

Walker, S., and V. W. Bumphus. 1992. The effectiveness of civilian review: Observations on recent trends and new issues regarding the civilian review of the police. *American Journal of Police* 11:1–26.

Warr, M. 1990. Dangerous situations: Social context and fear of criminal victimization. *Social Forces* 68:891–907.

Washington Post. 1981. Around the nation, addenda. *Washington Post*, December 30, 1981. http://www.lexisnexis.com/us/lnacademic/results/docview/docview.do?risb=21_T2190475714&format=GNBFI&sort=BOOLEAN&startDocNo=1&resultsUrlKey=29_T2190441879&cisb=22_T2190475716&treeMax=true&treeWidth=0&csi=8075&docNo=3 (accessed November 4, 2004).

Weber, M. 1922/1968. *Economy and society*. 3 vols. Trans. E. Fischoff et al. New York: Bedminster Press.

Weitzer, R. 1999. Citizens' perceptions of police misconduct: Race and neighborhood context. *Justice Quarterly* 16:819–46.

———. 2000. Racialized policing: Residents' perceptions in three neighborhoods. *Law & Society Review* 34:129–55.

Weitzer, R., and S. A. Tuch. 2004. Race and perceptions of police misconduct. *Social Problems* 51:305–25.

———. 2006. *Race and policing in America: Conflict and reform.* New York: Cambridge University Press.

Westley, W. A. 1953. Violence and the police. *American Journal of Sociology* 59:34–41.

———. 1970. *Violence and the police: A sociological study of law, custom, and morality.* Cambridge: Massachusetts Institute of Technology.

Williams, H., and P. V. Murphy. 1990. The evolving strategy of police: A minority view. *Perspectives on policing,* no. 13. Washington, DC: National Institute of Justice.

Wilson, J. Q. 1968. *Varieties of police behavior: The management of law and order in eight communities.* Cambridge, MA: Harvard University Press.

Wilson, J. Q., and G. L. Kelling. 1982. The police and neighborhood safety: Broken windows. *The Atlantic Monthly* (March): 29–38.

Wilson, W. J. 1987. *The truly disadvantaged: The inner city, the underclass, and public police.* Chicago: University of Chicago Press.

Wilson, W. J., and R. P. Taub. 2006. *There goes the neighborhood: Racial, ethnic, and class tensions in four Chicago neighborhoods and their meaning for America.* New York: Alfred A. Knopf.

Winant, H. 2001. *The world is a ghetto: Race and democracy since World War II.* New York: Basic Books.

Worden, R. E. 1990. A badge and a baccalaureate: Policies, hypotheses, and further evidence. *Justice Quarterly* 7:565–92.

———. 1996. The causes of police brutality: Theory and evidence on police use of force. In *Police violence: Understanding and controlling police abuse of force,* ed. A. W. Geller and H. Toch, 23–51. New Haven, CT: Yale University Press.

Worden, R. E., and S. E. Catlin. 2002. The use and abuse of force by police. In *Policing and misconduct,* ed. K. M. Lersch, 85–120. Upper Saddle River, NJ: Prentice Hall.

Wright, R. W. 1945. *Black boy.* New York: Harper & Row.

Zajonc, R. B. 1980. Feeling and thinking: Preferences need no inferences. *American Psychologist* 35:151–75.

———. 1998. Emotions. In *The handbook of social psychology,* 4th ed., vol. 1, ed. D. T. Gilbert, S. T. Fiske, and G. Lindzey, 591–632. Boston, MA: McGraw-Hill.

Zhou, M., and C. L. Bankston III. 1996. Social capital and the adaptation of the second generation: The case of Vietnamese youth in New Orleans. In *The new second generation*, ed. A. Portes, 197–220. New York: Russell Sage Foundation.

Zuckerman, M. 1990. Some dubious premises in research and theory on racial differences: Scientific, social, and ethical issues. *American Psychologist* 45:1297–1303.

INDEX

Note: Page numbers with an *f* indicate figures.